SPIRITUAL REVOLUTION

SPIRITUAL REVOLUTION

PREMANANDA DEVA
LAKSHMI DEVI

MOTILAL BANARSIDASS PUBLISHERS
PRIVATE LIMITED • DELHI

First Edition: Delhi, 2002

ISBN: 81-208-1859-8 (Cloth)
ISBN: 81-208-1860-1 (Paper)

Also available at:
MOTILAL BANARSIDASS
41 U.A. Bungalow Road, Jawahar Nagar, Delhi 110 007
8 Mahalaxmi Chamber, 22 Bhulabhai Desai Road, Mumbai 400 026
120 Royapettah High Road, Mylapore, Chennai 600 004
236, 9th Main III Block, Jayanagar, Bangalore 560 011
Sanas Plaza, 1302 Baji Rao Road, Pune 411 002
8 Camac Street, Kolkata 700 017
Ashok Rajpath, Patna 800 004
Chowk, Varanasi 221 001

Printed in India
BY JAINENDRA PRAKASH JAIN AT SHRI JAINENDRA PRESS,
A-45 NARAINA, PHASE-I, NEW DELHI 110 028
AND PUBLISHED BY NARENDRA PRAKASH JAIN FOR
MOTILAL BANARSIDASS PUBLISHERS PRIVATE LIMITED,
BUNGALOW ROAD, DELHI 110 007

Dedication

Ravi M. Khanna
(202) 619 - 2762

Dear Sri Premananda Deva and Shrimati Lakshmi Devi,

It is my privilege and pleasure to be your friend and associated with you both. Your presence is much needed here, and both your Cosmic Conscious experiences are invaluable to bring about the spread of enlightenment in America... and since you both imbibe the spirit of India serving as spiritual Ambassadors to help bridge spiritual India with material America for world peace and upliftment.

Your friend eternally,

Ravi M. Khanna

Ravi Khanna
Voice of America
Chief, South Asia Desk

Foreword

For those of you who are looking for spiritual shortcuts, novel innovations or exciting trends, you will not be satisfied here. For only humble aspirants of the Divine path will resound with these truths. *Spiritual Revolution* is a stepping stone that will help you develop a deeper understanding of yourself and the world around you.

We must all wake up to the truth of our existence and the Divine role we are here to perform. We must no longer succumb to the lethargy of our human experience. It is the supreme challenge of any spiritual man or woman to rise to the occasion of knowing ourselves and embodying the divine Will on Earth.

There are several things that make this book special. It is written by two illumined beings. Having had direct experiences of the highest planes of consciousness, their writing is in no way based on scholarly supposition, but on their own discoveries of spiritual truth. They are writing in collaboration with, and as instruments of, the Brothers of the White Lodge.

At this critical time for the world, this book proposes answers to the present day dilemmas we are faced with individually and on a worldwide scale.

It is a work directly from the Cosmic Mind to you, the reader.

Acknowledgements

We wish to express our gratitude to Radha Neumann, Savitri Bach, and Agni Willmott for their conscientious work and faith in our spiritual endeavor to make this book possible.

A very humble thanks to the Brothers of the White Lodge Koot Humi and Master Morya for choosing us as recipients of these Divine words of truth.

A special thanks also to my guru, Ananda Devi, who initiated me into Cosmic Consciousness in 1960, which precipitated so many wonderful events and especially the publication of this *Spiritual Revolution*.

— **Premananda Deva and Lakshmi Devi**

Table of Contents

Part II Metaphysical Truths

Premananda Deva's Master, Ananda Devi, provokes us to deepen and refine our spiritual inquiry and mastery; with her superconscious clarity of discernment, she instructs us on how we may live in the truth.

Part III Vision

Premananda Deva and Lakshmi Devi speak of their own metaphysical experiences, and give practical methodologies for the true inner spiritual transformation. By destroying the ego individually and collectively, and surrendering to the rightful spiritual forces on the Earth, we can turn back the tide of earthly disaster to resplendent Divinity.

Part IV New Future Society

The vehicle for these philosophies. Here are a series of ideals and commentaries on how to create a blueprint for a more perfected society.

Appendix

Glossary

Contact information

Introduction

This book explores facts about the reality on Earth. Certain unseen spiritual forces should and must be respected. These divine forces have just as much right to dictate to humanity at large as elected human powers. This is not just abstract law from beyond the grave, but something that has been in effect for thousands of years.

The truths in this book are discourses between the highest consciousness and the mental plane. They discuss methods for purification, for examination, and for elimination of the present problems on Earth, for a master plan.

America has a large role to play in the destiny of those on Earth. Premananda Deva captures and expresses them here in this book. But this is not the case of one person having all the answers, for we can all have access to this Divine Law, which protects and joins each and every one of us. The Divine Law must be manifested on Earth more urgently than ever before, as those in power fail to recognize the fragility of the physical Earth. They choose to let the material and economic systems influence everything.

This book can serve as guidance, as prophecy, and as a manual to those who sincerely wish to use it; to see what is in the nature of themselves in the universal plan; to discover what human beings can do to assist the Creator for the manipulation of more goodness on the Earth.

This book is not about creating another belief system. Rather, it contains tried and proven methods to enhance life, and to see that everyone has his or her niche in the grand schema or plan. Once you decide to make a difference, it can be so. Choose to see the truth. Choose to see yourself. Choose to see the divine Soul in you. If this path can guide you, so be it. If these explanations can lift you up, can give you answers to your questions, allow them to do so. We must accept that there are souls who have been searching deeper and more profoundly than us, not to our shame, but to our advantage, for healing, for understanding, and for the truth.

This book seeks to give the Eastern man reassurance and recognition of his direction, continuing in the tradition and in the spirit of his forefathers. Also, the pitfalls of the Western style of life will be enumerated, including critiques by a Western Yogi and his disciple. It richly describes the esoteric and exoteric techniques for self discovery and explains why the world is fast heading away from a true direction — that which is spiritual — in order to pursue materialism and capitalism.

This book warns both Eastern man and Western man — to take action, to inspire him to embrace the truth, to live by the truth, and to revolt against the hypocrisy in our lives, which is too easily accepted by all peoples.

We should not all rush headlong into the tidal wave of a Westernized kind of living when this can only offer a very limited civilization, one without a true connection to the Divine. There are no true centers of initiation in the West — they are only found in the East — and if we are not careful, these centers of initiation will also have to withdraw to the invisible planes of existence.

For the more strident the Earth becomes in spirit, the more difficult it will be to live here, the way it was intended. The Earth was created as a Divine manifested paradise.

Let us never forget this,

Let us join in a spiritual revolution to gain control of our lives — and live for the Divine, as divine beings.

Master Koot Humi and Master Morya

Premananda Deva — J. J. Kennedy

Premananda Deva studied with a great avatar Shrimati Ananda Devi who was French. They worked tirelessly for thirty-four years to promote their philosophies based on their esoteric knowledge.

He experienced the great Supramental Descent in 1961 and was initiated into the spiritual by Ananda Devi, learning the invaluable methods that have enabled him to transform others very rapidly into their cosmically conscious mind and being.

He is dedicated to this cause and serves the Masters of the White Lodge in every capacity, giving himself over completely to their works and plans. He is a master akin to the ancients who seeks out those who are ready for enlightenment in this lifetime. So few are prepared to surrender themselves to their Divine nature, as it always has been on the Earth.

And yet, beyond this role of initiator, he is a beacon of light, a pioneer living in truth consciousness imparted to him by masters who are no longer living in the physical form.

Lakshmi Devi (S. Kennedy) is his closest disciple and an accomplished medium. It is through her grace that we, the masters, can speak here in this book.

May those of you who read this book understand the significance of the messages and see how spiritualism *must* play a more prevalent role in the world's activities.

Premananda Deva's Lineage

All the ancient civilizations recognized the line of descent and, in particular, the lineage of the Guru-disciple relationship. Premananda Deva studied with avatar Ananda Devi for thirty-four years. She was initiated by two of the 20th century's enlightened souls from India, Sri Aurobindo and Sri Ramana Maharishi, and was also an instrument for the implementation of a world plan according to Djwal Kool, a Brother of the White Lodge.

Premananda Deva (like his master Ananda Devi) is unique, because there have been very few true masters born in the West. He is a Yogi and is capable of initiating those who are sincere about entering into their cosmically conscious selves.

He is a Yogi who works integrally with the world, keeping abreast of the socio-political state of affairs in the world. He is concerned that the spiritual forces should regain their rightful place within the society, as a whole, and that harmony should — must — prevail on the Earth between the nations. His outlook and critique of the Western Society is founded on the ideal that materialism is a toxin that has caused so much disharmony in the West, as it leads to the aggrandizement of the ego nature in man.

It is with this premise that we introduce the book, for our plans for the divine Perfection are far reaching and all encompassing.

The true inspiration emerges from within us — to see that we are capable in changing ourselves and the society in which we live. Yet if we presuppose that the Divine/God is already working out His will and everything is as "God willed it," then we are shirking our responsibility and fast losing sight of the plan for perfection and a perfect world.

As spiritual people or aspirants, it is our role to manifest these changes, not to stand idly by as our society and the world abide by the rules given to us by rulers who are ignorant of this large schema or grand plan.

For there *is an order* that can directly affect the mechanics and fabric of our lives and our society — this is where the true divine work lies — here at home around us. For the spiritual world is not and should not only be about retreating into the inner self, withdrawing from life.

In Deva's Own Words...

There is an old adage that says, "When the disciple is ready, the master will appear," and in 1960, while I, Deva, was living in New York, my mind was a whirl, my thoughts spinning. I was unable to control and stop my mental maelstrom of disorder. No sooner had I met with and surrendered to Ananda Devi, then my mind became stilled. And in a matter of a few weeks and months, I became no-thoughted, or one-pointed, to this very day. I had never heard of the spiritual life before. As I entered into my new life, upon our first meeting, I sat at her feet for five hours, listening to her cosmic experiences. Suddenly, I was lifted out of my body, into an early gleaning of higher consciousness.

Days and weeks passed, and my initiation intensified. I entered into the blissful state of child consciousness, soon afterward Cosmic Consciousness, where my mind was filled with blazing white light; I saw auras everywhere. By May 1960, the ultimate experience occurred, and I entered into the enlightened state of Nirvana, or the Supramental. When this occurs, there is an uplift and a descent of the highest consciousness; the body feels as if it will quake under the impact of this Shakti energy rushing in. The body becomes light, the voice a bare whisper, and the mind has great clarity. To this very day, about forty years later, I still live in the realm of truth and joy; and I have known the world of all goodness and beauty and love, and have recognized that we are the possessors of harmony and justice.

Over the years, my mind slowly merged with Ananda Devi's, consolidating my old, human, frail ego self, now diminished, into a newly transformed cosmically aware being.

We formed a team, Ananda Devi and myself, in the Indian Cultural Center in New York, which had been founded under the patronage of Eleanor Roosevelt and the then President of India, Dr. Radhakrishnan, and Prime Minister, Morarji Desai. Visitors came, such as Marianne Anderson, Elizabeth Arden, Philbrik of the FBI, and Ambassador Quasin Sakey from Ghana. We worked daily healing, initiating for world peace and helping to implement The World Plan into the life stream of humanity.

In the summer of 1962, we moved to Paris, France, home of Ananda Devi and founded another center. Here people such as Jean Seberg, James Baldwin, Ambassador Habib, as well as Langston

Hughes, were frequent guests. We continued working selflessly for others until the death of Ananda Devi in February, 1994, at which time I closed all operations and moved to India, where I met Lakshmi Devi, who was to become another enlightened Soul.

Deva and Lakshmi Meet

We met in the Himalayan mountains in Dharamsala, the Tibetan refugee camp and home of the Dalai Lama. We went into a retreat for about three months, until Lakshmi achieved Soul Realization. We now work together, as Ananda Devi and I had done, creating the New Future Society, under the guidance of the Brothers of the White Lodge, Master Koot Humi (K. H.) and Master Morya, the masters who inspired and initiated Madame Blavatsky, the founder of the Theosophical Society.

During our stay in India in 1997 in the city of Bangalore, we were fortunate to have been blessed with a visit from the Masters. Lakshmi Devi had acquired the gift as a medium a few years earlier. So as I, Deva, was reading an actual letter from K. H., from a biography of Madame Blavatsky, suddenly Lakshmi stopped my reading, and she became a vehicle for the first time for Master K. H. then Master Morya (up until that time she had been a medium for Orpheus, her own spirit guide). I listened attentively, as K. H. and Morya spoke directly to me, telling me that I was to return to my homeland (U.S.A.) and to continue in the footsteps of Madame Blavatsky and Colonel Olcott, this time in the Washington, D.C. area, to make the necessary changes in America, to bring about a more kinder, compassionate, harmonious, and peaceful society.

Because I had lived with Ananda Devi, my guru, for 34 years, I had learned to trust and accept ideas coming from the higher consciousness and trust my own intuition. And because Lakshmi Devi had surrendered in the Indian fashion as my disciple and had achieved both Cosmic and Soul (Atman) Consciousness, I was confident that the message was to be followed implicitly.

Master K. H. said this was to be my third and last mission.

Therefore, we established a spiritual center (ashram) in the Washington, D.C. area, where we have been initiating others who are sincere and awakened to the severity of the present day situation we are faced with in the world.

Spiritual Experiencing

An individual who undergoes metaphysical initiation should most certainly realize extra-human experiences, assuming, of course, serious attention and application are paid to esoteric methods delivered by the spiritual teacher.

Over a period of time, say many days mounting to weeks and even a few months of initiation, this would produce significant inner changes — *a mind's revolution,* in other words.

Once we have recognized that there is an "upper realm," a spiritual realm of consciousness, we should take it upon ourselves to be ready to pursue this experience. For once our mind, spirit, and nature have become immersed in this higher nature/consciousness, we are forever changed. We are changed in our mind and in our inner spirit, which turns our aspirations upward. We begin to think with a vertical moral obligation, seeing our human ideals as mere figments of the past. When we are cosmically conscious, we enter into a realm where our state of being is more divinized. Our surrender to this spirit at all times changes forever our outlook and attitude toward others and the world.

These experiences are essential for all human beings. Whether or not it occurs in this life cycle — it eventually has to occur for the natural passage of man and his celestial union and destiny. These experiences are natural and simple and yet astounding to the human personality who finds himself entering a new element, a new self beyond the limitations in which he previously existed. The spiritual path demands that we go beyond intellectual knowledge and enter *into* the source of knowledge to attain true wisdom.

What will be described in the following pages are the effects and prerequisites of spiritual experiencing, for it is possible for anyone to experience this if the correct preparation has been made within. This can and will transform your life. You will align with your higher self. Every little nuance in your life will be affected for the better — you will be shedding the human consciousness and replacing it with the Divine.

Spiritual Experience and Direct Relevance in Life

When one plunges into the spiritual life, everything — everything — falls into harmony. Instead of being the recipient of the past, you forge ahead, creating positivity and annulling karmic acts. As the inner harmony is established, the outer life — relationships, decisions — becomes clearer and easier to understand and grasp. One becomes more and more the master of oneself, able to cope with the pitfalls in life with more equanimity and strength.

The personality of our spiritual man and woman is one of action, spontaneous, joyful, and dedicated to a life of giving. By surrendering to our Divine nature, all that is in conflict is dissolved, and we are left free and liberated. We must live as the Divine planned, as "Warriors of Truth."

Part One

The Masters' Plan

Purge the Hypocrisy

This book will shock and surprise many spiritual seekers. For, within these pages, we intend to reveal secrets about the spiritual way of man.

It is the intention of the Divine to purge the hypocrisy that is man's life here on Earth, to shake his foundation, to prepare him for his birthright, the passage to the Soul. For without directness, and a frank commentary on man today, man will continue to be lost on the Earth.

The world course presently has very little plan and promise for the spiritual man — the sensitive, courageous, non-conforming individual. The fabric of our lives today is driven by the hands of both the political and corporate Titans who shape and contort the nature of our existence, stimulating and directing us away from the Soul's direction and quest.

For us to gain world unity, we have to somehow influence a large number of nations to agree on the direction of the Earth and to sympathize with the other nations' objectives, seeking to fulfill the needs of our brother and sister nations and peoples.

For too long, the Capitalists' dream was one of a free Democracy where, under the cloak of liberalism within a free market, we could avoid moral conduct and rule by mere brute force, influence, money, and power. (Seizing the weakness of voters, alluding to satisfaction for all within the "free" Democracy, promising us a standard of living and a way of life that is irresistible.)

No one can question the advantages and advancements that the Western Democracies have delivered. Man, for the most part, has his basic needs fulfilled: enough food, shelter, and clean water to drink. Yet, behind this wholesome form of civilization, there are many falsities. We will analyze ourselves within this growing culture of Western Capitalism and Democracy, and give shrewd and straight solutions to this extremely precious time in man's history, where he is coming closer and closer to the *imprisonment of the spirit*.

As we incorrectly close the door to our *duty* as a citizen, a nation, a corporation, we allow the demands of our *egoistic rights* to rule.

The Doctrine of the Universal Brotherhood was first introduced through the writings of Madame Blavatsky, a great seer who attempted, with the Theosophical Society, to launch a revitalization of the Western and Eastern world. She reintroduced ancient philosophical ways of thinking, conduct, and action. Indeed, many great thinkers of this time, *e.g.,* Edison and Einstein, respected the monumental classic *The Secret Doctrine*, which revealed a voluminous amount of secrets about existence on Earth. These secrets, precious and sacred, seemed not to perturb the ever-demanding Democratic materialist in his search for perfected Utopia and enslavement in his own creation. Man has to become disillusioned with the civilization he has produced, before he will take action either within his own mind or in the world around him.

Man is an offshoot of his Divine maker and, in his absolute self, he is the Supreme maker, and yet, we are intent on stunting our growth, inhibiting our plan, and discovering nothing: all for a few thrills and to secure the fears installed early in life.

Man *must* transform his mind and spirit. He *must* explore the depth of himself, which is infinite. Why? Because this is his true calling and nature. This, in turn, will uncover his inherent dilemmas, where he will discover why he makes the wrong decisions. This will bring order in his life. Then he can tap into the possibilities the Divine offers us here on Earth.

Revolution

There is only one decision we have to make, the one to achieve enlightenment now. All other decisions are made for the Earth, made for ourselves to live in the birth and rebirth cycle.

Once this decision is firmly implanted in our mind and it seizes all parts of our being, then the Divine will act, will assist us in the effort, and will allow us to fulfill our Soul's destiny. All other decisions will fall short of our own expectations and lead us through life's journeying with the Divine farther and farther away, the more we try to ignore it.

To be divine, one does not have to deny oneself and one's role in life — quite the contrary — one has to allow the Divine to govern, and whether or not this requires change, then so be it.

To think like a spiritual man or woman, we have to be ready to stop all that is false within us. This may seem to be an insurmountable task at first, yet we should be aware of the formidable power of the Divine Nature. We must always act, think, and be with the awareness that our divine nature is waiting to tell us what is right over what is wrong. We should recognize the Divine's plan and directives for us here on the Earth, allowing our intuitive self to control our pragmatic intellect.

We can only affect others when we have given over our egoistic wants for the grace of the divine action within us. We can only listen to the sound of our Soul and its directions when we have finished listening to the demands of the Ego mind. Then, and only then, can we give to others in a spiritual way. We have to be careful that we do not play the role of teacher or Guru before this purification process is complete. Too much intellectual knowledge can damage the "plan" here and can misguide you, for this is only another trap, another pitfall.

Those Masters (who have rightfully attained this name) are always waiting for souls to open themselves to be initiated, to move to a higher level of operation in the Divine Plan. We are all acting out our role in the cosmic play, it is just to how much of an extent. This is why at this time in the Earth's progression, when man is being given the possibility of communicating throughout the world with such rapidity, we have to be extremely careful that the influences of those who lie very low in the scale of the Earth play, those with egoistic intentions for Glory and Greed, do not gain the master controls. This is why, at the present time, it is urgent that more divinely inspired people gain a higher level of thinking, acting, and contributing for the pieces of the puzzle to be put together. We simply have to open ourselves to the possibility of acting for this purpose.

The time is now for revolution. Revolution of a spiritual nature — we have to revolt against our own participation in the undivine, unnatural, and adverse forces around us that we are allowing to consume us.

And yet, how can we be completely sure of what is more or less divine? That is why we require knowledge and guidance from those souls who are more advanced than us — those who see clearly the correct passage we should take as concerned spiritual adherents. Especially as we are in the process of destroying the last remaining, living ancient spiritual civilization — India — on the Earth today.

The true nature of a spiritual warrior is to take action, to defend, to make waves — all for the cause of Truth on Earth. For once we represent the Divine, we have to discern that which is true and that which is false around us. We can measure this — gauge it — by this test: Does this activity, object, way of being lead me toward the Divine, toward my spirit, to serve the Divine, or is it in direct contrast to it? The policies in my country, my city, my neighborhood — are they based in selflessness or selfishness, in ignorance or in wisdom? We will discuss further the levels of truth and falsity in the Western and Eastern cultures with the intention of guiding and inspiring you to act.

Greed and Materialism

To evoke a true spiritual revolution within, we first have to detach ourselves from greed and materialistic values. Greed is not good; it never was and never will be! Greed contradicts a universal law.

Capitalism's main foundation depends upon the insatiable greed that fills our minds and hearts until every little nuance of our lives and our thoughts become self-obsessed.

This excessive seeking for possessions is a sacrifice for truth, for the more we disregard others and our duty to give, to be of service, to think, act and live for others, we are living away from our true nature, our divine nature, existing only for the direct cultivation of the ego, the desire mind, and the ignorance of our human self.

Western society's progression into "civilized living" is based on the common beliefs that business, profit, and the economy will fuel goodness for all. The belief here is, as long as we are physically and materially sound, then all else should be ignored, all else should be disregarded.

Yet we all know intuitively that a life based on aggrandizement of one's ego's desires is not healthy. For the ego's nature is insatiable, never pleased, and always hungry. A "hungry ghost" is a man who lives cultivating only the physical life — and on a larger scale, a society that only cultivates materialistic aims and goals can only breed misery — and never be sated.

The course of capitalism and the implications for the world at large can be extremely bleak. Western man's egocentricity and obsession with power, world domination, and acquisition of the world's resources and control, mainly stems from his lack of ability to cultivate his spirituality.

The Eastern man, for so many thousands of years, with his metaphysical practices and philosophies, has created a race of people who are in harmony with the Earth, with the animals and, most significantly, with the Divine.

The Western man, however, is leading an extremely ignorant and dangerous life, disregarding the fact that we are not just physical, one-dimensional beings.

Indeed, this egotism has the capability of pushing away Divinity from the consciousness of *all* people on Earth.

Egotism is driving man insane and causing him to murder, rape, steal, and live forever cursed against his spirit.

Our work is to inspire people to cut loose from this greedy, egotistic sickness that is covering the Earth far too fast and furiously.

Spiritualism and the Corporate Sector

We have to engender more of a spiritual force in this barren wasteland called the corporate sector. For it will be through the corporate world that direct changes will manifest politically and globally.

Now that the corporate world has gained such influence and international power, we *must* insist on a new morality for the business sector. We have to engender a higher philosophy for working and conducting business.

The workplace today is completely unnatural. Human beings were not created to live where there is no joy, no beauty, no unity, and no community. The world of business is too detached, too cold, and calculating, worshipping the almighty dollar and profit margin.

We should change this; we should propose a correct plan of action, which would firstly instill unity and camaraderie among the workers: harmony where each person is respected, and his psychological welfare is taken into consideration. Where each becomes as a part of a "family," a force collectively, where he knows he belongs, and where he is appreciated.

This healthiness is just as important as the work performed; for the way we live life is the nature of our study; it is the ancient way to spiritual living. We must see that everything we do and think has to be done with our divine spirit in mind. Nothing can be compartmentalized (with the excuse that "this is for the profit motive.") Otherwise life becomes absurd, and the people who work in this kind of environment shrivel up and slowly die, moving far from their true Soul nature, making decisions that are wholly non-spiritual on behalf of their company. The life force within them is not being renewed nor cultivated. This is the secret of a spiritual man. He must continually seek to renew himself in the light of his higher divine nature and evoke this into the physical domain.

We should try not to emphasize dissatisfaction of our particular work but try to enhance it at all times — provoking change, suggesting to those who will be open to new ideas, new solutions for the improvement of the workplace, for the people who work there and, most importantly, to try and re-examine the nature of the company's philosophies: Does this company give back to the community or nation from whence it derives its profits? Do the people who manage it have high ideals? And perhaps now that some corporations have so much influence and power, isn't it only correct that a percentage of the profits (particularly the salaries of the highest paid executives) be put back into the support for employees, needy people, the country?

A truly spiritual state or governing body would command this of its corporations, that they have a duty to provide and look after its citizens for the good of all.

But as long as we stay quiet, as long as we deem this work too large and impossible a task, the more people will suffer, will be used and abused, both as a result of working in this unhealthy environment, and as a recipient of the way the corporations (that are non-spiritual) treat the people and the society at large. We must stop becoming automatons and incite change.

Why Does Death Occur?

Death does occur in our physical world but not in the spiritual world — therein lies its significance.

How can we master this process? And consequently, is immortality attainable?

Depending on our preparation when we die, when the physical body dies, we are thrust back in our spiritual nature and consciousness. Ultimately, if we accept that the sensory world is illusion and the Divine manifestation of the true reality, we are, at all times, existent in the death process. For the passage back to the Soul should be our preoccupation while we are living here.

It is possible to go beyond and experience the death process while our physical body is still functional. Once we have conquered the mind, brought it to a standstill, concentrating inwards, we can easily leave the physical body and enter into the inner astral realm. This astral exploration is an elementary phase in our spiritual experiencing. Therefore, we have to reach and attain a high level of consciousness while living, so when the physical body dies, we have already consecrated ourselves for the death process to be smooth and complete.

It is the death of the ego that has to occur, what we have to conquer both in the living and dying states. For our ego will perpetuate our resistance to complete immortality and spiritual freedom.

Why Is Life Here on Earth?

Inside of every little fragment, cell, and entity here on Earth is the divine force of energy. It imbues and is the invisible force that instigates all the earthly activities. Behind this force is a mind, a divine mind, that governs and directs the evolution of the physical development of all species. Behind this is the Ultimate Reality.

We are connected in such a phenomenally powerful way with this Ultimate Reality, and there are reasons beyond our mind's thinking capacity that gave birth to this creation for us.

We must pursue the experience of this Ultimate Reality, to again reach union with this primal force. The Earth is here as one of the easiest ways that we can, as human beings, reach our original state of Divinity again. When we die, we will be back in the nebulous state of the spirit. But here on Earth, mastery is much more accessible.

Life here is so sacred. We just have to answer the silent call in us to see this, to live according to this premise, and to align ourselves to our duty to the Divine.

We should seize our life's opportunity, our direction as divine subjects to utilize this paradise for our goal — Liberation.

Spiritualism and Our International Agenda

As decadence reigns, we should see it as our duty to be cognizant of the forces in power who are manipulating the world. As spiritualists, we should not shrink away from this role. Instead, we should become active in the orchestration of a more sacred Earth.

It is our role as divine "agents" to put back the world in alignment with the Divine Plan.

We should be conscious of international agendas and observe the current behavior of all nations, treating this as part of our extended nature. Our aim is to, within our realm of possibilities, take it upon ourselves to expose the less truthful leaders and nations and try to deny them their influence over the rest of the world. Take, for example, America: who claims that, with the ideals of Freedom and Democracy, she has a Divine-given right to dictate to whomever she pleases. Behind this front, she has a huge Military Industrial Complex waiting to become a comrade in arms with those who wish "freedom," to extend her "hidden" empire for the glory of fulfilling her pockets.

Kofi Annan, U.N. Secretary General, recently stated that America, as one of the world's wealthiest nations, gives the least percentage of its Gross National Product to the poor. What does this indicate? It shows that on one front, internationally, she pretends to be a savior upholding justice but, beneath this, there is a great vacuum in her character and nature.

Let us compare this to India. Internationally, even though India is the biggest democracy in the world (while China holds favored nation status in the U.S)., she is looked upon as an errant child. The media concentrates on her nuclear drama with Pakistan, completely ignoring what is significant. She is a spiritual nation. Yet, she is supposedly polytheistic and, therefore, not as credible compared to the common Christian monotheistic ideals, for the West fails to recognize the Hindu philosophy of Brahma as the first principle. So India is still looked upon with disdain as heathens, the uncivilized ones.

It is our role to educate people who have the influence in the world, to adjust current philosophies that seem to be *so* important. For example: If you are materially and militarily powerful, then your nation should be respected. If not, then of course you should be ignored.

Whatever happened to America's allegiance to her founding fathers' vision and idealism as put forth in the Constitution of the United States?

We have to set the record straight. For if we are going to spiritualize this Earth, its politics, and current democratic themes, we have to sway the general populace away from the exaggerated "Ego Freedom" bred in democracy where man has no allegiance to any principle as long as he pursues success. We must address the balance of our existence and admit that we have much to learn about the nature of man from countries such as India. Hopefully, India will not allow herself and her countrymen to be fooled by the glamorous facade portrayed with the might and infrastructure of the Western world.

The spiritual force does *not* reside in the physical — it is behind this and is embodied through the devotion of the people and the people's dedication to the spiritual, adhering to high philosophies and thought (not necessarily through religion) that breeds a healthy nation and world.

The Perfected Plan

The perfected plan involves the alignment of all minds on Earth with that of their higher divine mind, a consecration of human beings to surrender their notions of rule and law to their God-like nature. There have been civilizations on the Earth that understood this and cultivated their existence to this. They were devoted peoples and, to name a few, Egypt, Mesopotamia, Assyria, Mayan, India, China, and Tibet. This is not to exclude other peoples, but rather to highlight the more prominent cultures that we have knowledge of in the present time.

A divinized civilization has its foundation based upon spiritual principles that pervade through every layer of the society, from the political or governing elite to the social nature of its inhabitants. This civilization respects what is sacred in man, seeking to provide a cultivation of his divine reality throughout his daily life, no matter what his profession or position. It is through the dedication to the Divine that every layer of society acts and rules according to what is right and true. There can be no deviation from this; there can be no acceptance of the cultivation of the basest aspects of human nature, for this would defeat the purpose of existence and incarnation. This kind of civilization would be the result of a perfected plan, where we all allow our "free" will to be joined with our divine will — where we turn our minds toward our sacred Dharma or purpose.

For as long as we remain untransformed and immature, as long as we allow the powers who are governing us incorrectly to steer us away from perfection, we will become more and more lost, unable to utilize the Earth. We have to prepare ourselves to receive the descent of the highest force and energy into the consciousness here. This super energy, if received on the Earth, could have such a powerful transformative effect on, not only the human race, but also the entire world.

The Kali Yuga

For those of you who are unaware of the Goddess or Archetype Kali — she is one of the most feared Goddesses in the Hindu pantheon. At one time on Earth all peoples worshipped the Gods or Archetypes and mostly all civilizations had a representative that was destructive. For change to be implemented, to be sure that the light or Divine consciousness can descend on the Earth, there has to be destruction. Destruction of false systems and forms instigated by man that do not have any celestial bearing. According to the ancient Yogis and Hindus, now is the time on Earth of the Kali Yuga, the time when the Divine has to wash away redundant patterns in order to make room for the new.

Many faiths refuse to recognize the destructive face of the Divine, ascertaining that since God is almighty, that the state of the world is meant to be, that the "ruin" of our Earth environmentally, socially, culturally, and politically is "God's will." This could not be further from the truth.

We are *all* God. We are the makers and breakers of our own destiny. If we ignore the Divine's plan for us here on Earth, unfortunately, (or rather fortunately for us in the long run), the Supreme being, the highest aspect of us, will seize the opportunity to eliminate, to disregard what is unnecessary.

Yet we must all play a part in this action; we all have to become Divine Ambassadors, precipitating positive changes, disregarding what is false around us, in our lives, in our minds, and in the area of society in which we participate.

We must judge what is right over what is wrong. We must be strict and disciplinary about the important factors in life. We should not allow typical behaviors and constraints of our society to hold us back, to render us ineffectual. We *have* to activate ourselves, cultivating a healthy attitude that as individuals we have the possibility of becoming divinized, and with this divinity we can influence and change existing institutions, whether they be governmental, corporate, or educational.

Why should we consecrate ourselves to this aim? Because this is what is being asked of us — we are being called, as warriors — to clandestinely influence others. We have to allow the Kali force to work through us — for she is ruthless in her destruction of evil — and so we shall be fearless. No matter what others think, we have our work and our direction. The spiritual revolution will carefully and fairly make these changes for the good of all.

Directing Your Force

As we enter into a spiritual life, we naturally become more aware of our loving nature, our propensity to give and live in a spirit of goodness and kindness. Yet we should be careful that the wrong people are not recipients of this divine energy, so that it is not wasted and misdirected.

When you are in pursuit of purity and inner purification, it is important to surround yourself with those who are pure in their hearts and minds toward you. For in your endeavor to become more spiritual, to create a new personality of a divine nature, it is important that those around you are accepting and positive. If they are negative, resentful and egotistical; if you find that you are being inhibited and your spiritual self is not allowed to be expressed in your home, this can be + contrary to your spiritual aim and goal, and where earthly relations can actually hinder your spiritual Dharma.

This is when you must make decisions and prioritize the divine calling in you as opposed to being victimized by those, even family and friends, who cannot relate to your path.

Of course, we cannot simply eliminate people present in our lives because they don't respect our spiritual aspirations. We must try to change this person, carefully and subtly inspiring him also to take this direction toward spiritual inquiry and action.

Many times, particularly in the Western world, where true spirituality is rarely recognized, (rather only religion and belief systems are acknowledged), we may find ourselves alone, unable to relate any more to the thoughts and actions and people of our former "life." So we should try to make the best of a potentially difficult situation, and if you have tried and failed to convince those close to you; if they refuse to be influenced, it is best to leave them where they are and move onward.

We should direct our force, our energy, to those who are truly our spiritual brothers and sisters, creating a new spiritual family of like-minded souls, ready to work together for collective fulfillment and destiny.

The Master

Who is the Master? The Master is within. All of us have unrealized Masters in our consciousness, this God-head of perfection.

The very fact that we are unrealized requires that we seek this realization, this unveiling of our true identity. If we can accept that we are unrealized, we should be able to accept that there are those existent in the physical and non-physical realms who *are* realized, who are Masters. Within the Divine Order, there is a blueprint to facilitate realization; and mastery where one becomes a receptacle of high consciousness. The Master is a clear echo of the God force in man.

A true Master should be able to transform and initiate another person into his masterhood; although it is not the duty for a Master to take disciples, this can be one of his roles. A Master in today's world, should be aware not only of man's perpetual state of ignorance and the necessary techniques to eradicate this and awaken man, he should also be knowledgeable about the international and national situations — seeing himself as a necessary instrument able to discuss with either politician or industrialist, able to direct plans for the improvement and orientation of our society. A true Master, connected with the Cosmic Mind, knows the plan for the balance of powers on Earth and how to conduct these plans and what steps have to be taken.

* * *

The Disciple

We are graced if we attain this title. If we are accepted by a Master to pursue a path of discipline and devotion to the ultimate destination. We say it is an honor, because to serve one who is illumined can only be a blessing; to be in the presence of a Master takes us closer to our Soul and leads us to our Dharma or path.

We are all disciples until we can end the duality of our mind and attain perfect surrender; no matter what the situation, we have to command this of ourselves, allowing our true self to quiet the boisterous and rebellious ego nature.

The Woman

Ask not of the human nature in this description for this is known — mother, wife, sister, daughter. What we seek is the divine worker and companion. What we seek is the divine woman manifested. A creature, a daughter of the Mother Goddess, and her role to embody beauty, serenity, goodness, joy, and harmony — the male characteristics should accompany the above-mentioned qualities. By this we mean strength, courage, an assertion of the male mind and force from within.

Yet, should this change the outer body? Should we forget to uphold the form given to us at birth?

A woman has truly captured her sacredness if she remembers the value of celebrating her femininity combined with her masculinity in her dress, her manner, her mind, and her actions. (This is something that the Western woman should heed.)

If she resists this, determined to redraw or redefine her role, then she will push away her Soul's true nature manifesting in the physical form. Absolutely everything we do and how we present ourselves is of the utmost importance. As women, we must be sure that we are correct in our alignment with our divine archetype or force, in this case, the Mother Goddess.

* * *

The Man

As a man strives to prove his identity and place in the world, he should be careful not to mistake the ego's projection for his true nature. Too easily the role playing projected on the Western man is tailored to his ego. In the East, we find men who are much closer to an inner harmony — more female and refined and more subtle than their Western counterparts.

The divine man should take into serious consideration the true spiritual aspects of existence and plan the world around him accordingly. For too long in the West, the male has failed to seek harmony with his female aspect or energy within. He is driven by sheer brute force, carving out a male-oriented world that is consequently disharmonious — devoid of the female force.

It is time to reshape the male: he should step down from his assertiveness and arrogance and act according to his intuitive, natural self. With humility, he should observe the Eastern, specifically Indian male — for there he will find a spiritual male, one who is not afraid to explore his higher self, his devoted self, and bow down to the Mother Goddess.

Fears and Desires

When the Divine gave us free will, we decided to forget our principle creator, hence the human condition. We chose to reap the benefits of the senses and lavish in the fruits of the Divine's efforts and works. When we became full of desire, we began to fear what the world would be like if we could not fulfill our desires.

Then we just feared and didn't even know why, but deep down we were suffering from the angst of dissociation with our Soul. We had created a new personality, a poor replica of our true personality, which is only reinforced, the further we stay away from true inquiry.

All fear can be eradicated and all desire can be redirected, fueling the creative force or fire, for a divine purpose and allowing our true personality to blossom, not just to repress these ego traits, but to vanquish them for good, as you are elevated toward your Soul.

* * *

Likes and Dislikes

As long as we allow our petty obsessions to shape our spirit, we will keep ourselves locked in the illusion, unable to find out who we are without these constant attachments to our behavior.

We can even cultivate likes and dislikes for our "spiritual ego," which can be dangerous, dictating to ourselves which way and in what manner we should commune with the Divine.

Likes and dislikes must be ignored; then true surrender can be established within.

Animals and Ecology

It is important that animals and ecology be treated correctly, respected and honored.

The foolish lies, that animals are devoid of a Soul, should be stopped and, of course, the arrogant way man is refusing to respect his ecological balance with nature has to be rectified.

When will we learn?

When our water dries up?

When our air is so polluted we need to wear masks?

When will the outrage begin?

When will people stand up and revolt?

* * *

Yogic Attitudes

A Yogic lifestyle involves simplicity of the mind and simplicity of living.

One can embrace the attitude of a Yogi when one has tested oneself, entering all the fires of the Earth and come out untainted.

Our mind should not be attached to any aspect of the Earth, but pass through, keeping the purity of the Soul.

When we have a craving, to abstain or gorge ourselves in life, for the most part, the Buddhist's middle way is preferred and conducive for a spiritual temperament.

A Master Yogi, however, should not and does not have to abide by the human decisions of what is and is not divine. If he is illumined, he can choose any aspect of life to initiate and test his students.

Therefore, Yogic life to a spiritual Master is a continuing form of initiation wherever he is and whatever he is doing.

How the Masters of the White Lodge are Governing and Directing the Earth's Plan

Behind the scenes of the play on Earth, behind the so-called power machinery of our world, there are, and have always been, divine directors, observing, guiding, and urging mankind to steer itself toward the divine plan. The Maha Cholan Master Koot Humi and Master Morya, the two Masters who are the writers of this book, are deceased, but they still operate from a more subtle realm of consciousness. These Masters, and others of the same caliber, are the true governors; they are enlightened.

For them to implement the Divine Plans, we all have to become open and willing instruments; and then, through us, they and the divine can work.

* * *

How to Become Attuned to These Plans

With your mind concentrating on this one thought, ask with sincerity to be in touch with these Masters. Make yourself silent and offer up your life and its works for theirs.

We should not, however, wish for immediate results. The Masters are cautious and choose their workers carefully. Humility, devotion, surrender, and dedication are significant qualities that we should embody continuously, being ready to change our lives for this cause, ready to submit all that was the old personality before, for the possibility of this blessed work.

Why Western Spiritualists Are Confused

Confusion is usually party to assumption. And, here in the West, we assume about the spiritual realms and have not learned through direct experience. Our culture is not founded by great rishis, nor does it function, governed by wise men.

There are so many here who are not true Masters, who act as if they are, presenting their ideas, their formula for inquiry and the healing arts; yet they themselves are not purified nor deified to act in such a manner. Knowledge can be worthless in the wrong hands.

How can we learn about the spiritual path from mock leaders and false teachers? Our only salvation is to turn away from Western spiritualism and investigate the highly perfected formulae from India and the East.

* * *

What We Have to Learn from the Eastern Man and What We Are Refusing to Acknowledge

Of course, ultimately there is no East or West; yet as the races have developed and chosen their directions, the advancement of the Eastern man, his philosophies, his mastery over the inner realms, and the elevation of consciousness throughout his race is a complete contrast to the man of the West. The Westerner has conquered almost everything but the inner realms, ironic really, for this is the only "place" worth investigating. From discovery of the Soul, all order will arise and not before.

Refusal as a nation and as spiritualists to recognize this achievement, will be our downfall. For the Eastern man almost believes, due to media hype and materialistic colonization, that he is secondary, that he is poor, that his heritage is quaint and charming, but really can the "leader" of the world — America — take it seriously?

Because Western rulers fail to surrender to their divine selves, an injection of a dangerous spirit is being given to the consciousness of the new generation of Indians and Asians. They have the materialistic bug — the glamour bug, the greedy bug. Let us hope that the traditions and the wealth of knowledge that these civilizations stand for will not be buried by the tidal wave of arrogance bred here in the West.

May the Eastern man heed this warning: *Do not sell your Soul!*

How to Conquer the Strife in Our Mind

As the mind is the extension of the spirit, instead of listening, worrying, and contemplating the disturbances in the mind, we can remedy this by calling upon the spirit to put an end to all confusion.

We should be careful when entering the spiritual path that we do not try to purify the mind through intellectual reckonings; we can be sure of failure, for the human mind does not know the answers, and the intellect cannot produce them! It is through the silent master of the spirit that resolve can be sought and the intellectual and emotional probings conquered and found.

There are different "layers" of the mind and we most necessarily have to strive to attain our Overmind, and eventually our Cosmic mind — this clear and inspired divine mind is the state that we have to seek.

* * *

The Ego Nature

Before we attain a unity of our higher spirit and our earthly self, Jivatman, there is a division in our mind — thoughts are sent by and to us from two distinct voices. If we study ourselves closely we can hear at times these two voices. One voice stems from the individual ego self, whose integration and destruction is the work of the spiritual man. This voice, unfortunately, guides us incorrectly, clinging to the intellectual side of man and to the negative attributes of human nature. This voice, too many times, acts and reacts to the Earth play and steers us away from the second voice in our mind.

This second voice is mainly silent. If we allow the ego voice to be quiet, we will hear the true self and can connect with our inner true voice. Our "true self" voice is connected directly with the intuition and will always steer us correctly in our lives.

To combat the lure and lies of the ego, we have to proceed as if we are surgeons, diligently rejecting and detaching from this unnecessary voice and dictator. To be freed, from a divine perspective, is to be able to negate what is primarily human, directing our mind and consciousness upward toward that which is divine.

We must withdraw from the false voice, especially if it is trying, either through fear or ignorance, to resist surrender. And it will, at first, resist, because the ego never wants to die — it wants to claim its self-importance and individualism. Nothing can be attained if we pursue the "empowerment" of the ego.

If we adhere to the sensory mind that draws us closer to terrestrial existence, we will fall away from our real endeavor and spiritual purpose. Our mind is not a play thing, and what we think is not without consequence or meaning. The mastery of the mind is a deliberate and significant aspect of our spiritual task.

When we listen to the whims, to the self-absorbed thoughts, we are lost! We must seize ourselves and be determined to conquer the stray and malaligned echoes from the earthly illusion.

If we wish for Divinity, we have to engender and dynamize ourselves to capture the ego every time, to reject what we recognize as false and evoke the truth from our spirit. As soon as we have closed the door to self absorption, we will be given help and signs by the Divine to assist us in our task.

It is the mind and the emotions that are two of the greatest hindrances for the sadhak, the student.

The emotional self plays tricks with its demands and vacuums. Yet it is only through perfected purification, and, if you are lucky, in the presence of a Master, that you can fill this vacuum and quiet this turmoil for good. For as long we pine perennially for redemption, for whatever reason, we cannot turn our mind, still our mind, and answer the call from our Soul.

In the beginning, we can easily be confused by the demands of the ego — not knowing that it is he, the false self, calling out — forsaking the sound of the true self and the true voice. We must be sure not to become too absorbed distinguishing which is the true and which the false voice.

It is here that we should direct our concentration away from the individual mind and seek to find the answer from the higher, intuitive mind and spirit.

The intuition is, in fact, our real friend and guide; and the intellect a mere tool and of a lower nature.

Intuition

Intuition is the Master of the intellect and not vice versa. It is the more silent of the two aspects, and we can be sure that our intuition will guide us correctly, which is more than can be said for the intellect!

If one listens to intuition, one can capture the messages sent down from the Soul directing us here on the Earth. We can know things intuitively long before we can justify them intellectually. Indeed, the divine way of living should not adhere to human beliefs nor ways. It is a force of its own. If we allow ourselves to live by our intuition, we will exist with a much simpler outlook and way of being.

The Child Consciousness

Great Masters delivered this form of initiation to the Earth in the hope that those souls who were ready could glance into their own child conscious mind and remember the freedom,. abandon, and bliss that is so inevitably accessible to them. This is a rather new form of initiation, and it is a technique using the inner personality that is inherent in man already, to lead him back to his celestial side.

When one allows oneself to play and be the child again, he reserves nothing of his inner ego. In fact, the entire purpose of this exercise is to exorcise the false from within; abandoning all to the play.

It may seem a superficial procedure but, in fact, it is extremely serious and profound. In the 20th Century Jung spoke of this; Ananda Devi, Premananda Deva, and Lakshmi Devi have all experienced this.

It is possible to bring a sadhak to a deepened state of child consciousness by creating a chamber where everything of the physical needs are taken care of — food, water, shelter, etc. Then, in the company of a spiritual guide or teacher, the sadhak, with complete surrender and conscious suggestion, can enter and stay in the child conscious state for hours, days, even as long as a week.

This can be a tool for rapid and lasting purification. The sadhak has again returned to the paradise of the two-year old, even a one-year old infant.

From this state, the sadhak can be led consciously back to his adult age, with the careful guidance and penetration of the teacher. This is the time to purge traumatic events that previously shaped and formed the old encrusted ego personality.

The "adult" mind has now been fused with the Divine child mind. This becomes the foundation — the base of the Soul consciousness, from which we "build."

For without a lasting and complete riddance of the old phobias and forms, the divine energy, shakti, will have difficulty residing within you.

The Necessity for a Master

Ask a Western man about this, and he will almost certainly, with exceptions, tell you, and he will even write about out, how he *does not* require the presence of a Master for Initiation and Illumination.

How foolish is he! For every Master has had a Master, visible or invisible. And the man of the East knows this universal law to be true. It is just typical of the Western Democratic man to think ignorantly, "I can do it by myself!" and yet, he has not. Yet, every generation in India has produced a Buddha or Realized Soul.

The Master is a divine blessing for the sadhak, and a living embodiment of truth consciousness, who guides, protects and, by his presence, can Initiate.

If we deny the necessity of a Master, we deny the hierarchy that exists between us and the original Brahma. Do we suppose that with our "imperfect" consciousness, the Divine will allow us to commune with its highest aspects. We must be careful not to fall into any traps that we set for ourselves. For as we open our spirit and experience energy coming into us (do not allow the ego to become attached to these experiences), it is then that a teacher is necessary, for the refinement of our earthly consciousness for Initiation, to ascend and eventually to allow the descent, and continuation for the integration of the Soul Self on the Earth.

Initiation

Initiation is the process that facilitates our entrance and integration into a higher level of Divine consciousness.

Initiation comes to us when we have prepared ourselves enough to attain Illumination.

The highest consciousness will send us an emissary, an Illumined One, to facilitate our ascent.

Initiation is essential for Soul Realization. It is the Master's gift to the sadhak, and it is only through initiation that one can be Realized.

Initiation is not merely the passing on of mantras or rituals, but the immersion of the sadhak's spirit, with surrender, into the Master. He becomes one with the Master — their mind and spirit become ONE — and then, the sadhak can be transported into a state of consciousness sent to him by the Master.

Initiation is essential for Soul Realization.

* * *

Lila

This world is merely a stage, and we are actors in this play. On the spiritual path we have to be ferociously serious, for we certainly cannot become realized without a determination, and a faith, that we *will* master this reality.

The Earth is a "celestial playground," a platform for our entrance into the Lila, the cosmic play, which is the realm of truth and absolute divinity.

Purgation

What we have to purge is the ego and its stubbornness and refusal to obey us. We have to be ready for battle; for this is the hardest enemy to fight — the ignorance within. We have to judge ourselves, registering the false from the true and choosing to limit our concentration to the real. We must seek this vital purgation in order to precipitate purification.

* * *

Purification

Purification is the goal — once we are pure in our heart, mind, and spirit — only then can the Divine spirit occupy us. When our vessel is empty, when we have unlearned all earthly learning, when we have sought to distinguish arrogance from humility — the gift of giving over selfishness — then our divine Self can embrace us and allow our true nature to be free within.

* * *

Fire

Fire is an essential aspect of change. It is one of the primordial cosmic forces that we should acquaint ourselves with and strive for in order to precipitate transformation.

The Physical Body

The physical body's condition is very important, because it is the vehicle for the spirit and Soul. Yet one must not become obsessed and preoccupied with this and forget about the sixth sense, the Divine.

* * *

Healing Force

Healing forces are always abundant in the Universe; it is just a case of knowing how to harness them and having the correct disposition to direct them. The living force, Shakti, has the capability of healing any and all ailments, and the potential for success of this transfer of energy depends solely on the practitioner. If he has not been purified nor initiated, this can be a hindrance for the patient.

Self healing and the power of the individual is limitless. We can rejuvenate the quintessence of every cell. Such is the force of the invisible realm over the visible.

* * *

Abandonment

One must not, in his attempt to become spiritual, make a belief system out of any of his activities in the physical realm, whether this be eating, for example.

Abandonment is an essential part of the play for a sadhak, and we must be sure to sometimes break even so-called "good" habits in order to test ourselves and experiment with our spirit inside of us.

The Nature of Brahma

Brahma is the first principle, the creator, the originator of everything we see in the physical, derived directly from the invisible. We are all Brahma. We never disengaged from Brahma; we only projected ourselves into a manifestation on the surface of Brahma. It is our work and duty to return to this original state, to return to our original nature and existence.

* * *

The Divine Mother

She is the Mother of this Universe; she presides, destroys and creates at her will. She is the female principle of "the maker."

Her force, not honored in the West, has always been a significant part of worship for all the ancients and even today in the East. It is this worship and devotion to the female principle and her living force, which descends to the Earth, that has kept the cohesion of ancient practices alive and for so many thousands of years. This has held the fabric of ancient civilization. For what is seen above, is then ingested psychologically in the people below. It is this very factor, missing from the Western belief systems, that has caused so much disharmony and upset. The repercussions will be felt for hundreds of years if we do not again recognize the Divine Mother as an essential part of the higher principle.

USA, Europe, Africa, Asia: What Should We Expect?

Expectations are projections of what we would like to come to fruition. We would expect that the world at large will start to re-examine herself and move toward a more complete way of being. Humanity cannot survive alone from the support of the military and economic might. Divine principles were certainly not considered when Western man adopted his directive for living toward the profit motive. Indeed, the faults of our present condition in the West can be directed at our complete disregard for pursuit of elevated spiritual guidance that religion had us believe was too far away to attain or even strive to adhere to its principles. So Western man has decided to play "God."

The Europeans, the forefathers of the Americans, may have had a little more dedication and respect for the individual's search for freedom. Yet America, the so-called land of the free, actually is the land of hypocrisy, where the expectation is to become successful materially but all else be damned. We can expect more so-called "superior" policing of the world, the moral adjudicator, the military stronghold, the successful materialist. We can also expect more insanity and bereavement from the Americans who follow blindly the powers that have gained control over their minds.

The Europeans will follow in America's footsteps; their voracious greed is also on par with the Democratic giant.

There will be two kinds of Africans: the city dweller and the native dweller. The latter will stay in his spiritual self, close to nature and pagan rituals. The city dweller, the farther he moves into the mentality of the materialistic West, will lose sight of his heritage and his spirit. This is really the deciding factor in the direction of man: He must never lose sight of his racial and spiritual foothold, which was given to him at birth. If he eliminates this from his consciousness, he will be losing his divine passage.

Asia, and the countries that are still steeped in the ancient philosophies of Hinduism and Buddhism (in all of its forms), have an advantage. We can expect an exciting melange of East and West, the ancient and the modern together. Asia, and specifically India, is the Mother and the teacher of the rest of the world. Whether or not she recognizes and realizes this (after so much repression firstly by the Islamic invaders and then the British) has yet to be seen.

The Asian man must take the advancements of the materialistic Western man, and put them in their place. Materialism is the sickness of man. We have to discern, when it is the right time to stop the adulation of Western morals and start reorganizing our philosophies for living. Then the military, the corporate, and the political fields will have their rightful position — one that does not wreak havoc on the minds of the people worldwide.

For if we are not careful, the entire world will fall under the spell of Western materialistic values and the state of man will become more and more desperate. We have to act now, to reinstate the correct balance of powers, the correct Divine plan on Earth.

The East must proudly show her brilliance and not surrender herself in the wrong direction.

The Illusion — Maya

What if everything you believed to be real were an illusion? What if this "real" illusion were a playground — an intangible revelation? If we search enough into the antiquities of the Vedas and the Upanishads, we would find here written the secrets of existence. We would find souls who had gone beyond the manifested illusion into the Source, into the reality, and answered the call of the Soul that beckons us into eternity.

For this world, this physical Earth, is but illusion. We are echoes of the cosmic voice of "God."

* * *

Gifts from the Divine

A gift is an experience that takes us out of our "world" into the Divine, out of our closed minds into the eternal expansiveness of illumination. This gift is to be respected. It is a message, an invocation from our Soul, that it is time to further investigate ourselves, time to dedicate our inner world toward a "Life Divine."

Spiritual Revolution

Revolution from within is the first prerequisite for the pursuit of Illumination. One must reject the false in order to live in the truth. If we are to divinize our society, we have to provoke a revolt from *inside* the people.

Connotations of revolt usually imply a state of anarchy, but quite the opposite is true for spiritual revolution. One elevates oneself to become cognizant of the divine order and plan which, when obeyed, always directs us toward the good and away from what is bad.

Spiritual Revolution in the right hands can prove to be much more favorable than conformity in the wrong hands!

One's courage is the deciding factor. We have to become warriors of truth, crusaders for liberation on every level of our society, from the political, to the corporate, down to the layman. We have to dare to be different and choose to liberate our entire life to the good, to defend and represent spiritual change.

Unfortunately, in the past, those seeking the spiritual life have mostly shunned the *integral purpose* of the spiritual man. True and profound change can only come from those who are inspired, those whose intent does not hide a hidden, selfish agenda.

It is time now to activate spiritual men and women. Wherever you are, and whatever role you may be performing in life, you must give yourself, not only a human agenda, but include also a divine agenda. Set your goals realistically; communicate with others who also are of like mind; working together, we can make a difference. Working freelance, if necessary, clandestinely influencing and inspiring people to become aware that we can change society from within. Each one of us has a phenomenal capability to precipitate change, bringing back spiritual ideals into our lives. We should not allow the forces in power (on Earth) to dampen our determination or will. If we agree to defeat ourselves before we have begun, then the Earth will continue to follow its destiny of materialism and ignorance. The time is now, and we must prepare ourselves for battle!

Perfection on Earth

This physical manifestation is an Illusion, a passageway for realization of the Real behind the senses. Many of us forget why we are here on Earth. Many of us do not believe perfection is attainable.

This world was created out of perfection, as we were created out of perfection. The physical illusion is here to assist us in our quest for this remembrance.

We must return, while still in the world, to our most natural and regal self. We have to adjust and readjust until the alignment with our invisible perfection is possible, allowing the light to demystify us, wiping away all human solemnities and replacing them with joy and truth.

* * *

The Supramental Light

The Supramental Light is unquestionably the most powerful force that man can occupy in his celestial union on Earth. This light has the force to change all life on Earth. This force has yet to descend on the Earth completely, for the receptacles here are too few.

The light radiating from this consciousness supersedes any imaginings we can conjecture. It is a wish from the Supreme to allow this consciousness to descend, through Cosmic workers, to do its work. It can be pictured as a divine ocean of magnificent force that can only be received, and is only allowed entry on Earth, into those instruments who can distribute this energy as the divine wishes.

When it descends, this force crushes the recipient. It is an unparalleled experience, a flow from the pressurized waterfall of Divine energy, which enters and transforms one's spirit, mind, and body. The master spirit possesses you and you become a slave to the highest light and work for humanity.

Collectively, we should strive to become conduits for this supramental consciousness by evoking this refined force down into the "heavy" consciousness of the physical plane. We can change people from the inside out by spiritual osmosis.

This way, the Supreme will fulfill its plan, as we become beacons of light, radiating and pulsating with this force.

Sri Aurobindo, Ramana Maharishi, and Ananda Devi

To give examples of the most perfected Souls on Earth in the 20th Century, we have to recognize *Sri Aurobindo*, the Avatar from India, who was initially known as the freedom fighter behind India's independence. He brought to the Earth the dawn of a new era for spirituality — his philosophies, surpassing and elucidating — where perhaps no one on Earth had before.

With a direct link to the superconscious mind, he wrote great works such as *The Life Divine* and the epic poem *Savitri*. It is from Sri Aurobindo that we learn of Supramental consciousness and the reason that this consciousness has descended on Earth, for the betterment of mankind. This spiritual titan was a complete Yogi, who surpassed even the Rishis of the Vedas, and serves as the highest example for all neophyte sadhaks.

The great, smiling, childlike eyes, and the luminous face of *Bhagavan Ramana Maharishi* never failed to inspire all who came into his presence. Merely by gazing at his photograph one can understand the meaning of Illumination and how it may pervade on the Earth.

Had it not been for Ramana Maharishi in 1947, Ananda Devi would never have entered her Atman. This tells us that we human beings require Initiation, that helping hand, from an Illumined one who lives in a higher spiritual consciousness. The Earth's density is too great, even in the invisible realm, to do it alone.

Ananda Devi, after suffering as a student in a pension in France, had a supreme determination to discover what was in life and beyond. Sri Aurobindo came to her in the dream state at age sixteen, and by eighteen she had experienced Cosmic Consciousness. Preparing for a life of brilliance, she fought all of life's battles utterly fearless in the face of adversaries and problems. Ananda Devi never lost sight of the Ultimate objective, which was to remain in the truth, loyal to the truth consciousness, and the world plan given to her by Master Djwal Kool in 1949. This catapulted her into the world scene in France, India, and America, contributing from high planes of consciousness to the elimination of the Cold War and intervening in the Gulf War. She personified the Superwoman. A Supramentalized being in life, she experimented and formulated techniques for the Initiation of the Western man into the secrets of the East.

Ananda Devi initiated her primary disciple, Premananda Deva, an American, in New York City in 1960. Soon afterward, Deva experienced Enlightenment and continued his studies and work with Ananda Devi for thirty-four years until her passing in 1994.

Premananda Deva's Role as Initiator

A true Master will serve to bring disciples to a state of enlightenment, and this is evident in the teachings of Premananda Deva. Being aware of the purification and preparation required for the Westerner in the spiritual, he is finely tuned with techniques for the destruction of the ego, bringing his disciples to the state of Cosmic Consciousness. He has the refinement and devotion of the Eastern Spirit with his Western mind.

He is extremely rare on the Earth, and is an essential cosmic worker, who has the capability of steering America, and the world, back in the right direction.

Lakshmi Devi, Deva's closest disciple, was initiated by him in 1994 and experienced her Atman. She is an inspiration to women and an example that liberation is possible in this lifetime. As a medium of the highest order, Lakshmi is the channel through which messages from the Brothers of the White Lodge pass.

Messages vs. Prayers

We may consider prayer an art of communion with our spirit and the Divine, yet prayer is a poor form of surrender. We must not want to take from the Divine, when we firstly have not given! We have to observe and study the mind and be cautious that one is not asking from the Ego consciousness.

Yet if we have a sincere calling to the Divine for guidance from our true self, we may receive answers. We have to strive to ascend to the Divine, and only then can we be ready to receive a message from the higher spheres. Only then, will any kind of answer come, when spiritual transformation is our highest goal and mission.

Rituals and Discipline

Since man has worshipped the Divine, he has sought out inspired communion to ensure that the higher forces would descend into him, regularly, sustaining a harmony, psychologically and spiritually. Unfortunately, there are few true ritualistic practices left on Earth. Indeed all the ancient civilizations practiced rituals. Today, we can experience the Sanskrit mantras and pujas of the Yogis, Hindus, and the Buddhists, which can evoke a high consciousness, merely by the pronunciation of sacred words (along with other practices).

Yet ritual should be accompanied with the practice of pratyahara, a withdrawal of the senses, to ensure that one does not become dependent on the ritual, as the sole means for purification. Discipline, in the form of concentration and contemplation, is essential along with dedication and surrender. Added to this, we have to enforce the destruction of the ego, so that the true self and spirit can flow through us.

We have to become desirous of discipline in order to check ourselves, to prepare our entrance into the Divine Self, harnessing our unruly human projections: allowing the true, free-flowing force to possess us, then life itself becomes one long, devoted ritual to the Supreme.

Discipline from the Master

If one has the grace of living and serving under a Master, he will have the opportunity of observing a Soul who no longer lives in duality. The Master represents the true self, the Soul, and we will only see a separation between us and him if we live in the world of duality. It is his role, then, to bring the student to a state of oneness. To effectively do this, the Master will require from the student a spirit of complete surrender at all times: no matter what the task set before the student, he must not obey the ego spirit within but embody the spirit of truth.

This way, the powerful spirit of the Master can fuse with the student, and the two minds become one: of one thought, one spirit, thus ending the duality.

If the student, however, chooses to disobey, to resist, to show contempt, anger, sadness, etc., it is the role of the Master to discipline, and aid the student to direct himself back to the true nature again.

The Master does not have to accept any students. Out of compassion, the Master will attempt to guide another back to his Soul.

Discipline from the Master is the voice of truth consciousness, reminding us to persist in our purification. Many times, we may be tested, to see how attached we are to our egoistic traits. The Master can see, at all times, even at a distance, the state of surrender within his student.

The Master serves as a beacon of light, and from him the shakti-energy will pour forth into his students.

Destruction of the Old Forms

The "old forms" will prevent us from uncovering the true knowledge within. We were born with all knowledge. Indeed, our Soul is the container of all knowledge, but we, the social animal, have acquired many sheaths to cover up our pristine Self.

If we decide to become permanently attached to our old habits, emotions, thoughts, mannerisms, fears, anger, desires, and projected plans for our lives, we will most certainly never know our true nature, our true self, our Soul.

We must see *destruction* as an essential part of the spiritual life. For without the destruction of the false within us, how can there be room for the true?

It is a battle, and the hardest one we will fight as humans, but the reward is also the highest and the reason for our incarnation on Earth. Any other pursuit will bear only illusory fruit, and we will die again and again from lifetime to lifetime, simply to learn that we must pursue the true reality and attain immortality. This is how serious "destruction of the old" is.

* * *

Complacency and Emotional Scars

One can become complacent; even on the path, he can slip into a state of satisfied delusion and take on the appearance to himself and others that he is spiritual. We must be very wary of this form of arrogance, for it will stunt the growth and direction of your spiritual Dharma.

Emotional scars must be overcome for a completion of our spirit nature. One cannot project anger, depression, self-pity, and fear onto the Divine. There is no room for self-absorbed emotions for the true divine subject. He must create a catharsis and be able to detach himself from the traumatic event or person and *forget* this part of the earthly personality.

Once he has rejected this enough and willfully projects himself toward the creation of a new self, a spiritual self, he conquers the Karmic cycle. Then the spiritual force can be born in you, and it is the beginning of a life of joy, purity, and a oneness within.

Lies of the Persona

The persona is the ego nature; this persona is the voice in the mind that can only live in negativity. It will try to fool us; to get its own way, it will try to justify and intellectualize itself into existence. It can produce many personalities, just to coddle its wants and desires. Indeed it is the *enemy* for the spiritual aspirant. It is the enemy within. But we shouldn't be alarmed, because this part of us is also part of the illusion. It is made from the illusory, sensory world and belongs in this world. We have to dehypnotize ourselves to stop listening to the persona's voice. We have to firmly turn our mind away and delve deeper within to find the true voice, to discover and uncover our true self.

The lies of the persona may fool others, but the Soul knows at all times and judges us at all times. There is a permanent state of judgment from our true nature that we all have to obey. It is this obedience that will be our salvation.

* * *

The Spiritual Man

The spiritual man never hides from the truth. Indeed, he will reveal and provoke truth from those around him. One may not see the inner workings of the spiritual man, just by his exterior faces. For it is within that the spiritual man guards and protects his spirit, only to be revealed at the auspicious time to those he deems ready to receive it.

Indeed, the physical face of man does show us the map of the Soul, and the spiritual ones exude beauty, joy, and strength. Their eyes are powerful and can see through you in one glance.

The spiritual man will, at many different times, manifest the divine archetypes within him — from stern to sweetness, whatever he deems correct — for the delivery of whatever Dharma or action at that time.

The spiritual man can also camouflage himself, all for his divine mission, moving in any circle — from the political to corporate to the layman — with facility. He is the master magician, able to present himself, fitting into every occasion with guile and adeptness. He is equipped by knowing the workings and nature of those in front of him, and always will charm, and attempt to captivate for the sake of his divine role. He never shrinks, never refuses anyone. He is all-compassionate and a ready warrior. Using his perfected mind and intelligence he inspires and directs all who are willing toward the correct direction.

Judgment vs. Hypocrisy

The Soul contains our innate knowledge of right and wrong. When we were born we contained this knowledge, but slowly society projected its views of morality and behavior upon us. It is our goal to recapture our innate judgment and discard society's program for us.

In the West, the society around us is based on lies. We are the containers of these lies. We have to start by judging ourselves to seek Truth. We will find significant evidence that those around us are caught by the lies; we also have to judge them. For if we do not judge, we will harbor a psychological impurity inside of us, which will perpetuate our sickness.

There are two forms of judgment, and it is imperative that we distinguish the correct from the incorrect form.

The correct form, as discussed, allows us to step out of our personal psychological drama and precipitates correct thinking and purity within. Once we have eliminated our programming, we can start to become a free thinker and free spirit.

The incorrect form of judgment originates in the ego-consciousness, which determines the action of others from its belief system and psychological imperfections. This judgment belittles and harms others for the sake of superiority and/or sadism for the human ego.

Unfortunately, many religious institutions have misused this latter derivation of judgment, which leaves people feeling confused and psychologically deranged.

If we do not judge from our Soul's perspective, we will perpetuate a hypocritical society and way of being. Certainly, one does not alienate those judged as wayward or wrong in his action; rather, the spiritual man chooses, by virtue of devoting himself to be a divine representative, to treat everyone with sincerity and consideration.

It takes courage to judge, and it is an act of cowardice to live in hypocrisy.

Archetypes and the Spiritual Man

Before two thousand years ago in the West, before the advent of the dissolution of paganism, people would not worship each other — they worshipped the Gods, the *true* divine archetypes, who emanated beauty and force originating from a divine source and when they communed with these archetypes, the mind and spirit of the people became one with this force sent down from the respective archetypes. They were divinized because of this devotional practice. They were uplifted and purified.

To compare this form of devotion and method for the divinization of man with modern man's hollow obsession with his false icons, illustrates how he has fallen away from his true direction, en masse.

To recapture man, we have to become the new archetypes, appealing to him, presenting a side of ourselves that is beautiful and pleasing. We have to become the representatives of the Gods and Goddesses incarnate. Creatures that personify perfection, exuding light, joy, and wisdom.

This is how the spiritual person can well serve the Divine; by appealing to the likes of man, he can then master him at his own game!

Creating Sacredness in Your Life

If you are lucky enough to have been born in India, born in the East, then you are already surrounded by the sacredness of a civilization that has been existing for thousands of years. There are temples throughout this land that are a reminder to the people of divine existence. Indeed, the Indians are so fortunate, for if they observe and respect their heritage, they can constantly be uplifted by their ancient systems and philosophies, which have created a way of life, within the people and society, that is sacred.

It is only through the intervention of Westernization that life will become less sacred and more mundane.

In the West, however, the opposite is true. There is very little in our society in daily life that directs us toward our spiritual existence. As children, we are introduced to bankrupt belief systems that only derange us psychologically, insisting on the separation between divinity and man.

Individually, we have to create sacredness in our lives. For we cannot look to society to support us in our endeavor. We must place our "world," or life, as much as possible into alignment with the Divine.

We have to simplify our lives, making our house or home a sanctuary, with a special assigned area of that home for our spiritual practices, creating an altar, which we can visit daily. The body must become our temple, and we should try to live a pure life, surrounding ourselves with things of nature and objects of beauty, when it is possible, creating an environment that is harmonious.

By preparing our outer place of habitation, we can promote an inner calm and silence of mind. Then the Mahashakti will descend around us and inside of us, when all has been directed toward her.

Karma Yoga — The Art of Service

When we realize our true nature, our original Self, beyond the ego's demands, we will exist in a state of service. We will be all giving, a devoted subject to the highest principles.

But before we can arrive at this state of purity, which very few souls attain immediately, Karma Yoga, or the philosophy of service, is an essential way of eliminating bad karmic acts and accelerating the eradication of unwanted traits. Service is a way that we can stop thinking of our own obsessions and frailties and start thinking of others and their needs. It is one of the most effective methods for purification of the human self, allowing our true inner nature to express itself in action, thus giving us the opportunity to reign over our lower nature.

It is important, however, that one does not attach oneself to the work done, nor to the fruit of the works, for this will defeat its purpose. (The ego will continue to grow.) We must give willingly of ourselves to override and defeat any traces of attachment to action and ego.

If one is serving a true spiritual Master, this can advance progress rapidly, for not only does one derive the benefit of individual purification, one also is blessed with the force (shakti) being received from the Master, and the two selves, the true nature and the ego nature, become unified.

The philosophy of pratyahara, the withdrawal from the senses, the observer of action, has to be introduced during these acts of service. So by disciplining oneself innerly, even the simplest act takes on a sacred spirit, and one matures from the earthly pawn to the divine subject.

Ancient Techniques for Governing Our Civilization

Idealistically, Plato's idea of the philosopher-king is the most practical solution for rule. India's Dr. Radhakrishnan of the 20th Century is perhaps the closest one who arrived at the perfect union of philosopher and statesman.

Ultimately, there has to be reintroduction of this premise back to our governments, or society will continue to crumble from within. Today we do not have wise men in control, we have puppets, demagogues, arguing for the interests of the corporate sector.

From the perspective of the metaphysical and divine powers, these rulers are not the true governors of the world. The true leaders are the realized Souls, who can bring down from the superconsciousness, the right direction for guidance of their respective nations and the world. From behind the scenes, Sri Aurobindo was the true instigator of India's liberation. India was freed on his birthday, August 15th, a sign to him of his work and effort.

So, from behind the scenes we can occultly change the events in the world even between nations. From another level of consciousness, Ananda Devi and Premananda Deva both worked to bring an end to the Cold War and the Gulf War.

We have to keep abreast of current world events and world leaders, concentrating on them — projecting our ideas for world peace and for the upliftment of man — this is how we can serve as conduits for the Masters who exist in such rarefied consciousness that they need our assistance and occult power and determination, here in the heavy strident earthly plane.

The Psychic and Spiritual Realms

Too often we confuse these two aspects of the Divine. The psychic force is the lower power of the spirit. When one has accessibility to psychical phenomena this does not automatically ensure the spiritualization of that person. It means that they have had an opening, primarily in their intuitive chakra — or third eye.

If you are experimenting with out of body experiences, for the most part, this is an exercise of your psychical powers, which may or may not lead you to your spiritual self, depending on your motivation behind these experiences. One must be careful that he doesn't lose himself in the phantasmagoria and the pleasure of astral discovery, for this too can be a trap and an eventual hindrance on the spiritual path.

If you are experiencing an opening, however, in this area of yourself, do not suppress it; merely see it as the beginning of a spiritual awakening and apply the further disciplines of pranayama, mantra, guided concentration, and contemplation to try and awaken and consolidate your entire being, to take you to the realization of the spiritual realms.

Divine Wrath

As the West falls farther away from her true merited direction, she glides silently into the abyss where most demonical forces try to mutate what was perfect.

It is a Universal law that we have to progress upward and not downward. Thus, it is significant that the West has directed herself away from ascension. Why, we may ask, does she do this? Because she has been instructed by demonical forces, for many centuries now, and they have gained control over the minds of the people.

This calls for a radical adjustment. We have to rectify this injustice to Divine Law. We must call upon the wrath of the Divine to break the spells so carefully grafted by the collective unconscious mechanisms.

It is through a meeting of the force of the Divine in its darkest wrath, through natural disasters, death, disease, and poverty that man will reexamine himself. Henceforth, this is the path that America is beckoning upon herself.

Extreme though this may sound, this law has been in effect since man came to Earth: That if one defied the divine code and practice, the Divine would literally destroy man's false creations to make room for more souls and civilizations to be born in a fresh and pure state again.

To make sure that man followed the divine order before, he was given archetypes to follow, a blueprint for living and dying. This plan worked successfully for the ancients, who could easily contact the invisible realms and meet with their respected Gods and Goddesses. There was an understanding that this was a method sent down to man and that he was obligated to organize his life and society ruled by the Gods.

Psychological Studies

Psychology is a relatively new field of study for man. Indeed, psychology, for the most part devoid of any spiritual adjudication, renders man confused and weak.

The aim of psychological studies is to prepare man to conquer his mind. Psychology today, in the West, is far too preoccupied with a stultified analyzation of man's dilemmas and predicaments. This upsets the Masters, for there is time wasted on Earth and man is left in a perpetually disagreeable state.

Psychology actually only bears any kind of significance when it links itself with man's higher echelons. Once man has discovered the root evils within himself, he must disengage himself from the personality disorder, which occurred as a result of the "evil." Then real progress will occur, not a contrived checking and analyzing, but a real elimination of the old self, to gain the momentum to pursue his right and natural course of behavior.

Man's gift for himself is the game of psychological study; he perpetually amuses himself with the physical, rendering this service without true purpose.

The true answer to our divine calling would be a marriage of the psychological schools and esoteric occultism. One should see the esoteric as a necessary appendage of psychology. After all, psychology is merely the study of the mind in its infancy, compared to the true work of the spiritualist, who conquers all deficiencies and weaknesses — allowing his most perfect nature to rule. He becomes a Superman, a being of light, and a messenger from the Divine.

When one speaks from this level of consciousness, he knows how to eradicate the psychosis and neurosis out of others. He can delve into the weakness of others by allowing them to see their putrid personality, revealing to them the reasons as he pierces all the masks, rendering them unequivocally defunct.

It is our job, as Masters, to initiate this law revealing the ego mask for purification, to take in our own hands the deep dark natures and then revel in their idiocy, and then splendor will reign.

One must be completely freed from all ailments before one can concentrate on this revelation — for this is the real psychological work, the revealing and eliminating of the false masks, the false ego and its false projections.

If we placate the false ego and listen to the twisted and undeniable hypocrisies, nothing will have been accomplished, merely a glossing over of what is already there.

The spiritualist is a warrior, and it is his mind that he chooses for his territory of battle.

This work asks that we all have to become warriors and stop merely pretending to take arms, testing our sincerity constantly.

Existing forms of multiple personality disorders can be greatly improved with the application of a spiritual discipline and a renewed interest for the individual in the spiritual world and life. It is here that devotion, meaning, and direction give no reason for the extraneous characters to manifest.

Our work is to bring individuals out of their false reality to the true spiritual reality of this world.

All people who are sick, mentally and emotionally, can be cured. They have to be put on a special rehabilitation program for their spirit, where all of their creativity and latent spiritual force is allowed to blossom. It is the wish of the Masters to create clinics specifically for spiritual nourishment — to make people aware that there is unity within them and that this errant society must not divide them anymore.

It is the intent of the society to make people mentally unstable to perpetuate a dependency on the organism of the scientific body of medicine.

Society creates psychological disunity to be sure that every aspect of its tentacles is obeyed and makes people enslaved and sick. One becomes obsessed with even the most mundane of works, for example, cleaning, as a result of the paranoia of the scientific community and the producers of cleaning products. This causes neurosis in the people.

So, it is the nature of the society itself that causes the mutation of the Ego consciousness, which no longer resonates with its Soul or truth.

Letting Go — Wu Wei

When one sees the light of his Soul, he exclaims innerly, "Why did I lose myself unanointed thus?" When here nothing bothers me; I am free; I am pure; I am one. Here I know myself, and I know that nothing can touch me when I am here in the highest peak of me. Here I see my little self below, and I wonder no more, for I am letting go of everything false and constructed, and I am flowing, ever moving, still and ebbing with the divine chorus — the silent song of mysteries unknown and known eventually.

The Chinese wrote "wu wei," and this epitomizes the naturalness that we live in when we are at one with our highest self. We do not only ascend into our highest consciousness, we eventually descend with it down into the Maya, the physical world, joining the Soul and the human self, Jivatman, and here we learn to walk, talk, think, and live as a new personality, a divine personality, guided by our intuitive self, never allowing the rigidity of the individual ego to trap us again.

* * *

The Importance of Surrender

Surrender is a game the Divine plays with us; the more we surrender to her, the more she gives in response. It is a dance, a code — as we send messages of surrender from below, there is a call and echo from above that answers. Surrender is an ode of love from the spiritualist to the Divine — a leap into intuitive knowing that the spell of withdrawal and withholding is being broken, that one is becoming a true "giver," — with no constraints or rules laid down, no moralizing just plain and simple surrender.

Then the Masters can direct you, not before; then the Masters can use your offered vehicle for their work, and then the doors will be opened for you on Earth and your work, your Dharma will become apparent.

Degrees of Sanity

Define sane. What the spiritualist may know to be right, the society may think wrong. What the spiritualist does in the face of evil may appear to be out of the ordinary, may appear to be overzealous; yet what can be proven wrong when one lives and dies in the truth?

It is insane to listen and act according to the programming around you. It is insane to refuse your natural course of purification; it is insane to watch the world around us listen to the dictates of false leaders. It is insane doing nothing to prevent this decay, nor feeling obliged to do anything.

Where do the boundaries of sanity lie?
Surely not on the Earth but in the sky.

* * *

The Western Outlook and its Effects on the World

Without damning the entire Western culture, it is the opinion of the Masters, seeing the destructive forces released and ignited by the Western man's action, that causes us to write with such vehement alarm.

The Western world and culture is not and never has been spiritual. At least America tried to build on the European ideals, but unfortunately, she too has gone the way of her ancestors and has lost her direction. Indeed, she has mastered the physical domain; she has "trod where no man had trodden before;" she has mastered the art of business and of war.

But she has not guarded herself against the influence of unwarranted and ill-directed forces within her society. Indeed, she encourages even the most corrupt of organizations, not judging their intent, just to perpetuate the balance of the economy and to make her one of the most wealthy countries in the world.

Sadly, this lack of discernment of these titanic lower forces in society has encouraged a decay within the people. Western man no longer has a bearing on his spiritual life, because governing forces — in the political-military-industrial complex — neither seek out true divine alignment nor wish to discover divine potential.

Soon we can expect this form of moral, societal, and spiritual decay throughout the world as she follows blindly America's spirit. A force that advances the physical world, only to sacrifice the spiritual world.

Human and Divine Heart

When the mind is still, we can truly hear the voice of the heart.

When the human heart is still, we can truly hear the voice of the Soul, and when we hear this silent voice, its touch opens us to the heart of the Universe, and we become lost, drunk with the taste of litany lost — and we are but slaves to the beat of this drum, never to fall again to the murmur of the mere shadow of the true light.

The light dost fill us to awaken and shake out all dusty webs of attachments we do not yet know are false. Triumphant, we are starting to live in the large wheel, the large egg, the large self of us.

* * *

Challenging Old Beliefs

"Break the molds of the past, but keep safe its genius and its spirit or else thou hast no future."

— Sri Aurobindo

Old beliefs are a failing for us if they do not have significance in our spiritual purification.

It can only be a strength to eliminate the debris that causes us more trouble than its worth.

Yet we have to challenge ourselves to the very *core.* We have to settle the honor to our Soul and ask for no more assistance until we have superseded our own misnomers. When we have succeeded, we can then truly know the meaning of strength and be satisfied no more with weakness and avoidance of the reality within.

Entering the Light

The "Light" is a term frequently used by many and, yes, it does describe the entrance into the spiritual realms. But we spiritualists must understand more in-depth, the route we must take to *Live* in the light.

"Light" represents the energy, the consciousness, the Divine. "Light" represents a world different from our own here. "Light" is what we must call into us if we are to begin.

When we enter the light, all darkness subsides. We are taken out of our human consciousness and elevated beyond all individuality into an existence we have not known consciously before. We then exist for the light, we are suspended, animated, and devote ourselves to this consciousness, for this is all that we are. There are no forms; there is no thought; it is just a state of being.

When one enters this early step of awakening, one must know that this is only the beginning, that one has been graced and has chosen oneself to experience this elevation of consciousness, and this ascension is an essential part of our nature.

The ascension seems limitless and then, depending on the preparation and the experiencing of the Soul from previous incarnations, there are differing levels of entrance into the light. Indeed, there are many states where one loses his or her sense of individuality and you are *One* with the Universal consciousness and, depending on your preparation and sequestered will, the gates of the Divine will "show" you what you are ready to receive. Then you will begin to really and truly understand the nature of existence.

Joy and love here are abundant, and the truth about everything peels away at the falsity of individual consciousness, as if it has been carried with you all along.

Now, we are *all* capable of these experiences, and indeed it is our duty to pursue them, but the Divine will only grant them to those who are seriously adherents to her law. For she will not risk the possibility of unwarranted trespassers in her kingdom, and it is our duty to cleanse our impure "hearts' desires" when requesting these experiences.

The Energy and Force

This force, Shakti (as known in India, Chi in China), must be revered. There is absolutely no point believing, because you have awakened momentarily, because you have seen something of the realms of truth, that you are now the Master. Indeed throughout man's history there have been many who have fallen in this spirit of folly.

The path to complete enlightenment has its perils for the man who has seen the light and then magnifies himself in the physical world, untransformed. For this upliftment of consciousness does change us. But we must remember that we have returned from our ascension down and back into the impure vessel — and so it is our duty to pursue pure aspiration in order to justify our blessing of light and to continue the work that has only just begun. We have to vigilantly try to stop the chatter of the human mind to precipitate further experiences, culminating in a Cosmic Consciousness and later in Soul Consciousness or Atman. Eventually, the goal is to bring down a descent of this light; the pinnacle is the Supramental light, into the human self, to transform the human mind and spirit, ending all duality and destroying the ego nature, making room for the true personality of the Soul, to seize us and free us.

Changing the West: Why?

Why indeed! For the most part, the West has fulfilled her Dharma, introducing science, modernizing and cultivating a physical stronghold, and a military force capable of governing the world. However, during this period of creation she failed to abide closely to Universal laws, *e.g.*, obedience to the Divine plan without egoistic incentive, and so the kind of man she produces is sadly, incomplete.

The West's main mistake, and fundamental to her philosophy, is *arrogance* — believing and instilling the spirit of superiority over the rest of the world within the dominance of the religious orders she endorses. Indeed, there is very little room for sympathy and understanding of our formulae and philosophies.

In fact, due to the incomplete religious doctrines, Western man has simply disconnected from any kind of divine reverence and guidance, which is and will be his downfall.

Western man is ignorant of his spiritual origins and fearful even to pursue his own investigations. It is this fundamental severance from Truth that perpetuates all forms of ignorant action and conduct within the body of society. Man has become so sick and disoriented that he has developed serious diseases and has failed to be able to unite even the family. There is so much contempt here that never seems to be eradicated from the psyche of the collective consciousness in the West, so that Western man falls short of his true potential.

For sure there are small pockets of individuals who are trying to imbibe this divine spirit of change and rebellion, but this very rarely changes policy on a larger scale.

The adulation of violence, for example, is a definite sign of sickness — the adulation of the false archetypes and prophets from Hollywood with the "media machine" shaping the minds of children.

We must change and modify the Western world before her philosophies of materialism and greed, dictatorship through Democracy and free trade, make few people richer and more people poorer, and all bereft of the spirit.

It is our role, our dharma, to concentrate on *spiritual revolution* for the transformation of this society. We must all become active participants, introducing spiritual ethics and policy into every aspect of society and ultimately concentrating on change in the highest levels in the government, in the military, and in the corporate world.

We can no longer give our thoughts, our minds, and our intentions away, merely because the body of influence we are attempting to transform appears to be inconquerable.

Spiritual people are the ones who have the real power and force. The leaders in our society are merely puppets.

Democracy

The perfect system of society would not only act for the good of all but for everyone's Spiritual liberty. Democracy acts for the liberty of its citizens, only it is a social and physical liberty.

The Democratic state produces a governing body that is prey to a great deal of impure forces who seize the reins of power and usurp the sacred veil and duty that all governors have when leading the people.

Democracy now is not necessarily just a vessel of liberty from all injustice; it has become a vehicle where many anarchical forces — namely heavy materialism — and all of its repercussions on the mind of man, have opened the floodgates occultly to dangerous forces.

These forces have, within a century, taken us into more duality of the mind; our concentration is solely on our physical existence. To gain back the Unity of our personalities, our families, and the fabric of a healthy society, we must not permit the strongholds of Big Business to influence the way we think and behave.

Surely, true liberty does not come from the homogenized culture that is being purported worldwide! For within this excitable phenomenon, we lose the beauty of curiosity and the creation of our own true personality and inquiry on an individual and national level.

Democracy has to command herself. She cannot allow the whims of the corrupted few to take humanity away from its Soul. It is a crime for the people, who are so caught up in their egoistic wants and desires being encouraged by Western Democracy. Very few people give even a thought toward their duty as divine subjects.

A New Government and Leadership

We can influence and change our leaders if we are inspired to do so, and this inspiration will come from our allegiance to our higher selves and the spiritual direction. As spiritualists, it is our role to provoke change, to precipitate a catharsis on a grand scale.

We have to activate ourselves; even if we have never participated in this kind of action before, we cannot allow any more corruption to spread to the rest of the world like a gangrene. The New Future Society will still perpetuate the fundamental democratic rule, but it also will include a strong adherence to certain philosophic and spiritual tenets — not religious, but spiritual. The rulers of this society will be governed by boards of wise men and women, who will have no direct communication nor allegiance to the corporate, military, or media structure.

These wise people will have been trained in special schools and chosen because of their selfless attitudes and dedication to the improvement of our society. They will be philosophers of rule, the most perfected people, not just intellectually but spiritually, not affiliated with any belief system nor prejudice.

This new form of government or leaders will have to emerge sooner or later, resulting in complete annihilation of the malevolent forces existing today.

Spirituality and Religion

Spirituality has a very different approach to unity with God than religion. It states that it is the birthright of every man to ascend and realize himself in the image of God, that every man was made in the likeness of God, and that there is nothing to prevent man from this pursuit, for he is already existent in this state. It is just a case of remembering and capturing this enlightenment again.

During the acquisition of his Godhead, man may choose any path he deems efficacious for this purpose. He does not have to obey a doctrine; he does not have to pass through the blessings of certain archetypes he just goes ahead and does it. Simple!

Religion, however, presents a formula for union with God without explicit detail or direction. You must believe and not question, not allowing the individual to know God without entrenching himself in the doctrine and belief system presented. Despite the fact that this belief system has no scientific formula for entrance into a higher consciousness, nor does this system give techniques for purification.

Now it may seem that the ideas in this book represent a belief system and, yet, they do not. In fact, here we cannot possibly encourage anyone to *believe* in anything specifically; we propose a way of life. We propose that you experiment on yourself, using the techniques illustrated in this book to conquer the mind and harness the spiritual forces within you.

The brave will take the spiritualistic path, the ones who dare to depend on recognition from God through themselves, standing alone, bare before the Truth.

Man as the Center of the Universe

We are all at the center of the Universe.

The Universe is more than a physical domain; it is the very quintessence of creation and we can experience the Oneness with this force.

We are the key holders, the potential Masters, who unlock the secrets of all time.

It is within us, the very fiber of everything that has existed and will exist.

We are not just an individual body; we are united with the complete, vast, unfathomable mystery.

Why Spiritualists Must Enter the Pragmatic and Rational Fields of Society

The spiritual life does not just encompass one's own experiential union with the Divine; it also requires of us that we work on behalf of this force. For too long, unfortunately we have allowed the non-spiritual people to take control of the machinery of society and the Earth. Now it is time to take back the reigns of control. To stop the damage that is almost irreparable in some instances.

The spiritualists are still seen by the mainstream Western world as people who are not realistic, who do not have direction, nor basic intelligence. It is time to set the record straight; it is time to assert the rightful role of the spiritual man and woman.

We should not lose ourselves in the pleasure games. We have to fight, to become real warriors of truth, inspiring change. Proving to the materialists with guile, intelligence, and pragmatism, that our ideals *are* realistic and that they are worthy of being enforced. World peace is a realistic aim; do we have to push it aside just to accommodate the arms producers?

We have to fight fire with fire, for these materialists are so convinced, they are so determined to do business as they please. That is why the spiritual people are being asked by the Divine to go to the places where they are most needed, into the eye of the storm, to change the military industrial complex and to chip away at its bastions of enforcement.

Sacrifice

Sacrifice is a law unto itself. Sacrifice is a love unto itself. When one imbibes the spirit of sacrifice, there is no room for egoistic ways. One becomes the instrument for the whole, no longer losing oneself in individualistic demands.

When we sacrifice ourselves to the Divine, we offer up everything, so that her work becomes ours. We see life with meaning; we feel her breath as our own; we hear her thoughts; we act with her cadence, and everything that once clouded our view of life is crystal clear; undoubtedly, we are on a higher path of existence.

The ancients would make a habit of sacrificing their most prized possessions to evoke the forces to descend and protect them. What really do we sacrifice, if Earth is an illusion and our attachments mortal? Is it not the sacrifice of the Divine that allowed us to project ourselves out of bliss? What about Her sacrifice? What about the beautiful Earth that we live on? Out of hard labor, the Divine has sacrificed for us, and we reap the benefits. Have we forgotten so soon? Is it not our duty to sacrifice ourselves? Yes, yes it is. Now let us begin.

* * *

Leadership

Leaders are born, not made. They are born with an awakened Soul, and they are spiritual. Those of you who read these words are the leaders of our society. Why? Because you are searching for more than the exoteric; you search for the esoteric meaning of life. Every one of you has the potential to lead. It is time now to activate yourself. To investigate yourself. To inspire others to live a spiritual life. It will be the role of the New Future Society to train people to become more perfected instruments and eventual leaders.

For the battlefield awaits, and we are the warriors ready to fight with wisdom and the Truth.

Living with a Master

When a Master is fully adept at his role, the disciple can arrive at a state of complete liberty. When you live with a Master, you see the nuances of Truth in a living being, and you only want to be in the presence of others who live and abide by the Truth. There is a spontaneity and a naturalness that graces the Master and, far from losing your personality, you gain the possibility of expressing your true Soul's nature, for you will be guided to live by the master Soul within you. All duality dies, and a unity is born.

You will be the receiver of the Shakti energy living within the Master for he/she serves as a beacon of light, beaming out continually this super force, especially into those closest to them.

* * *

Detachment

Unkind to our pleasure, undesirable to our likes, the Spirit and Soul reign above all insignificant terrestrial constraints. Alluring to the Soul? "No!" he cries, "I am above all that ye see. I am above even the individual me! I am absorbed in longings eternal and cannot be bothered by the workings human. Can you find me by looking hungrily? Can you find me by possessing possessively? Can you hear me by hearing outside of you? No, it is impossible. Thereby, I decree the philosophy of Detachment from the sensory world — such a charm, but a trap until you attain my Soul's glory invested in you. Then, and only then, will you see the immutable in the terrestrial and the boundaryless within the boundary, and you are free even here, down here in the maze of solid dreams."

A Kinder Democracy and Capitalism

When capitalism forces the democratic rule, when Democracy answers the cries of the heard minority, global hunters of the mighty dollar, how can a system be fair? How can a system live up to its Divine expectations? How can it do justice to the inadequacies of so many people's lives?

Such a dangerous system. Preaching power to the people, and the people long since starved of true spiritual nourishment decide that we should all form a democratic state with the advantage of physical prosperity as its governor and individual satisfaction guised as Liberty!

It is so apparent that capitalism has long driven down the wrong path, away from a considerate force in society for all. It takes care of titans only and the people are forgotten. So much for Democracy, if it allows this delinquent child of capitalism to throw away a perfectly good opportunity to rectify the world's serious agendas — to utilize this power that they have gained to change and contribute back to the people, back to the Earth, and back to its higher nature and mission.

Does the society have to break down any more before we express the urgency of kindness and duty to do Good?

Long live Democracy and long live Capitalism — in another form, of course, because this form is far too complacent, greedy, demanding, careless, and inexcusably devoid of a Divine direction.

Karma and the Western Denial

When one desires something it is usually due to an avoidance of accountability. This is exactly true of the Western man who refuses to be accountable for the way he is living, thinking, acting, and relating to the Divine.

The law of Karma dictates that we shall "reap" whatever we have sown. When we are affiliated with a group of people, a family, a city, a state or a nation, we are branched to that respective group's karma. That is why, as nations, we can be subject to natural disasters — a penance for misconduct and disrespect en masse to the Divine.

The more we deny the law of Karma, the less we will try to be spiritual and aligned to our Soul, pretending to ourselves that there is no one to be answerable to, no one to be judged by. But alas, this is wrong.

Scientific superiority, military superiority, technological superiority over the rest of the world, this does not absent the West from building a heavier and heavier karma.

When will she learn? When will she start to see herself? When will she want to be accountable?

Let us start by reminding her. Western man, do not forget your divine scales; do not tip away from your Soul. For the feather is light; the Egyptians were right. It is the judgment that we all must highly regard, before we govern with philosophies imperfected.

Heart and the Mind

As long as fear and disbelief do not cloud either the Heart or the Mind, as long as these centers remain constantly open to transformation, the aspirant is safe. If, at any time, you start to fix yourself, to create yet another mental image, the "Formless One" cannot be united within you.

Imagine your heart full of divine love eternally; there lies your self in your perfect state. Imagine your mind so luminous that it allows the highest comprehendable source to possess and flow within it. There lies you in the perfect state.

We are all existent in this state now! So why are we pretending to ourselves that this life of lamentation is eternal? When this is the only part of ourselves that is finite!

The heart and mind are gateways to the "other" side, to the magic and blessings of the Soul and its harmonious place in the origin.

Schools of Initiation

Schools of Initiation have mostly all vanished from the physical Earth. These places are very different from most of the present "schools" of spiritualism here in the West.

When one enters a true school of Initiation, he places himself into the study for the pursuit of, firstly, discipleship and ultimately mastership.

Only a select few Souls on Earth are ready for this pursuit, and the Divine herself chooses them carefully. For this training is purely Esoteric.

The adherent learns how to master his own mind and will derive his highest state of consciousness through direct initiation from the Master of the school. The adherent then becomes a Master of psychology of others; he can "see" the complete personality of others and how to transform this person in a very short period of time.

The highest schools of Initiation exist in the "invisible" realms where even the Masters themselves are initiated by more powerful adepts into the essential reality and the implementation and orchestration of this reality.

It would be our privilege, as Brothers of the White Lodge, to encourage many of you to align yourselves with our schools of initiation, for here is a pure form of entrance into the Supreme Creator. We cannot guarantee your transformation, unless you understand the significance of these Initiation Schools.

Initiation is the pinnacle of one's spiritual path; it is when you are considered ready to be taken completely into the consciousness of the Master. Your spirit and his/her spirit are unified on the highest levels of consciousness. You then engender the embodiment of that Master's particular force and Dharma.

It is our goal to create more schools of Initiation on the Earth level, to initiate and prepare as many people as possible to participate in spiritual work, so often ignored on an international level, and stand as a force defending the Truth and the Divine.

Part Two

Metaphysical Truths

Beyond

Beyond time, is the Abode of the Immovable
Beyond the body, is the Being
Beyond Death, is Life
Beyond Form, is Beauty
Beyond the object, is Love
Beyond my Being, is the Absolute

In my Being, the Absolute resides
In the neighbor, there is Love
In the Universe, the Soul of the Whole
In Space, the Image of the Whole
In Time, the Evolution that leads the Beings
Slowly and imperceptibly to perfect
  Coincidence
To Joy, to Plenitude...

Joy has come into my being
The Mystery of the World is discovered...
I smile to the "Being..."
The symbol is no more a Reality
It fades away before the Essence of All
  Things:
Silent, mystical adoration that comes from the
  depth of my Being
And penetrates it totally
And impregnates it into the Absolute...
Identification.

by Ananda Devi

In Quest of the Absolute

"To believe and to know are as far from one another as the zero and the infinite."

— *Ananda Devi*

To be aware that *we do not know* is real discovery and the beginning of wisdom. Why not recognize the Truth hidden in this apparent paradox and abandon all beliefs, all accumulated knowledge, all preconceived ideas about Truth and all anticipated ideas about what is even unknown to us. We must be in a state of perfect "nescience," of constant opening of the mind, in a spirit of discovery toward the "Unknown." As Kabir said, "It is the spirit of research which is of assistance to us; I am the 'slave' of that spirit." This should not only be done once in a lifetime, but at each moment. Each moment of our life should be adjusted, controlled, and governed by the divine movements of Shakti, which governs the whole world and whose movements are "unknown" to us before it is manifested and have to be constantly revealed to us, and this revelation is made in the Present, for we are as yet unable to realize the immense harmony of the Universe in its totality; we are, however, always able to conform ourselves to it, to follow it, and be impregnated by it. Then, only, can we participate consciously and enjoy this sublime harmony, for a spark of the life of the Universe is within us. Once we have become aware of it and are awakened to it, life is no longer limited to the phantasm of mere individuality, but we are able to communicate integrally with universal life: We are able to merge in it and to be one with it. Everything has to be known, discovered, and achieved in the present, so it means we have to be alert. Let us be aware of this only through identification with the consciousness of the Shakti. When this consciousness is awakened within us, we are able to become an instrument dedicated to the service of the Shakti, then only do our eyes become Her eyes, our mind, Her mind, and can She pour into us the flood of Her tremendous energy. The more we become receptive and *passive* to Her, the more dynamic we must be in the *world*, that is, receive from Her altogether ideas, impulses, powers, and convert them into action in the world of Creation.

We must be conscious of the necessity of training ourselves. The speed of our motor must be given over as an instrument of execution of action. Our speed should be adjusted to Her speed if the Shakti is to be given a free hand. She is action in the Present. She does not need any *time* to create. It is this adjustment which makes a perfect instrument, willing to be more and more perfect and open to Her. Only then can come greater consciousness, a greater knowledge. An awareness of the Cosmic Plans can be awakened in us and can transcend our individuality with its limits and its short-sightedness. Some have realized the necessity of being "passive" but not the necessity of being "active." Poise and efficiency are obtained only through complete awareness of what She expects us to do. The more this type of instrument is created in larger numbers, the better for the whole. Only after creating these instruments in a sufficient number can we hope to set the cycle in motion and recreate "the golden age" of the old tradition.

There is constantly an absolute movement, which is the perfect expression and manifestation of the Absolute in our world. It is possible for our mind to be constantly imbued by this greater Mind, which alone is able to control the movements of our body. Through this, our action in the manifestation, in life, will be given a new direction and a new impulse and, thus, will reflect the absoluteness of all things. Each movement of ours may be a movement adjusted to the Infinite, symbolized in the famous and allegorical dance of Shiva. Each gesture of us becomes the manifestation of this absolute life. It is the most intimate marriage of the Transcendental with the Ephemeral, aimed at losing the sense of our ego, of our individuality in as much as we succeed in merging with the one consciousness, which is sustaining, creating, preserving the whole world in harmony, as a manifestation of its own joy.

Your Closest Friend

The Divine is your closest friend.
He is the *true* friend.
He is a *silent* friend.
When no one else stands by...
He, alone, is there, attentive
and considerate.
Ever ready to help, soothe
and succor...
He will never abandon you...
Even in the midst of the most
drastic circumstances
He will always be with you
You will always be with
Him.
He is present, eternal, and
Real.
From this mystical marriage
is born your Soul.

by Ananda Devi

True Surrender and Our Role as a Divine Instrument

"Being true to oneself (or sincerity) is the law of Heaven — to try to be true to oneself is the law of Man"

— Ch'eng

For those who want to reach the state of integral union with the Divine and who are already engaged in the ways of Yoga, the necessity of "surrender" to God is acutely felt. This becomes, very soon, our main preoccupation and purpose.

It is at this stage that we must be particularly attentive and careful to the way we understand this "surrender."

There are, in fact, many ways of understanding surrender on the human level, but, in truth, there is only one real and authentic "surrender."

It is in finding this true "surrender" that relies the success of our whole enterprise, as to the goal we want to reach, which is a complete realization of the Divine within us.

If we look among the people who are in search of the Divine, *i.e.,* those who have taken consciousness of their Soul to accomplish the will of the Divine into them, we may notice that many souls have been misdirected and still now are.

This is because once the average human being has heard the call of his Soul, he is urged by a very strong desire to take refuge in Her and forget everything that constituted his former existence and conditions of life.

This is based upon a very normal reaction, which leads him from one pole to the opposite one, from materialism and the world of ignorance to the most exclusive spiritualism whose natural end is asceticism and complete denial or simply rejection of the manifested world.

To take refuge in Bliss, Love, and Beauty; whereas, he only knew suffering, hatred, and ugliness, to retire from the world, to forget even the existence of such a world, to unite his mind with God and be completely and forever absorbed in this contemplation of ecstasy, to live in the Impersonal, in the Impersonal Brahman, that is what he is longing for.

However, this Power, the Divine Shakti, is ordering the Actuality in the World through a subtle and elaborate occult transformation of the World. It is an awakened Force, active. It is not a static Force, only retired in Bliss. It is Bliss Love indeed, but also Action, Fullness of Being, Power and "Lila."

Man, being in a body, belongs to the manifestation and not only to the Purusha. He is a part of the Life of the Universe. It is why a passive enjoyment of God, without the acceptance of His creative aspect and manifestation has been and is one of the most dangerous ways of thinking where many Souls, among the best, have fallen, depriving the world of their very important contribution. This attitude, when largely expanded, has resulted in the monopolization of the World by the "Asuras," or malevolent forces.

What is significant about the Buddha's teachings is that he refuses to enter Nirvana as long as there will remain a human being in the bonds of ignorance upon the world. This surely means that Buddha is constantly keeping His eyes opened to the World, not living away from the thought of the world, constantly irradiating Forces and Light to the World, serving the World.

On the other hand, some are inclined to immolate, not their own life and normal participation in the human society, but their "ego" which is confounded, in their half-illumined mind, with individuality. These human beings become very empty of all true Will, Power, and Energy, and they get confused, because this abandonment of all the Powers of their being leads them to stagnation and spiritual inertia.

It is only when we are already sufficiently opened to guidance from above that we can find another more adequate solution to the problem of our life upon the Earth.

In the Bhagavad-Gita, Chapter VI, verses 5 and 6, Lord Krishna says to Arjuna:

> *Verse 5:* "Through the ego, you must deliver the ego. You must neither depress nor lower the ego (and Sri Aurobindo adds, as an explanation of this: 'may it be by complacency or by suppression'), for the ego is 'the friend of the ego and the ego is the enemy.'"

> *Verse 6:* "The ego is the friend for the man in whom the (inferior) ego has been conquered by the (superior) ego; but for him who is not in possession of his (higher) ego, the (inferior) ego is an enemy, and it acts as an enemy."

What is exactly the human ego? Where does it come from? Why is it asserting its supremacy over the whole personality of the human being?

If we scrutinize the human ego more deeply, we will see that the human ego, with its ordinary train of defects, is making personal assertions and legitimization upon the True Self, whom he sincerely believes himself to be, or that the True Self of the integral personality with whom "he" is dealing, is Him.

When we have the chance to "reintegrate" our True Self, we become intensely conscious of this fundamental error and know that the True Self, with whom we legitimately use the "I," is not the same as the "I" we use in the ordinary consciousness of the human ego. So becoming conscious of this capital difference, a part of the influence or usurpation of the human ego disappears. In fact, we feel compelled to keep our ego no longer as "he" is.

However, at this stage of spiritual awakening, if we succeed not to be too petulant and excited by the first revelations of Truth, we will be able to receive a greater knowledge.

This knowledge will show us how to effectuate a "transformation" into our human ego, not an annihilation of our instrumental being and nature.*

But how are we going to make this transformation?

This certainly is the most difficult part in the course of the Sadhana. But this difficulty will be greatly reduced if we observe our ego with a very objective eye, and we will see that his defects are but the exact contraries or prismatic reflections of all the transcendental qualities of our Real Self.

It is through egocentrism that man is becoming more and more conscious of his individuality, of his unity, and this unity is already a projection of the Soul's unity, and behind, the unity of the All. It is why all the defects of human nature, when analyzed, can lead man, by their conversion, transmutation, to his Soul first and then to God.

If we take ambition as an example, a man who is greatly ambitious will work for his own advancement through egocentric activity, and as soon as he succeeds to prove to himself that all the human greatness is surpassed by the greatness of his Real Self, he will be convinced that the greatest endeavor that man may undertake is to realize this mighty Self. He will immediately turn all his energies and activities to pursue

---

* Sri Aurobindo; *The Synthesis of Yoga*, p. 104.

this higher aim and, at this stage, his very ambition, once converted, will be the source where he will find strength and energy to realize his new ideal.

The main confusion comes from the fact that, in the beginning, the ego is absolutely convinced that he is the real and authentic center of consciousness of the individual and "he" does not perceive that all the marks of respect and consideration should be returned to the Soul who, alone, is the true substance and legitimate representative of God in the Universe (the human ego being only a virtual image of Him).

Everything in the ego should be analyzed, clarified, argued until we succeed to manifest the Divine Perfection.

The average human being has arrived at the state of evolution where the manifestation is taken for the Principle and the infinitesimal part of this manifestation is confusedly considered as an equivalent of an authentic center of the Truth-consciousness.

And we surely have to arrive at such an extreme point in our conclusion before turning our attention toward the real and effective center of our being, as the true manifestation of the Divine.

It is a natural passage and stage.

So why consider any longer our human ego as an enemy? He is no more our enemy as soon as we realize what "he" is exactly and from where "he" is indirectly proceeding. Let us make a friend of "him" and so help his transformation lest he should become a real enemy if we are facing him aggressively and really creating opposite forces against the realization of our true aim.

To avoid this, let us try to find the secret meaning and true correspondence of our defects, and when having found them, we will return to our True Self, and the transformation will be done in the easiest and quickest manner.

In everything, we must learn neither to be attracted nor repulsed; it is also true for our human ego.

We must not be short-sighted but have a complete understanding of the transitory formation we represent and try to help this transformation with our conscious will and more illumined mind. But this is not the whole of the dangers man has to face in the way to Divine Realization.

There are other kinds of misinterpreting surrender, as pernicious as the preceding ones, especially in the true understanding of "surrender in works," all of which concerns the outer life and our own action upon it.

A very common confusion comes from our unmatured thought: We arbitrarily separate our outer life from the inner life and, thus, in the beginning of our attempts to establish "surrender" into us, we most often fall into a passive acceptance of the events of our life thinking that they are the perfect expression of God's Will. In this case, we surrender ourselves not to the Divine or a so-called Divine Will, but to our own ignorance. The effective control of our Life and events in Life by the Divine comes only when the Soul has arrived at a certain mastery of the Earth-plane, no more under the influence of the Asuras or blind forces.

When the Soul has succeeded to control these forces and establish Herself on a more peaceful plane, only then She can feel that the Divine is taking the events of Her Life in hand more directly and that She has less effort to make, because most of the work is now being done by the Divine.

She is able to get a greater and greater certitude that the events of Her Life are a certain and direct reflection of the Divine's Will. The direct conduct of Life can only be taken by the Divine when the Soul has arrived to leave this "whirl" and cease to be like a "cork" upon the sea.

To cease to be that cork, we must, with the greatest possible courage, face all the obstacles in Life, with the greatest faith and aspiration toward the Divine who, alone, is able to help us to get rid of these currents. Then we will succeed to reach a more peaceful and quiet land, and only then begins the implementation of the effective direction of our life and events guided by the Divine. Not before.

The Soul must gradually increase its worship and confidence of divine protection and help. This worship is naturally increased as She becomes conscious of the Divine's direct intervention in the organization of Her Life.

A greater communion of thoughts and action can be established as soon as we are under complete control of the Divine.

This is the real beginning of the establishment of surrender in works to the Divine. It must not only be an attitude of our mind facing the event. It is an *active* surrendering, not a passive and superficial surrendering. The danger is that we may confound them and take the one for the other.

It is when the Divine Shakti has taken everything in hand that we can say that we are conducted by the Divine. The proof of this should be found in a lessening of our struggle in life and in ourselves, our more complete dependence, reliance upon the Divine.

If we try to impose this attitude before its natural coming, we are committing the greatest error and condemning ourselves to a dangerous stop in our spiritual progression.

We must remember that everything that is arbitrary, which is produced unnaturally, is not good for us. There is a smooth, sensible and direct way that can prevent us from falling on one side or the other of the razor's edge. And our goal is to keep a tight equilibrium between the two opposite poles — to be neither attracted nor repulsed.

This is the way we must always have in view. There is no other way to arrive at the real destination. All other ways are leading us not where we want to go, but to artificial paradises of the Soul.

If someone is escaping life, he will find the same problems and difficulties again in this life, or in another, until he understands that what he is asked is to know that the real richness, the greatest possible joy and the end of our research for Truth is Life; that God is in Life.

If we escape this, we do not realize our destiny is to become a living example and a true and perfect instrument of the Divine in the World.

Our ordinary human life should be divinized, because even in accomplishing what is necessary for human being, our main aim will be to reach the Divine and experience His attributes and forces through the daily ordinary life-game, which will be "revalorized" to our new eyes and understanding.

"The Power or Powers that will come would not be considered as 'our own' like in the past, but as 'gifts of the Divine for the Divine's 'purpose:' then we proceed to the organization of our life in the way the Divine intends to organize it, so that it will be 'fit for the Service of the Divine.'"*

We must use our new equilibrium to listen more attentively to the voice of the inner Guru who will show us exactly what we have to do as positive universal work.

Through Life, the inner Guide, who is our Real Self, can express Himself and reveal Himself to us in all His clarity, light, immanence.

God is an inner realization through the teachings of Life and experience, for how are we going "to be thoroughly transformed and unified by living only in the internal life, without any test of the

---

* Sri Aurobindo; *More Lights on Yoga,* p. 52 & 53.

transformation and unity by external contact and the ordeals of the external work and life?"*

To surrender to the Divine effectively means to surrender ourselves to the Power of the Divine, to the creative faculty of the Divine, to the great liberty of expression of the Divine in all domains, to the vast richness and fecundity of the Divine in His creations. The Divine is all abundance, plenitude of everything, joy.

We must not have a cult for poverty, sufferings, and diseases. We must not believe (even for an iota of our being) that the way to find God, or the Will of God, is *obligatorily* our own maintenance in those sufferings.

Of course it seems, in the present, that it is the inevitable share of worries of the many. But a Power must come down, a new strength coming from supramental consciousness, to be developed among human beings; and those who are destined to bring it, should be awakened from all inertia, ignorance, and superstitions. The mass should receive new ideas and, consequently, a new power so that it should have a new means at its disposal to transform its present circumstances of Life into new ones which will not be "suffering, poverty and disease" but joy, abundance of everything — in the way of Nature, which is all abundance — and health.

It is these ideas, new for our epoch, which surpass all ordinary human understanding, either in the Orient or in the Occident in the World of nowadays (each of them having realized only half-truths or made half the way to the complete synthetic expression of a Divine Life) which are essential to the transformation to be worked out in ourselves as in the world.

The new equilibrium, the Salvation either of Asia or of the Occident are based upon a harmonization, a fusion, or melding together materialism born in Occident and the World-shunning asceticism largely expanded in the Orient. It is most important to help this transformation. It is why "those who are able to see, to develop, to re-create themselves in the image of the Spirit and to communicate both their idea and its Power to the masses"* should have these ideas present in their minds, so as to give, on the mental spheres, a strong vision of the Truth to be intercepted and realized.

---

*Sri Aurobindo; *More Lights on Yoga*, p. 50.

*Sri Aurobindo; *The Human Cycle*, p. 306.

Nothing must be denied of what is in this world, neither the materialism of Occident, nor the ascetic passivity of Oriental Sages who are in the other half-Truth.

But what we must know and what we must be more and more conscious of, is that everything now should be "transmuted" into a new synthesis until the forces are no more constrained from both Orient and Occident should be brought together in a great spiritual and mental assimilation through a few minds specially prepared for this work and illumined by the Truth.

We must accept the facts, and then, make a new synthesis on our present human level as in the work on a wider Cosmic level. This is the *"fin mot"* of the message of Sri Aurobindo to the world. This is a work which must be done, which must be continued in ourselves as in the world, because there is a community of action, an interaction which, perhaps we do not perceive at the beginning but which takes the whole of our interest later on and is always increasing. This is a part of our work. It is why we are not only asked to realize the Truth for our own liberation and self-satisfaction but, in doing so, we make a part of the work, for the whole of Humanity. It is in taking contacts with the world and other souls, as with the Divine Inner Guide, that we most easily will edify a more and more perfect expression of the Divine for the World.

Now the time has come for a deep transformation, a transformation that is more important than those we may have kept memory of.

It is a new language, a new transcription of the Eternal Truth specially adapted for our time, which must be used. We must remember that the intelligence of God is always creating and essentially creative.

That is the Real Truth. There is no other way than to identify ourselves to that spirit of creation and adaptation to the situation of the world, in a positive act of the mind.

We must not misuse our energies in deploring the present state of conditions, but we must use our possibility of seeing the present, inevitable wrong side of things to help and favor the transmutation to be done.

And this transmutation is as inevitable as the present inevitable wrong state of things.

In conclusion, to establish the true surrender into us, we have "to give ourselves entirely to the Divine alone and to nobody and nothing else."*

---

* Sri.Aurobindo; *Lights on Yoga,* p. 37.

All evil comes from our belief that we are thinking in the right way and sure that our actual vision of the Truth is the definitive one.

We are not, as a whole, sufficiently conscious that to be free from all ignorance on our way to Perfection, is not as easy as one may think. We must use constant discrimination in our present elaboration of the Truth and constantly project upon it the Light of upper stages of consciousness coming from above.

This collaboration, of course, should be acquired only if we are conscious of needing it and willing to accept a sincere and continual self criticism.

There are terrible mistakes, which have been professed for a long time, concerning the means to be employed to get the mastery over the ego and ending practically to the ruin of the personality and its dynamism upon which is based our whole evolution toward the complete realization of God.

But so many souls have been misdirected, and still now are, that the vision of all these poor souls abused in their own credulity to have realized themselves or to use the true means to do it, is just a pity.

One day or another, in the soul's pilgrimage, every one of us has to face the terrible attraction of this delusive paradise where the real problem of our true evolution is the lure of easiness and simplicity.

But, as in any paradise in which the soul is imprisoned, it is enjoying a certain happiness and peace there.

The only remedy for us is to constantly have in our mind the danger of all the possible errors that assail us and intensely pray to always have a clear mind and perception of the constant rectification that comes from above as a counterpart.

It is a sense of equilibrium that we have to acquire and put into practice.

We must also remember that if we do not make the effort to be a source by ourselves, a direct channel with the Divine, we will never be able to do anything valuable for others.

It is in seeking to be this direct channel that we will establish true surrender, transmuting all our powers, energies, and personal will into a new synthesis that will be able to accomplish the dynamization of our whole nature so as to receive and keep the considerable power and flaming light of the Supramental Consciousness as the anterior human form is dissolved.

The Conscious Being

...is like an actor on the stage or a medium used by various entities; the entities are the different tendencies, desires, wills, etc. to which we identify ourselves simultaneously or successively and which work autonomously each one for themselves — as if independent from the central being. As the conscious being is the mouthpiece of many different aspects of ourselves, we have to be cautious: unless we believe in everything which he expressed and are deluded. Sometimes the conscious being is a hypocrite: He denies the very things that are dear to the inner being on some plane or other.

The voice of the Soul is naturally the only one that should be of importance to us, but, in most cases, it is the only one ignored. We have to learn how to listen to the voice of the Soul, let it express itself through the puppet that is our conscious being: so that the conscious being should be at all times the intermediary of the Soul and not a delusive intermediary. To believe that the conscious being is always true is a great illusion.

We have to constantly criticize ourselves, put everything in doubt, question, open a way for another issue. Let the opponent within contradict what is believed consciously — challenge it and, if we are in doubt, we should refrain from concluding prematurely.

Let the mind work freely on the problem, until the solution comes; the certitude is born. To find Truth is a path paved with many doubts, many argumentations within oneself, and a way to learn to live temporarily with conflict until they are reabsorbed. It is an exalting experience.

Law of Recurrence

According to this law, there is a tendency in each of us to reproduce in part, or in totality, the destiny we had in the past. Unless we can overcome this extraordinary attraction toward repetition of the same acts, we cannot free ourselves from what certain people call Karma, which is partly a phenomenon of the Law of Recurrence. Until we break our karmic pattern, we are not in a position to create for ourselves a new life, original and composed by our intelligence and creativity of entirely new themes and motives. As to the conception of Karma, it is a most ambiguous conception. We ought to differentiate between the Action-Reaction resulting from past lives, which is essentially what we would call the Law of Recurrence, and action-reaction, issued from the actions that have taken place in the frame of this one present life. We have to recur to a deep analysis and study of these past influences. The sannyasin is the one who has succeeded in breaking off the bonds of the past and who is revolting according to a completely new line of destiny.

Most people repeat their past. They have no *future* really. The future is a mere repetition of the past.

What has to be broken is this repetition. When it is broken, an individual is *free* to be what the "Gods" wish him to be.

By ourselves, we are not powerful enough to break these recurring phenomena. We have to open to a new Power, a greater Power, a Cosmic Power, to be able to achieve this. Then our mind is being transformed, as well as our destiny.

Analyzing the Reality of the Ego Nature

"Schizophrenia is to identify with the Ego."
— *Ananda Devi*

There is a process by which we can recover the superconscious state. We all know everything. We are the architects of the world, but we have lost consciousness of this. This is what is called to live in a dream, to be not fully awakened.

The ego, in its most negative aspect, looks at itself as being a static entity, something finished that cannot change. There is no evolution, no outlet. There are only two alternatives: pride or despair, over self-estimation or the realization of a sad, morbid, fatal state of affairs. The ego is static, not dynamic. This is why the ego is outrageously susceptible and its susceptibility is painfully pricking it all the time, because whatever defect is seen through it, whether by itself or someone else, it is considered as being definitive, fixed, shaped forever, crystallized.

The ego is created when we project ourselves in the outer world. This is a movement turned toward the outer, toward the surface, toward the artificiality, which has reached its quintessence in the Western mode of life, toward the things and objects of creation.

The ego nourishes itself on this false identification to which we give credit.

In fact, the ego is a non-entity, it is a usurper and hypocrite and is not the master of the house — it has to be dismissed. Instead of prolonging *ad infinitum* the life of the ego, why not first cease to nourish it, starve it, embellish it, adorn it and increase its knowledge, ability, and talents, always developed and acquired toward differentiation and infatuation?

We must simply come back to the reality of ourselves, to the essential reality, which does not care for all these superficial adornments, as it is the *Reality in itself.* Why not let the ego be dissolved and reintegrate the universal Prakriti? It is a product of the Earth-plane, not a product of "Heaven."

The thought-forms which are at the origin of the ego should be dissolved with the energy they have canalized. It is a magic creation not a real one, it is a Homunculus, it is a ghost that has sometimes succeeded in maintaining an existence of its own. It has known many passages on Earth. It may be very powerful as a mental being, it knows much and sometimes succeeds to glimmer and shine as if it were Truth.

It is the "occult" being *par excellence* and all the more difficult to destroy.

It is not the agitated mind, the mind which rushes around which can help us to find Truth. It is not even in being impatient to find Truth that we will find it, but rather by being at peace, by working for peace in ourselves and by achieving a state of complete relaxation, abandonment and "opening." The "inquiring" mind, which is still, which is ready to discover, to find out, is what is required.

A withdrawal of our attention from the surface is as essential as our stabilization in the deepest layers of the Reality within.

The state we seek is primarily a state of *peace*, and it is only by the cultivation of peace that we may harvest its fruits.

The difficulty, at the beginning, is to understand that the ego has to disappear, because it is *not real*. It is only when the ego has dissolved itself that the Real may be manifested and may reappear at the surface of our consciousness; this is what is meant by "integration." After achieving it, we re-establish the true relationship between the world "within" and the manifestation.

After reaching the stage where we are fully and consciously able to discriminate between the world of Truth and the world of Falsehood, we must proceed to investigate the totality of our phenomena of consciousness. We must *trace* falsehood and follow it through each corner of the labyrinth of our ego, in each of its intricacies, complexities, recoils. We must screen each movement of our being by an awakened and alert mind through the sieve of our critical faculty. Every thought, every action, should be sifted in order to let the right movements of the Spirit come into being, to let the Spirit become a living, conscious, and manifested Reality in our world.

If we could utilize this alertness and give thorough attention to observe every hour of our life and to scrutinize each moment of our being, we would win the challenge of life.

Let us be *sincere* with ourselves; let us *seek* Truth, in order to discover Truth within ourselves, and then we will deliberately abandon the wrong movements of the lower nature with which we were associating.. This is the price of Truth, but having found it, we attain total happiness.

If we consider what we call "ourselves," in its totality, we find that our conception of the Ego is not clear. We actually face an entity much more powerful than imagined, because it has its roots on a plane of which we are not completely aware, and of which very little has been said so far except, perhaps, in the tradition of Ancient Egypt. The notion of the "Ka" perpetuating its life after death of the physical body, may refer to the existence of the super conscious self, which is not to be confounded with what in other traditions is called the "soul." This "Ka" or occult being is the one who incarnates from time to time; it is much more powerful and integrated than the "ego" of the surface that we only know and of which it is a manifestation. It is as illusive as the present ego in regard to the Transcendental Real and the Atman. However, if we really intend to proceed to disintegrate this occult being, we shall find it extremely difficult, for this entity has nourished itself on many experiences through any number of lives and has been endowed with a characteristic will to survive, to embellish itself, to accumulate knowledge, power, and fame.

To reach this first center of consciousness is of considerable importance if we want to proceed to our liberation, which is annihilation of this occult being. This was one of the necessary achievements in the ordeal of initiation in Ancient Egypt and the first preliminary step. It gave to the Egyptian considerable ability and unsurpassed knowledge in the occult science. Needless to say, if we do not stop amusing ourselves with such creations, we consequently add to the power of resistance that the ego constitutes and weighs in the balance against our real and definitive salvation.

We today wish to perpetuate something of ourselves, after death, be it name, fame, or wealth. To die without an heir is often considered to be a misfortune as it means that sooner or later all that has been "ourselves" will disappear and not a trace of our passage on Earth will ever remain.

In certain civilizations, tombs are the objects of particular attention, so that the memory of the dead should be religiously kept by those who are living. It is evident that we make as many efforts as possible in order to assert ourselves and to survive by all possible means.

The ego is a process toward "becoming." To stop this process of becoming is to let the ego die. It is to bring out radically its total destruction which is thus bound to come sooner or later. It is to uproot its *raison d'etre.* If we cease to associate with the world of becoming, the Real will instantly be experienced and revealed, as the Real is in itself the world of "being." Only by stopping the process of becoming, will the ego cease to nourish itself. Its vital energies will dissipate gradually and, if the vision of Truth is strong enough in our mind to sustain the process until the final and total dissolution, we shall be "liberated."

Contact with the Real

As beings on the Earth plane, our problem is to find a way to the Real, which is Truth. There is a *state of poise* that has to be maintained in order to keep a constant balance in the very process of the play of Life. The equilibrium is broken when we become unnecessarily attracted by the objects of life and become attached to them. We then lose control of ourselves, as if we were forgetting the real significance of life, which is clearly and perfectly seen from the upper spheres. There is nothing wrong in a normal life with the natural enjoyments that life offers, as long as it does not interfere with our spiritual life. It is only when the "state of poise" is broken that we lose the "contact" with the Spirit and fall back into the world of delusion; so we must keep a constant purity of Mind in order to be able to resist the power of attraction of the world through awareness and a sense of discrimination between the normal and natural and that which destroys our fundamental equilibrium. The Chinese expressed this long ago and put it into practice in everyday life as the ultimate discipline and ethics transcending all other spiritual disciplines. This is the only possible way to live on the Earth plane, a real normal and ordinary human life, in complete attunement with the laws and reality of the Spirit.

If the capacity to concentrate at all times, meaning to be constantly aware and alert at all levels, is achieved, all the other side problems of the self are solved.

It is the lack of concentration or evasiveness of the mind that creates all the other problems and lets the door open to all — outside or inside — disturbing influences.

The body is endowed with a consciousness and it is that consciousness which has to be contacted and eventually summoned and called forth in order to effect what we would call a "treatment."

It is precisely this consciousness, once alerted, which can produce a rectification at the physical, as well as the psychological, level. The body must be stilled; in order to allow the healer to penetrate this consciousness and to have an exchange at the telepathic level, which can be established, more intensely, when a magnetic contact has been made possible between this consciousness and the practitioner through the Center or Chakra, which is related to the Solar plexus — the organ of immediate apprehension of all that is coming from the outside.

Judgment

"The Death of Dogmas is the Advent of Reality."
— Ananda Devi

We are our own *Judge*. Nobody is judging us but ourselves.

Naturally, this Judgment is being made at the level of the *True Self* who, alone, has the power of discriminating between what is *true* from what is false, between what is good and what is not good.

This judgment cannot come from the ordinary earthly consciousness, from the *ego,* which does not have the power to discriminate, for it lives a fictitious life that is in total ignorance as to the world of Truth.

The one who is in touch with the spiritual intelligence becomes a *mediator* between the powers from "above" and the Earth plane. He receives the necessary impetus allowing the transformations that are to be made upon the Earth. He channels the power of essential Goodness. The power that he receives is in proportion to what there is to be achieved and which he is perfectly conscious of, and he uses this power exclusively to implement the will of Essential Goodness.

The ego has no power whatsoever, for the ego lives in ignorance.

The ego must be transcended, so as to allow the manifestation of the *true* entity, which should be unveiled in its total luminescence.

The man who is genuinely turned toward the good, alone, can have access to these heights and can become the instrument of this Divine Power-Consciousness. To find again the *true Power:* the one who is responsible for the entire creation, in its magnitude, its beauty its magnificence. The salvation of the Earth will come *from the people* themselves, when more and more individuals awaken to the necessities of the time and to a sense of the responsibilities in regard to the human community.

These kind of people *do exist* but a large number is not yet conscious that they *can* and *should* do something about it. They don't see *how* to operate in order to help.

They have been made, for so long, to believe that only those who are in charge of Society are the ones who can do something.

They think that they are helpless being in a position where they are not in the limelight. In fact, there are different levels of limelights, and the one who has succeeded in establishing a contact with the spiritual powers, who is ready and willing to serve as an intermediary between these powers and the Earth plane, can receive and channel the *real* powers, the *real* Energy, the *real* vision to achieve, more than all the efforts of those who endeavor to work with their own limited power whether political or of any other nature.

Only through these channels can the transformation penetrate ultimately the entire population of the globe.

These intermediaries are absolutely necessary and indispensable so that Humanity can receive an orientation, a direction that would spring from its bosom, thanks to those dedicated Souls who care for others and who are capable of establishing *contact* with the upper power. This contact is not a *fiction*, like the one the religions have tried to entertain in the minds of their followers. This *contact* is the result of an initiation, of an opening to the primordial Force. This is what Humanity is waiting and hoping for.

The super-structures, whether governmental or religious, have only succeeded to precipitate Humanity into *anarchy*, as we can see today very clearly, for they do not possess *true* power.

It is a most vital necessity for us all today at this present juncture, to act and prevent the powers of destruction from getting a hold of the entire world and finally succeeding to *destroy life* and the planet as well!

Man and the Spirit of Creation (Man's Unlimited Powers)

One-pointedness, in thought, desire,· action, is indispensable in order to achieve our purpose. Understand that the moment thought is created, it carries along its own creative power. If you come along with another thought and desire to be materialized, and if it is diametrically opposed to the first one, you will not create anything at all, and you will defeat your own purpose.

But if you carry through any one of them, without any doubt or hesitation, without any drawback, vacillation or postponement, you will succeed.

There is always a way to create, and we can create almost anything we want to create. Desire is the first step toward creation and response from the outside world will only come when we put our heart fully into it. But the difficulty never really exists. It is a phantom of the mind that we have to get rid of. Let us remember that as soon as thought is engendered, reality is being transformed.

It is henceforth to the very source of thought that we must focus our attention in order to eliminate all negative ways of thinking.

It is necessary to reverse completely our present, elusive way of thinking, redirect its emission, in order to use best our power of creation. No power in the world — if our intention is legitimate — can stop us from doing what we want to achieve. Thus, shall we create new coordinates of action, and a new life will open for us in the vast, limitless field of creation; we will reassume the Divine instrument — which is the creative Power of the Mind — the magic wand of the fairy — and will transcend the limited, narrow mode of existence in which we are groping in the dark.

We possess the instrument that would allow us to create upon the objective real, but it is as if we had ignored it and are not using it. Unless we realize our mistake, we will vacillate between pessimism and optimism, passing alternately from one to the other, and our life will reflect our belief in the difficulty and, at other times, our belief in our own power of creation, which is the guarantee to success.

All attainments at each and every moment lie within our reach. Man possesses full Power to create, and it is this Creative Power that is the very mark of his divinity. Man may experience and reach a stage wherein there are no more limitations; he is able to transcend himself and, by so doing, rejoins God and becomes "one" with Him.

It is given to Man to hope for, desire, and possess all that he wishes and longs for. There is no limit to his power of creation. It is in this certitude and in the utilization of his creative power that he becomes aware of his divinity, that he imitates God, that he is God. He participates in the creative movement constantly manifesting in Nature, for in the truest sense, creation ought not to be regarded as having a beginning (as many seem to believe), but it is present, real, eternal, and constant. Not for one instant does the creative movement stop, not for one moment does the entire Universe fail to be renewed. It is one of God's attributes to recover our Divinity; we must feel the creative spirit living within and manifesting through us, as it does through Universal Life. Let us be one with it. Let us be a part of this *élan*. Let us liberate ourselves from the inertia in which we are imprisoned, or, more precisely in which our spirit is imprisoned, for it has not succeeded in annihilating the creative power residing in us and entertaining the flame of life in every cell and function of our body.

We must participate with our full being in this creative impulse, mark, and seal of the Divine in us, as in all things.

Let us realize that nothing is impossible for us to achieve in this world.

Creation has an unlimited field in which we have our part to play, and the work we create can be unlimited insofar as our mind does not conceive of any limitation. For the scale of the human mind is most often far from being attuned to the scale of the Divine, and we are accustomed to seeing limits where there are none, an error resulting from our narrow outlook.

We must try to accommodate our vision to that of the Divine. Let us free ourselves from the categories of the mind, which make up our immature, primitive thinking, from the narrow confines of Time, for Eternity is in the Present, and the present moment, the Now, is ours forever.

Then this vast Universe suddenly appears as an infinite field of creation where the impossible does not exist and where Man can and must manifest himself totally and display his creative genius ... the same man who now seems to be aware only of his alleged limitations ... and it is in this belief, and only in this belief, wherein lies his actual limitation. But, in reality, such limits do not exist. All his aspirations can be realized; in fact, they must be realized. If he were to realize this essential truth, the illusory veil of the finality of his present conditioning, the false conviction of his importance, would vanish, leaving a clear untrammeled field with no obstacle. In his Spirit would evolve all freedom, expressing only Joy and true enthusiasm, with the astounding facility of seeing his smallest aspirations as well as his greatest enterprises being materialized.

Man's enemy is, then, primarily his incredulity, slowly destroying his genius, and blind ignorance, depriving him of all Joy on Earth.

Let us behold the Creation and take part in the creative effort no longer through sadness and suffering — as though one were condemned to death — but in the Holy Joy and the Divine Light, which are our true heritage. Heaven is not to be achieved in some indeterminate future time, a place inaccessible and improbable. Heaven is to be reached and actualized on this Earth in the Present. When it is understood and realized in this world, it will be an acquisition for all time to come, because that felicity can never be forgotten once it has been tasted. It is a real, eternal possession. The real poison of man — man in the process of evolution — is *doubt*, which derives from ignorance and blind forces.

To participate in this infinite creative spirit will lead us, if we surrender to it, to realize ourselves and give our full measure, which is in itself unlimited. We would thereby reach "God" through the sole and most direct way, which can assure us of its possession. For it is not enough to be mentally *aware* of God. We have to become *Him*, to partake of His Nature, that is to say, to conquer all those forces that prevent us from re-integrating "God" ourselves.

To conquer inertia within our own sphere is the first condition for this achievement. But to conquer inertia does not indicate that we should spend our reserves of energy in an unintelligent effort. We have only to open ourselves to the creative *élan* and work in communion with it for all that we want to achieve, including our inner transformation, so as to break the bondage of the ego.

To overcome the force of inertia would allow us to transcend the limits of Life and Death, to which we are, at present, subjugated. If we are sufficiently steady in our effort, we may escape decay, which naturally comes with old age, soon followed by death. For it is the force of inertia which slowly, but surely, leads to death. Let us no more submit to its power, but on the contrary, let us be guided, directed, impregnated totally by the creative impulse, perpetually active and dynamic, and thus shall we break the spell under which we are, at present, by our believing in the inevitability of the laws of destruction. In order to manifest the creative power and be "one" with it, we should utilize the Cosmic energy, which is without limit, by the genius and art of the Spirit.

A man is old when he no longer possesses the creative urge. This can be observed among the aged, and even among the young, who have been prematurely deprived of their reserves of energy due to some serious illness. Men could be relieved of the strain of their harassing labors by opening themselves to the divine Creative Power. Instead of doing so, they consume their vital reserves of energy, and a time comes when they no longer receive the ever-new and invigorating creative breath. They die of asphyxiation or of the irreparable lack of that vital breath, which gave them birth and engendered their physical life.

At whatever moment we realize the necessity of this opening to the Divine Creative Consciousness, we immediately experience the benefits of a suspension of the normal processes of destruction. This process of destruction is intimately connected with Time and the ordinary consciousness in the waking state, unaware as it is of pure consciousness and bliss.

At any time, it is possible to accumulate some new and fresh energy and reascend the chain of time; that is to say, to rejuvenate and rebuild our organism and different bodies in their initial and perfect eternal condition.

From this moment, Joy never leaves us; all sadness, disillusion, and anguish disappear from our lives. Those around will also benefit from this contact with the Divine, as a lamp shining in the night illumines all that is around, not only he who carries it.

This explains why there are some Yogis who are able to remain young for a long period of time. They have found the secret of partaking of this creative force. They are conscious of being "One Imperishable" unit.

The first step toward this achievement is to feel the creative force to be active, not from the outside, but within us.

There is no longer any need to despair, when we realize that it is in our capacity to create the object of our desire. Nothing is unattainable as long as we understand that we can create it.

God is love; He is also Power. Let us experience God in his aspect of Power, which is displayed and manifested in the creation, and test ourselves in the art of creation. Then we shall be permitted the most fantastic dreams. All that is necessary is to know that we can realize and materialize them. It is only when we realize what we are in the Truth that a force is released within us. We can experience in all its fullness the Divine Love and be a fountain of Love to others.

If we are not self-realized, our love is partial and limited. Those who have much to give, can give much. Those who have in plenitude can give without limits.

Without the experience of the creative power, Joy is not complete, or more precisely, it cannot be stabilized within the heart of man, for

God must be reflected in him also in his power of creation. This is why man must himself experience in the field of Creation, awaken his latent powers, and manifest them fully. The more he manifests them, guided by intuition and inspired by Joy, the more he approaches and tends to become a part of the Divine.

By the magic virtue of the creative Spirit, man is able to become a limitless source of Energy and Power to achieve. As soon as man has identified himself with it, the creative Spirit pours all the energy that man requires for his enterprises on Earth, which means that man does not encounter any more limitations regarding the problem of energy, of its accumulation and conservation.

He is able to create without any limitations and disposes of the Universal Energy without any restriction and bondage. Man comes to experience, in this state, a paradisiacal condition of existence in which he realizes "oneness" with the Father, and he is able to recover the wondrous Kingdom of God.

If we are part of the Spirit, if the Spirit has created the world, then it is true that we have created the world. To reconquer it, should be simple for us. Thus can we say that "all attainments at each and every moment lie within our reach."

This is why we must become one with the Real, love our participation in the Real. We must not evade the Real, which constitutes our one and only means of experiencing our latent Powers, of becoming ourselves again, such as we have never really ceased to be.

The real and the Play of the Real upon us is the unique means at our disposal of destroying the ancestral suggestion firmly established, on the conscious and subconscious levels, that the object is distinct from the subject; it is also our sole means of destroying the Illusion, the Maya, our ignorance.

Let us evade the Real, because what we call the Real, is also the Creation, the image of God, and God and the Creation, that is ourselves, are inseparable and indistinguishable.

As we cannot separate the consciousness of Being from the Joy, which emanates from it and the speculative Play, which is the result of both and which has created the Phenomenal World — the true expression of the Divine Joy and Fantasy — in order to become aware of our own divinity, we have to create in our turn and enjoy our creations, in the image of the Divine.

Then shall we find again our identity with It.

What must be changed is our way of seeing things, our manner of thinking, our mental process, being made up as it is, for the most part, of doubt, apprehension, and uncertainty.

We must also disengage ourselves from the collective suggestions which rule over our mind.

Think of the psychology of the child to whom all is possible and for whom all can be realized. Much more credence is given by him to the "marvelous" than to that which we call "the Real." He believes in fairy tales. Then, bit by bit, the impression received from the world of adults and our customary ideas about the reality — that radical objectivization of the Real — overrides his sense of the marvelous.

The connection between our thought-desire and its fruit — the realization — is no longer perceived, as it was so naturally during childhood. The fairy's magic wand, which is actually the creative power of thought, disappears, to be replaced by doubt and the complete objectivization of the external world which, so seen, then reacts upon the mind, which has given to it a distinct reality in itself, upon which it can see no possibility of acting, except through effort and work, wherein the idea of time and endurance is of principal importance.

A fundamental misapprehension regarding the authentic origin of the external world has, therefore, engendered a belief in this distinct reality upon which the human mind has no hold, or very little. This error can be comparable to the one that occurs in the mind of the child who is frightened of his own shadow. An autonomous existence is conferred on it, made of our incapacity for true thinking, our failure to realize our own powers, which we have allowed to slip into dormancy. We have forgotten them; we have denied them. Since we recognize no possibility of true, immediate action — that is to say, of the power of thought alone over the external reality — we have allowed it to react upon us, as if it were not our own psychic projection with its multiplicity of reactions — the "how" and the "why" of which we do not analyze. We become frightened by this "unknown" reality, and make sacrifices before the altars of the gods of "chance" and "fate."

When, at last, we understand our error and wish to try the power of thought, it is then quite difficult to free ourselves of our doubts and fears before a Reality that we have only to organize in order to bend it to our will, for our complete satisfaction.

We must re-educate ourselves, again habituate ourselves to believe in our own powers. We must destroy the counter-suggestions of our quasi-powerlessness in the face of the "Objective Reality," test our powers, and rely upon results obtained. Auto-suggestion must be used as a corrective measure. Then, as if by the effect of a magic wand, beings and things will be changed. We should again make use of this divine instrument, which we have for such a long time ignored, which is our own thought process, in its positive creative aspect.

The whole subconscious ought to be modified and adapted to this new leitmotif. Not even one of our previous thought habits ought to be allowed to remain, at the risk of diminishing and retarding our creative powers and their consequent desired effects upon "Reality."

We will be stimulated in this endeavor by the first fruits of this new way of thinking.

This is a new formula for thinking, adapted this time to the true Real and no longer the apparent.

In this way we shall have eliminated in ourselves the belief in a fundamental illusion. When we have through those demonstrated to ourselves the non-existence of a reality independent of ourselves, but, on the contrary, absolutely dependent upon our own mentations, we will no longer be slaves of the Real, but strong in our powers; and, in the use of our thought, we will play at creation as the Creator has made with the totality of the exterior world, in joy and complete independence. All is "play," and the play is the expression of joy. The child also plays, because in so doing he uses his creative faculties. Surely we can recall the true pleasure that we took in these creations as a child, and which we have not since tasted in all its intensity. We must rediscover the joy of creating through the right use of our creative powers. This is why art, which is play, can take us out of ourselves and out of our limitations. In this way, the artist is a creator; although he, too, is limited by one last illusion — he rejects the external world as a Reality over which he has no powers; a reality which he scorns, and which makes him suffer. He creates instead another world by using a different material. He works upon a form that is, actually, the image of the form of the objective Real.

Why does he not create directly upon the Real? Why represent the Real, when the Real itself is infinitely richer in materials, diversity; and, lastly, because the joy of creating in the real, with one's own materials, is much deeper? Only such creation and such creation alone allows the complete liberation of all man's aspirations, which art cannot fully and definitively achieve.

In the Real, man can live whatever role, at whatever level he wishes, according to his plan, and this plan need have no limits, reaching as it may to God.

Man becomes, at the same time, the author and actor in his own drama, and he plays, as have thousands of souls before him, under the eyes of the Creator, the dream of creation, in possession of all his means and powers as a true demiurge.

He has then the possibility of changing over completely, according to his own aspirations and desires, the objective world. The more expert he becomes at managing the objective world, the deeper will be the modifications he will effect upon it.

All those who have played a role upon the Earth have not done otherwise. They all used the creative power of their own thought, having the absolute conviction that their own certitude was enough to modify the Real.

In this way, man learns to know his true nature, which is Divine, that is to say, which was at the beginning of all things. It is by acting thus that he realizes, ever more fully, more consciously, more integrally his Divine Nature.

Thus, will he find himself again unchanged, throughout the ages, where it seemed as if he had lost himself, not marked by time, always the same, installed in his own certitude and enjoying contentment, which is also Peace and Serenity, realizing oneness with the Spirit, having nothing to do with the human mental world, which is the victim of all illusions.

Since we are, in essence, One with the Divine Mother, it is not surprising that she be Providential and gives us proof of her love. For her love, which we objectify, is our own will manifesting itself. In a word, we are amazed at the gifts that we make to ourselves. Imprisoned in the illusion, we are, in the eyes of the true superior consciousness, in the greatest mental delusion.

By always separating the object from the subject, we create an illusory world — a mental world — of which we become the victim. We create duality; whereas the only reality is *Unity*.

All our mistakes come from dualistic belief.

If we cease to believe in duality and realize this evidence, all will adjust itself in our mind; our foolish rambling will cease instantly, as in the case of a mad man who suddenly is brought back to his senses.

We become conscious of and enjoy the marvelous unity, which is in all things as it is in ourselves. The human theater ceases to have an existence in itself. Henceforth, the author and the actor become one in the eternal of the Spirit.

We objectify the external world, the egos, and, on the other side, the higher world, the Providential world, without realizing that all these worlds are but One, and that we, alone, can not act upon the one and the other, because they are both the fruits of our own thought.

In objectifying these two worlds, we extricate them for ourselves; we dislocate ourselves; we do not see the unity of subject and object, which make one Reality of which we are a center, a thinking and dynamic action.

We fail to make use of our own powers, because we are ignorant of them. We cease to know them and become one thing among so many others.

"Man's worst enemy is man himself," who acts as would a vastly wealthy man who would go begging from door to door, looking for a scrap of food, and thinking himself the poorest of men.

Symbolically, the external world represents to us the Difficulty, and Providence represents the assistance that we draw from the spiritual powers.

Why can we not understand, through a more direct and efficient use of the spiritual power, that the Difficulty is nil before the Spirit, but that the Spirit has created the external world and perpetually creates it, and if we commit the error of believing in the Difficulty, this Difficulty will materialize, because, whether or not we are aware of it, our thought has a creative power. If we affirm the existence of the Difficulty, instantly it exists.

In fact, we use the creative power within us *against* ourselves. We are afraid of the Reality that we engender, because we do not know how to use the mechanism of creation that we should use in one way instead of the other, positively, rather than negatively. It is necessary to completely re-educate the mind in order to think positively and in the true direction, for, as soon as thought is engendered, Reality is being transformed. It is henceforth to the very *source* of Thought that we must focus our efforts. It is necessary to revise our way of thinking, redirect its emission, control it, and learn to eliminate negative thoughts, so that we may only create the positive. Then the universe that we shall create around us — which is our very destiny — will be positive, in absolute harmony with our own wishes.

We possess the instrument, which permits us to create upon the Objective Real, but we do not know how to use it. We have to learn the true use of it, because until we have discovered it, we remain enclosed in a destiny in which pessimism and optimism alternate, wherein sometimes the events are the reflection of our belief in the difficulty and sometimes of our belief in the Providence that is of Success.

Let us realize that the phenomenal world and Providence are but One, and from this moment let us take up the reins of our own chariot and not give them over to anyone else. We were meant to be the conductor and nobody else.

These two worlds created by us ought to be commanded by us, since they are a direct emanation from us, a reflection of our own thought. The moment our thought turns toward the right direction, our destiny will enjoy an astonishing continuity to which we were not previously accustomed and will bring us all the satisfactions that we expect of it, since, through the re-education of our thought, we have found again the means of acting completely upon it, in another word, to create it.

Thereby we have the means of reabsorbing all that is our Karma. Our will-power ought to be able to counterbalance these past influences, as one can easily control and stop the movement of a machine that was before going at full speed.

So long as Man has not seen his error and is not able to use the creative power of thought, he can and should pray that he may be helped to find this greater knowledge. Once in possession of this power, what use is it for him to pray for it, for the realization depends only upon himself, since he possesses the instrument and he knows the way to use it.

To pray is to objectify the Providential World from our own self. In reality, the power, all the power, the greatest power, all that which we are in need of, the power of the whole world, is within the self.

It is not necessary to beg for it in order to obtain it, because we can freely use it through the effect of our own will through our own certitude.

When Truth is Seen

"The more we 'see' ignorance, the more we have the spectacle of ignorance, the more we 'see' Truth."

— *Ananda Devi*

To reach certitude on a particular problem is to discover its inherent, not apparent, *Truth*! This conviction leads to a *choice*. When we have made the choice, which is inevitably in favor of the Truth, then the difficulty disappears; its Truth is seen. There is no more conflict within. Who was trying to elude the difficulty? The conscious being riding the surface. This is the way to get rid of many of our wrong habits and set patterns. The subconscious is conquered only when true vision is reached, the conviction secured, and the choice made. Then the power liberated from this choice is considerable — it is the power of Truth — and no obstacle is great enough to stop its progression or diminish its power of transformation. To square the problem, face it and think until we reach the bottom of it in an impersonal approach, until we reach a certitude, is the key to solving our problems. It is an arduous thinking that needs courage and determination — for the easiest way would be to avoid the difficulty and escape — until we are able to uncover the truth lying underneath.

Once that is *"seen,"* it is automatically accepted; once accepted, human nature, with its accumulation of wrong habits of thinking and behavior at the unregenerated level, can be transformed, not before. Regeneration of human nature cannot be affected in any other way. Mere wishes do not do the trick. They have to be substantiated, supported, nourished by a clear vision of the Truth on the matter. Sometimes the fact that we do not want to remove our blindness is the only cause for ignorance. We do not really want to find out; we just pretend; we avoid thinking deeply, for we know at the back of the mind that we would discover the Truth that would imply on our part a relinquishment that we do not wish to make. This is why we were claiming our impotence to *control ourselves* on this particular matter.

The real thinker is bound to become a sage — otherwise he is a hypocrite. If he cannot put into practice the truth in which he believes, if it is not implemented within himself, it has no value. We can demonstrate the hidden truth to those who are still blind through implementing this truth in our life and being a living example of it so that the passer-by can see for himself that this is the truth. Truth can only prevail in the world if and when it is incarnated in the individual. That was the power of Aurobindo and other Spiritual Masters.

The people around could see Truth directly through their own realization of it. They were convinced, encouraged by this example and stimulated to follow this example. Mere talks have no effect. This is why religions and ministers who have no power (no spiritual realization) do not succeed in transforming Humanity in spite of all the words and the preaching they deliver incessantly to the masses.

* * *

Thinking Right

To save the world there is nothing else to do than to *think right,* even if we never express these *true* ideas through any other channel than the mental-waves. These ideas are issued instantaneously and emitted through the instrument of the brain, carried out by the power accumulated within us and at once considerably increased when the mind receives a Cosmic idea. A Cosmic idea is the result of a calculation in which two factors are involved: the true vision, the right thinking, and, on the other side, the needs of time, the necessities of evolution of each race, nation, people, and of mankind as a whole.

Removing Obstacles

First of all, how do we rid ourselves of wrong thinking so that the realization of the Divine within ourselves is no longer beyond our reach?

How to remove obstacles, face the problem, not be satisfied only intellectually with the vision of Truth, but go deeper and see that Truth, means to go to the bottom of an obstacle or situation. When we do that in an objective manner, then the obstacle is removed, the power of resistance abolished instantaneously, the things that we wanted to solve are solved.

It needs the primary courage to face the problem, not to escape it because we know that by facing it we come to conclusions that will be unavoidable; because of our weakness, we want to elude the whole thing; we do not reach impersonality in our thinking. We are partial to try to see Truth for Truth itself, no matter how we are going to be affected by this realization. Not only do we think it is impossible to reach realization, but we want mediocrity; we are afraid of leaving mediocrity like a pig who wants to remain in his own filth. When we have found a method within ourselves by which it becomes easy to detach ourselves from all filth, then we know that Perfection is possible; it is our concrete achievement of every day. This, by thinking, reasoning, clarifying for ourselves, seeking constantly, is the Truth in an impersonal, detached manner.

It is an act of cowardice that prevents us from thinking clearly. Subconsciously, we know that it will lead us to give up that which prevents us from living, experiencing the Truth, fear of losing whatever life has to offer. The ghost of the ascetic man, projected by the various religions as the example to follow, has brought about fear in man and has associated the discovery and living in Truth with that image of asceticism.

The Belief in Meditation

In philosophy, we use the same scientific attitude as in science — and also in metaphysics — a state of mind of expectation that leads to new discoveries.

Our belief that we know everything is stupid and unfruitful.

Truth cannot be found without courage.

There are some people who believe in meditation. What do they meditate about? They take a principle, a big idea, like the Love of God, and meditate about it.

They superimpose their mind on an idea that they select, and they think that by doing so they are doing some good to themselves.

A new being emerges out of that which may be to some extent a little more refined than the average type, but still they have enclosed themselves into a mold, a pattern. Even if that pattern is a better pattern than the previous one, it is still something that is there. The real inner richness of the individual has not been exploited, searched for, dug out.

Why not stop all this nonsense and do nothing of the kind? The real problem is to discover Truth and not meditate about something that we do not know yet, because we risk to meditate for a long time to come without much result. What has to be done is, on the contrary, to *discard* ideas: withdraw from the lower level of thinking associated with, first our day to day life, and the substance taken from our contact with the mind of others whom I would call the real "invaders of our mind." Get out of the lower spheres of our own mind and proceed in this withdrawal until we reach a standstill. When we have become a vibration of thought, refraining from being caught in the mechanism of thinking to which we were previously subjected, we will have succeeded.

To think of things that we know and that we have already identified cannot help us in any way except maybe when the time comes when we have to recognize the elements of thinking, already gathered, in a synthesis. But apart from this exception, we should not turn toward the past, but in the direction of the future. In the future, are obtained all the things that we do not know yet, and this is what we have to discover. Our attention should be in alert; we must keep quiet with our mind, attentive and in a state of expectancy. If we succeed in maintaining our mind in that state for a length of time, searching in the unknown, ready to capture or detect new ideas, the revelation of Truth is bound to come. For whoever has tried it, has received such a revelation.

It is to put one's mind in a neutral position, and this attitude has to be cultivated — not only when we experiment in this direction but every minute of our life. Every moment should be turned in the direction of the unknown in order not to repeat always the same gestures, but be directed by this greater Power of the Unknown, which is God himself.

Then, on our level, we can, at any time, transcend our condition and build up a destiny that will be drawn by an invisible hand and supported, actualized by this invisible Power. The Power of God himself. This is feasible, realizable, and possible at this present level of ours.

Do Not Set Limits

X: I am a writer.

D: Don't limit yourself; don't condition yourself; you are greater than a writer, but you don't know it.

Through the ego, you can achieve that much and no more; there will always be a plus. I discarded many things, which to many are of significance and great value in this human world, because I was looking for that Plus, and that Plus directly leads to the plane of the Gods, of the Heroes, of the Titans who have enchanted the imagination of the people since time immemorial, in every civilization. It is to live an existence of freedom, emancipation, Joy, and creativity. It is to touch the most intense powers of creation. It is those powers, behind the veil of our ignorance, which are creating — to touch even an iota, gives you tremendous bliss. It is sheer madness to choose the limited, the suffering, the grotesque, and the hideous, when you can accede to a Divine Life on Earth.

What people should know is that when they choose the Life Divine, they are not going to lose anything, but are going to gain everything; they will have everything in abundance; Human life, as conceived by many, is only a caricature of what should be our life on Earth.

Let us go beyond the intellectual knowing and reach the realm of the "seeing." To see Truth, the truth of a problem, to reach to the bottom of it, then we can never escape again from the consequences, the inevitable changes that follow once truth has been seen, faced, and contemplated. What men do not do is go to the bottom of the problem, because they know that if they go deep enough, they will have to change, to see things differently, and to act in a different manner. This is the very nature of Illusion, twisting the Truth and making us cling to the unreal and to the limited.

Men do not know that Perfection is not utopia or a thing impossible to reach, as commonly believed, beyond the reach of the human beings. Perfection is possible, and it is easy to reach, at least there is a way to reach it. It is a boundless achievement, once it has started, it does not end. Values are changed, scales are changed; we then live in a different world; the narrow, the limited is being replaced by the unlimited, the boundless, the ever-attractive, captivating reality that evolves and revolves in the limitless field of Creation. From that day on, you know that you cannot escape from that: One day or another it must come in your life. The dedication of yourself to Truth and the abandonment of the ego-consciousness, why not today?

"I will be always there present at every crossroad waiting for you," like in *Peer Gynt*. Here it is *life* and not death that will be there waiting for you! Don't postpone it, because Time is treacherous; you may never be able to do it; surrender when you still have something to surrender, something to offer, before it is too late!

X: But I am a writer, will I have to give up writing?

D: Who says that you will have to give up writing? You will not have to give up writing.

But it is the motivations at the back of the writing that will be changed, not the writing itself. You will write not in the same spirit but in a spirit of dedication, to serve the Divine and the purpose of the Divine in the world on the largest possible scale. Don't try to foresee at present what would be the consequences of this change in you. Let the transformation take place and stop worrying about its after-effects. Everything will unfold in the right direction and for the good of all concerned, in a natural manner.

First work out the essential; first things first; this is wisdom. Then the whole life of yours will be reshaped according to a new pattern — the very design of the Divine — to suit the purpose of the Divine.

Renunciation, or the act of giving up, is natural and never painful. It is like the child who one day gives up his toys, not because he wants to punish himself or renounce them in a spirit of sacrifice, but because they have lost all significance to him. He has grown up.

It would be useless and even harmful to give up without having the full desire of it or the understanding of why we should give something up.

X: You make things very clear to me; I see now what it is; you are living proof that the Message that Aurobindo has brought to the world is real, workable, feasible.

D: I see it every day; I am constantly experimenting on myself and on others and demonstrating the truth of his tremendous vision; these things are possible, and the transformation can touch and work on almost anyone.

To proceed from one evidence to another, enter the density of the forest, but never to be lost, to come to the core of the problem, continuing, pursuing one's road until we reach the supreme Logic *par excellence* and the beyond — which is the plunge into the innermost, secret, hidden Reality in order to know it through an ineffable, direct approach that is beyond the ranges of human perception as known and experienced by the multitude.

If this happens to me, this can be the experience of the whole race. Let us not give up when there is nothing left to give up. Let us give up when we are young; then we reap, when it is still time, the fruit of renunciation, which is immediately converted into spiritual achievements, like through the most subtle alchemical transformation.

Fire

When I want to convince someone of something, I reach the subconscious, and the work is done through the channel of the subconscious, and the conscious responds automatically. The fluid, or etheric, level is the meeting place of the mind and the will where the notion of "speed" intervenes and fire is the most powerful agent of creation or destruction.

The Fire has two qualities: developing what is real and destroying what is untrue and unreal.

In the atom, the elements of the atom turn at a certain speed, which is considerable. The atom itself is turning at a tremendous speed, which is also true in living matter and at the level of the subtle body. The motion of speed intervenes at all levels and the evolution of an individual can be measured and established in terms of a certain coefficient of speed.

On each plane of the manifestation, each universe is characterized by a certain condensation of the primordial energy and that condensation is, itself, subjected to the speed of an original motor generating the substance, characteristic of each plane. The more speed is increased, the higher the plane is, and the more fluidic and immaterial the substance is. At the level of Spiritual Consciousness, speed is total, the power is total, and the density is the lightest that it can possibly be.

Therefore, when we wish to change planes, whether we intend to ascend or descend, we have to modify the nature and quality of the vibrations of the plane to which our consciousness is momentarily attached, which is also to attune the subtle body to the intrinsic speed of the substance forming the plane we want to reach and where we want to maintain our consciousness.

Fire must necessarily be used when we want a change of plane and to uplift our consciousness to a higher level. Otherwise, how can we transform the nature and quality of the vibrations of the substance of the etheric body, which is the *sine qua non* element in this matter of projection, and change?

Fire, alone, can materialize and dematerialize, at will, the various substances of the entire Universe manifested. Therefore, Fire is the sole real agent of evolution, for it acts on the substances and their intrinsic nature and can liberate the primordial energy constituting these substances. Liberating the primordial energy is to operate a process of dematerialization. It is also attuning the etheric to the various planes of manifestation of the Universe. The etheric being the real vehicle through which we move, act and create, ascend and descend, at will.

Breaking the spell of the Unknown is performed when we live fully aware of all planes at all times. It is also to close the cycle of evolution and Life by fully experiencing the Spirit in its most outward manifestation through the Lila of things and our own consciousness liberated, free, expressing only the joy of the primordial wonder.

* * *

Subliminal Consciousness

The subliminal consciousness registers what is being said, for instance, during a lecture that the ordinary consciousness cannot register everything and understand completely what is being said, for the information given out might be too new and out of the field of knowledge of the individual who "listens" but does not totally register consciously.

The phenomenal consciousness is aware of the subject treated, during the same lecture. This is what is perceived consciously. The rest, which has not been captured entirely, is, nevertheless, registered at a different level of consciousness, but, though out of reach of the ordinary consciousness, it is, however, not lost at all. It is, somehow, put in *reserve*. It is the subliminal consciousness.

It is what allowed me to notice that, after an indefinite period of time, sometimes months or even years, the individual, present at the lecture had, in fact, "registered it all," but the emergence of the information collected was taking a certain time to signal itself to the phenomenal consciousness.

Brahmacharya

What is Brahmacharya?

A Brahmacharya is the one who has acquired full control of the senses and the sense-desires, not only in deeds but in thoughts, not only in conscious thoughts but in the vast domain of the subconscious, the roots of the sanskaras. When, through intense purification and a complete opening to the Divine, the roots of the sanskaras regarding all sense-desires are eliminated, the individual is able to know Brahma and becomes a teacher of Brahma. It is to withdraw all the tentacles we have prolonged out of our own Self into the outside world back into the Self again in order that we may become an integrated Self, collected, not subjected, to outside influences. It is to open oneself exclusively to the influence of the Divine with whom we may establish a direct contact through the chakra of the top of the head. It is to receive our life and subsistence, the necessary substance, our food, the only one, which can make us grow, from the Divine; our inspiration, from the Divine and only those impulses, which come from this channel once it has been created. It is to be an integrated whole, as much as we can achieve, before the complete transformation takes place, which is essentially a working of the Divine; it is our sole participation, consisting of not interfering, of letting go the old and the distorted without any insistence, of being the "witness" of the operation and assimilating it through understanding as quickly as we can without projecting our preconceived and most cherished ideas, which would again distort the vision and its full expression.

Brahmacharya brings about:

1. *Isolation* from the outside world and its influence. This does not imply, at all, an escape in some Himalayan abode or retreat, which would be improper, for the problem has to be solved once and for all and in the midst of all temptations. There must be a withdrawal from the power of illusion prevailing only when we open ourselves to outside influences. How can we transform ourselves in the image of the Spirit if we let ourselves, at the same time, be influenced by outside unregenerated powers?
2. A concentration of the total being with his powers to be used for the purpose of transformation. Nature does the same. During each winter-season, it retires, collects all its powers, so that nothing happens or is manifested during that period on the outside. A new creation is in the making, which spreads out and becomes evident to all in Springtime.

3. Relinquishment of all this in order to manifest the Divine nature. We cannot achieve the Divine, a World of quintessence, by remaining in contact and under the direct influence of the world of imperfections and indulgences, a pale reflection of all the attributes and joys of a fully emancipated Divine Consciousness and nature. We have first to cut the roots that bind us to the animal, lower, unregenerated nature.

Regeneration starts only with the acceptance and application of the principle of Brahmacharya. Then Divine Consciousness has full power to exercise its influence on the individual, once Brahmacharya has been adopted and put into practice. There is no longer any interference between the Divine and Man for his own transformation and regeneration, the meaning of which is to find again one's own nature.

Brahmacharya becomes then the key to our progression and ascension in permitting the reawakening of Kundalini. Man is then able to establish peace within himself. He is not distorted any longer between his two apparent dual personalities or natures. He has definitively made his own choice. He has chosen the *Divine nature*, which is the real nature in Man. The other one was only assumed for a time, the time necessary for the experiment through the species and to fulfill the purpose of the lower nature.

It is a work of intelligence, clear thinking, and deep reasoning that is demanded of man — a work of courage that makes him raise and definitively depart from the lower forms of Nature and the grosser and more material purposes of the Prakriti.

Yajna: An act made as an offering or a sacrifice. All acts practiced in another spirit create bondage and go against the purpose of Moksha, or the final dissolution of all sanskaras.

Sanskaras: Accumulated habits and forms resulting of ignorance and an attitude not conformed to the spirit of Yajna, which leads to bondage. The Soul Consciousness, which we want to reach, is of another nature. We have deviated from this fundamental nature of ours, and this has resulted in the building of a shell, which we carry like the turtle and keeps us bound to Earth. We acquire a density, a heaviness, which takes time and effort to destroy, when we realize the fundamental error it has originated from.

Establishing a Link

You have to develop an awareness of the straight line, the straight line of the spine, of the neck, and the right position of the head.

Then prolong, ideally, this straight line upward — build up mentally and fluidically a channel reaching as far as you can imagine to an ideal point above your head along the line which is the prolongation of the spine.

Develop an awareness of this line in all its length. Feel attached to the ideal point in space situated above, which represents the siege of your *real Self*, in the Transcendental sphere, like a puppet is attached through a string to its operator.

Now, from head to feet, establish a shell made of Cosmic energy, which will be like a fluidic veil all around you, and know that the source of your inspiration, of all power, energy of the right ideas, the right movements, the right impulses, is this ideal point above your head — that you receive everything from it, because it is the *source* of your being. Don't cling to yourself as you are at present. Know that you are nothing, only a transitory phase. Don't cling to your actual ideas, volitions, the movements of your lower and unregenerated nature. Abandon the levers of command of your actual consciousness to the *source* of your being of which you are not yet aware. When you start receiving, through the instrument of the conscious being, from this source, you will no longer live in a separate consciousness, but you will be united with your real Self; your actual consciousness will only be the reflection of the Self, *bringing the Self into evidence* in this world of Man, into the manifestation. Your actual nature will have been regenerated; the transformation will take place.

By establishing a deep relaxation of the body, the muscles, the nerves and filling the etheric body with Cosmic Energy, an unusual lightness is felt in the body.

When the lightness has been experienced and you become aware of it, then tranquility, calmness, and poise are reached and emerge naturally out of the Self. When that has been experienced, along with the prolonged sensation of lightness, upliftment of the whole body, which is the detachment of your being from the gross vibrations of dense matter, Joy emerges out of the Self — Joy which is one with the consciousness of our existence. It exists by itself and is intimately linked with the awareness of the fundamental Reality.

We must prolong this Joy, not deviate from it, but prolong the echo of it in our total being and consciousness; we must enter into it.

When Joy is reached, for no other reason than the mere fact of existence, an awareness of Real Existence, that which is seized in the deepest layer of our being, the fundamental essence of our Existence has become known to us again.

This is a very simple way. No exertion is needed; on the contrary, it is to be avoided; what is needed is a gradual and increasing awareness of what *is*.

It is to re-establish the *link,* which we have lost, with the Reality, and which is the *cause* of the *"Fall of Adam."* Then, when this link is re-established, we are no longer a "fallen," subject, "creature" of the Divine; we have reassumed our Divine Consciousness and nature.

Most of the time, you spend your life and are actually living in *hell*; of course, you have never been fully conscious of it. Although some of your moods and expressions clearly indicate that you are living on planes which are not happy planes, you sink into them, because it is to follow the slope of least resistance, and you do not make the effort to emerge out of them. I do not want to see sad faces around me. I want to see Joy penetrate all the parts of the being, even the most obscure, which have to be exposed to the light of the conscious, enlightened being. No dark corners, nothing left out of account, untouched, unmodified, and unregenerated: a gradual disintegration of the artificial ego formation that we call "ourselves" has to be effected, due to which Reality will emerge and shine again of its own sheen.

From above, along the straight line, which I have already mentioned to you, there is a continuous inflow of energy coming, from the plane above, to us on our actual level, which is the level of the Earth plane and Earth consciousness. This is the link that has to be established again, recreated again; it has to become active again and more effective; we have to become aware of it again; it is a kind of umbilical cord between the Divine and ourselves. Time can be used for our benefit.

We are incomplete beings; we are in process; we are not finished. We have to build up a wall of protection around us and emerge from the subconscious, deep, and somber layers of our being through which we drive into the collective obscure planes of the Unconscious. This sphere of existence, to which we also pertain, has to be abandoned or regenerated.

Not one *link* of the chain can be omitted in the unfoldment of ourselves from within; otherwise, the unfoldment stops. The process of unfoldment can be continuous, if we know how to follow the natural lines of unfoldment. There is an order in the unfoldment of various links.

Upper Pole or Magnet

Blossoming of Man into his own Archetype
Sahasrara Chakra
(The Thousand-Petaled Lotus; The Upper Cerebral Center)

Buddhi
Opening of the third eye (illumination)
enlightened irrational or intuition
Ajna Chakra (plexus of command)

Intellect
Siege of actual Consciousness of Man. Siege of the ego.
Vishuddha Chakra
(pharyngeal plexus (throat))

Heart (Psychic Being)
Affectivity
Anahata Chakra (cardiac plexus)

Astral

Solar Plexus
Chakra of relationship and recognition
Manipura Chakra (solar plexus)

Etheric

Assimilation, digestion, elimination
Svadhisthana Chakra
(hypogastric plexus (stomach))

Physical

Creative, reproductive force
Muladhara Chakra
(pelvic plexus of the sympathic)

Lower Pole or Magnet

Divine Work

The Divine, or the realms of the Truth, can be seized through dedicated work. To find out again the purpose of creation, behind the veil of ignorance, which is the purpose of the Divine, regarding the whole as well as each and every parcel of creation and to serve exclusively, with our total being, this purpose, and this purpose alone, leads us through the shortest possible way and the easiest way to the Divine. We will re-embody the Divine, or the Divine will re-embody us.

When we do not follow the path of dedicated work, or our work is not placed on the highest possible scale, time becomes an eternity of negativity. When we get into the real work, all our energies are galvanized; the ego-sense sooner or later is disintegrated.

* * *

Conversation

Conversation is not necessarily speaking but thinking together, and naturally the thinking brings periods of silence in between the words and the ideas expressed.

Deference impels us to follow the thread of thinking of those with whom we meet and to whom we owe respect due to their knowledge. To invade the mind of such a person and impose our own ideas by expressing them and cutting, at the most incongruous moments, the thread of their thoughts, is a sign of irreverence and would be interpreted as a sign of the coarsest and rudest type of uncultivated ego ever known. People of the East are more courteous than this; they know when to talk and what to say; they also know when to remain silent.

The Greatest Act of Love

To be present upon the Earth is to participate in the life of the Earth.

It is to contemplate the infinite Beauty and Perfection of the Creation, the miracle of Life, of the flower, of the animal, and of the human being in their manifestations.

It is to feel within oneself the thrill, the palpitation of the Universal movement of Life, which binds us together, in the most intimate manner, with every living creature on Earth, as a manifestation of the Divine Consciousness. The only regret one might have, after contemplating the wonders of Creation, which are offered to give us a taste of Heaven, is to consider that, in spite of the Beauty and intelligence displayed before our eyes, we are still very far from approaching the Source of all these marvelous creations, the Source of the primordial, essential, immutable Reality.

When, one day, the aspiration to reach the Source is stronger than anything that has ever seduced our mind and the longing to fill our heart with an everlasting joy is more and more pressing; all of a sudden, the feeling of "aloofness" becomes so acute, whereas, at the same time, a secret sense of identity with that Source of all things is being felt — that the separation is more and more painful to bear. Our heart is then divided between the joy and admiration which overwhelm us when contemplating so many testimonies of Love and Beauty and, on the other hand, the inexpungable regret not to be able to plunge as yet thoroughly in the "Universe beyond Time," which, alone — we know it intuitively — would totally fulfill our innermost being!

To return to the Oneness, to the primordial Source, to merge in it, to get lost in it, is the greatest act of Love we would be capable of.

A Re-evaluation of the Concept of Freedom

There is one way the Soul is able to play as She wants, and it is the way of non-frustration, *i.e.*, of freedom. To be like a bird under the Heavens, it is to have all possibilities at our disposal, as the bird has all the food he requires and can *go* when he wants.

Freedom is the possession of the Soul alone. Frustration belongs to the world of ignorance, mental, human. Only the one who has reached his Soul can be *free*.

The whole concept of freedom within the boundaries of America and the infatuation, which has been associated with and provoked by such a concept, have to be analyzed and studied in a new light.

It is a fact that the concept of freedom has been used most excessively and indiscriminately in this country. It has served as a powerful suggestion of the most stupefying narcotic on the people. Let us try to analyze the concept of Freedom in the light of what we may know of the nature of Man.

Man is dual. One aspect of man is the one identified with the Ego and the lower part of Nature — the unregenerated man; man, the slave of his instincts and passions; on the other side, we may also anticipate Man identified with his Spiritual Nature, man possessing a sense of duty, capable of perceiving his place in the world, the meaning, and purpose of his existence; in a word, Man has accepted, as the supreme Law of his own being, to recreate himself in the image of the Spirit and, therefore, curb his gross instincts in order to reach his own Archetype.

I ask this simple question:

Which of these two aspects is entitled to freedom?... and should we not make, for ourselves as well as others, this basic distinction first before selling the idea of freedom to every corner of the world?

What are the results, already produced and with which we have to cope, of such an unpardonable lack of judgment and discrimination?

In the domain of Art:

We witness a continuously growing degeneration of the Art of Painting. The concept of freedom there has worked against the very purpose of Artistic creation. It has resulted in the misleading of the masses, ignorant and all too easily ready to gobble with frenzy the biggest and most fraudulent bluff of all time: Modern Painting, in its most eccentric and exaggerated interpretations.

In the domain of Music:

A similar decline can be observed, although, because of the survival of rhythm to which can always be attributed a meaning and is never completely bereft of sense, as Painting is.

The idea of Freedom is responsible for the complete irreverence of young people toward their parents, toward Society, and a lack of the most elementary respect for the life of their fellow men, initiating hooliganism and murder.

Egocentricity is the leitmotif of this country in its pitiless "struggle for life," which is compelling everyone and crushing, in its formidable machinery, those who are weaker and cannot stand the pressure. Hence, the astonishing number of recruits for mental hospitals and asylums, growing at a rate that is beating all the nations in the world.

The terrible consequences on the mind of the people, in relation to the problem of anxiety, the impact of the fever for speculation and gambling, which has seized the country, has terrible consequences on the mind of the people, due to the existence of the Stock Market, spreading throughout the country the atmosphere, tense and always so depressing, of a casino and this on a gigantic scale.

The fact that *a false evaluation of the concept of Freedom leads to anarchy.*

On the youth, it has already started its process of disintegration. It has really turned upside down the minds of young people who are easily influenced and lack the proper discrimination, normally acquired with maturity. It has made them lose all balance, has opened the way to "freedom" of the senses only. See the situation in France, illustrated by the writings of Simone de Beauvoir, Francoise Sagan, etc., which describe only too eloquently the kind of deprivation that had followed the initial mistake of a wrong concept of freedom.

When the senses are loose, violence is not far.

Imagine, for an instant, as I imagine it with awe, that a hypnotic suggestion, comparable to the one exercised by Picasso in Painting, would affect and insidiously penetrate the world of literature and the art of writing, affecting communications among men and people; compare this with the clear, rational, lucid thinking that has been reached through so much labor, enriched and perfected by so many civilizations and, without which, civilization would not be. Without this, the world would really be a mad-house, in which no one still adhering to reason and common sense would be able to live. The danger is at our door.

In painting, it seems to have started like a joke, and the joke was later on taken seriously by more and more people. It even seems impossible to straighten things out, or for someone even to say *no,* to manifest his indignation and gather what remains of the sane elements around the pavilion of reason, decency, honesty, and real interpretation of Beauty.

This is against all this corruption that President Sukarno was elevating a strong protest, banning the "cha-cha-cha" culture from Indonesia.

Showing a great insight and prescience, President Sukarno foresaw the frightening consequences of such an intrusion in the life and culture of his people, who, so far, had remained pure, unviolated, unspoiled, as yet "uncontaminated" by the degeneracy of the West, which has lost its sense of values and would like to drag along with itself the whole world in this suicidal direction.

"Freedom" may indeed lead to anarchy, to all the evils that the great sages and seers of all times and all religions have warned man against. This time the infiltration has happened on a mass scale and is dangerous for the human race, as far as the spiritual destiny of Man is concerned, as an Atomic extermination.

Man is actually split, the lower self wanting to rule the higher self and to precipitate him into an almost inevitable destruction.

What are the remedies?

Man should be taught, again, that he has to learn the meaning of *respect* and *to surrender*, no longer to an illusory God, but to the Truth, to the Reality of himself, his total Self, his true Self.

A recognition of the Principle of Spiritual Authority has to be made. Not anymore a false authority, duping him, making a fool of him, enslaving him as in the past, but to the sole Authority of Truth.

Man today has to learn to know himself, to study himself more carefully, to sift his ancient beliefs through his own critical sense, not like in a desperate gesture, but in a constructive manner; for man has to recover a new sense of freedom ... freedom of judgment in the light of Truth. He has to abolish his own world, before he can rebuild again his metaphysical and psychological universe. The old slogans will not do any more. Old beliefs will have to be eradicated, so that man may save himself from all doubts, fears, and anxieties and be able to contemplate, again, the naked Truth, Truth without a mask, Truth without the ordeal of priesthood.

When the experience of Truth has come, in the secrecy of his own Self, Man, within, is liberated. He does not fear anymore; he *knows*; he does not have to believe, for he *sees*. He has found again the direction of the road on which he was proceeding, on which Humanity itself is proceeding. It is a road that leads to an always greater freedom and emancipation from all that is limited, vulgar, abasing, for the conquest of those qualities that were recognized once as the sole attributes of the ancient Gods!

Man has to uplift himself to the level of his own ideal; Man has to become "God" himself, through cultivation of perfection and adherence to the spiritual truths.

Paradise will be regained. This time right here, on Earth, at the level of Creation. Everyone is called for this noble task, but let us not delude ourselves any longer; the direction that a growing portion of humanity is engaging in does not lead to paradise. It will lead sooner or later to Insanity and certain Death.

World Situation

"To precede events, instead of being the witness, once the events are being actualized, is the characteristic of the Cosmic Workers."
— Ananda Devi

If one looks impartially at the present situation in the world from all levels of Society, it is a matter of great anxiety and perplexity for the *future of Humanity*. The main impression that an impartial observer may receive from the present chaotic picture that the world offers is the constant uncertainty in which we are living and which has been considerably aggravated due to the variety of the factors involved on a world scale. Now, should some difficulty arise in any part of the world, we realize the gravity of the situation, as the danger might not be localized in that particular part, but might provoke a general conflict. It means that, today, there is an interplay of forces in the world that have never been so strong. This is, no doubt, a sign in favor of the unification of the world, a sort of a greater synchronization of all the varied collective reactions on the conscious as well as the subconscious level. We may not actually associate for the good, but we may be sure that the association will work for the bad in favor of the forces of aggressiveness.

This is the most apparent sign of the modern world. As a counterpart, there has been a great and laudable effort on the side of more conscious and wiser forces expressing the voice of self-defense and instinct of preservation of humanity as a whole, joining with the more Super-Conscious impact coming from planes of consciousness that are not yet awakened in humanity, but nevertheless working behind the "veil of ignorance," watching in full knowledge the development of humanity in its present phase of evolution and irradiating the powerful Ideas coming from the Cosmic Mind — the real architect of the whole. We are actually passing through a crisis, which is due to the fact that we are reaching the end of a cycle where we have been ignoring the Cosmic mind. As the movement, which has generated this cycle through the normal play of the laws of nature and the pair of opposites, attraction and repulsion, one can observe that a tendency has succeeded to manifest itself practically throughout the whole world today, even more extensively in the West, leading to a gradual disregard for the principle of authority, which is the legitimate attribute of the "authentic Hierarchy," who serve as a relay from the Cosmic at all levels of Humanity.

Dissatisfaction has come, originally, because Power, at a certain period in the history of each civilization, has been usurped and abused by people who were far from being enlightened Souls and not the true representatives of the Hierarchy. This usurpation implies the rejection of the true and legitimate souls really qualified to direct the evolution of the world. This has been the main and most important factor, which produced the disintegration of societies through a slow internal process, following the decadence of the "elite" and their subsequent corruption.

Societies that were primitively based upon the principle of authority started to be corrupted when this authority was abusing Power and was not governing according to the vision and legitimate laws of the Spirit. Then an effort was made toward reestablishment of the broken equilibrium from the very bosom of humanity, born out of a feeling of dissatisfaction and an obscure awareness of the necessity and importance of solving the problem of how to find the real "elite" in humanity capable of leading it toward its ultimate good. The problem was even more intricate when humanity developed certain mental abilities on a mass scale and began to have opinions of its own. So it started to think about its problems and egalitarian ideologies emerged. Some people thought, at that time, that the solution of the problem of the "elite" was found, the representatives of the people being elected and the people being given the possibility of exercising their own free choice. But who was really choosing? The mind, and a very immature and inexperienced mind, very fresh from school, and certainly not an illumined mind. It was the mind of the surface, of the "ego," more of the time judging arbitrarily, asserting itself, thinking that it knows everything and has no need to ask for any assistance in regard to the problem of its own destiny. The representatives of the people also were under considerable pressure of all kinds from the society and were giving way and subordinating themselves to it.

This state of affairs still exists in our present time in democracies, on a smaller or greater scale. What has happened in Russia was still another experiment of the subconscious mind of humanity, always searching, seeking for the "ideal" solution and never satisfied with what it finds. The proof of it is that new experiments are still conducted in the same fields, social and economic, in different parts of the world. Everyone tries to suggest something to make his own contribution. It seems that this problem has been one of the most puzzling of all those that man has had to face. What has happened, for instance, in India in our times is significant, and the real, impartial observer should notice and be aware of the importance of the phenomenon that has taken place in India.

Here, for the first time in the history of humanity, we witnessed a "non-violent transformation" of the Society, which seemed, this time, to be moved by a force of intelligence and wisdom; not moved any longer by "instinct" or reflexes but a master of its own self, conscious and capable of a deliberate and constructive action. It is the genius of Gandhi to have orchestrated the mass movement in such a way that he never lost the control of it. A new elite arose under the impulse and effort of Gandhi. Those who were voluntarily grouping themselves around Gandhi at the time when the adherence to the movement of non-cooperation implicitly meant the holocaust of the individual to the cause of freedom of India, were no doubt representing the "elite" of the country, the real men of heart, intelligence, and good will. No doubt, those people were pushed a very strong and compelling urge to offer themselves to a suffering and humiliated India. They have, by virtue of their sacrifice, succeeded to canalize and to be imbued with the tremendous and specific powers of Shakti — always present, always at work, and always ready to transform and ameliorate the conditions on Earth.

Through the genius of Gandhi, the contact was established with the higher Powers, which alone can renovate, regenerate, and transform the conditions on Earth in the shortest possible time. For the first time in the history of Humanity, the hierarchy established a direct contact with the newly awakened conscious forces of Humanity. For the benefit of India, this contact has been maintained and the powers are pouring over the country, awakening the people and helping in the work of transformation of the Society. In some ways, the problem of how to find the "Real" elite was solved through the pressure of circumstances and the Art of Gandhi. No doubt that the initial purity of the Spirit through which the whole movement started will be preserved so that not only the transformation on the social and economic field will take place but the spiritual values, which have always been honored in India and have preserved her Spirit throughout the ages in spite of all obstacles, will still be as many centuries ago — the living force, sustaining, preserving, and guiding the collectivity.

Through this awakening, which gave way to the conscious power of transformation of the Shakti, much can be hoped for, as this is only the beginning of a movement which, if everything develops as it should, can spread all over the world and retransform the societies through the Power of the Idea, working out and being directly implemented through the mechanism of nature. A similar awakening should take place in each country of the world, so that the re-emergence of the right type of souls could be brought out as heads of Society as they are selfless and guided by a real love for their fellow beings and receive their inspiration from the cosmic plane.

There is obviously no other solution to our problem than this very emergence of the right type of souls called to govern the nations. The factors through which this emergence will take place in the different parts of the world are as yet unknown to us. It is a fact that, in most instances, those who are representatives of the countries do not represent the real "soul" of the country, but are only elected by a choice made by a majority, whose judgment is obviously subject to errors, wrong appreciations, and mistakes. Only those who have surrendered to the absolute good of the society, with selfless motives, should be asked to govern. To govern is not an ordinary job: one may choose to be a grocer, or a butcher, or whatever he likes of his own choice; but the function of the governing is of a higher order and not reserved to every one. Those who are ruling should represent the real "head" of the nation, not only intellectually but also spiritually. They must be enlightened Souls, people of heart, and good will; moreover, they should be capable, by virtue of their natural ability and personal evolution, to be in contact with the upper spheres and to rule under the guidance of these upper spheres.

So the process of disintegration has to be arrested first and the real "elite" must be rediscovered and placed at the head of societies so as to enable societies to find again their equilibrium, their true stature and stability.

This is a matter of concern for all of us, and we should do our utmost to help this movement toward a radical transformation of the societies. The "elite," at present, in most cases are not occupying governmental functions but are disseminated in various fields of activity. They should be conscious of their responsibility and be ready to assume a more important role in society. They should join together, unite throughout the world, constitute the real "Brain Trust" of the world, and establish the desired equilibrium in some future time. This is a very arduous and important task — one in which the best souls on Earth are requested to take part and are strongly called from the world within.

The Collective Unconscious

The collective unconscious is like a clay to be molded. The artist, alone, knows how to mold it according to a desired pattern.

But this represents a work and only the one who knows the form to be given and how to do it is the true master mind of this creation, which has to be ceaselessly renewed and pursued.

The collective unconscious of a people cannot be obliterated as if it were something unimportant that we should forget about.

The collective unconscious is a living reality, which is related to the past of an ethnic, the memory of which past goes back not to a few hundred years but sometimes to millenniums, even though this ancient past is not always present in the consciousness of those who belong to that particular ethic.

It is the collective unconscious that binds the people together; it is what forms a group.

In the "unconscious" of a people, there is, buried, their memory, their symbols, which constitute their identity, deeply rooted within.

To destroy the symbols of a people, under the influence of a foreign occupation, for instance, is to provoke the disintegration of the Soul of a people; it is to make them lose their reason to live; in fact, it is to wish them to die.

This has to be taken into consideration, when it concerns any foreign intrusion, whether ideological or even religious.

These considerations are, unfortunately, not always taken into account and have not been taken, particularly in our historical past, ours, and the one of other people.

It is that which explains, for instance, what happened to Ancient Egypt, following the impact of Rome, after the battle of Actium.

The symbols of Ancient Egypt have been threatened, and even replaced by those of Rome, which marked the end of the Egyptian civilization.

A civilization that had covered several millenniums!

An invaded territory, a foreign influence; dominant is a threat menacing the very identity of a people; it is to reduce them to slavery. By destroying their symbols, one destroys, at the same time, their Souls; what made their particularity, what was constituting their history, their very life.

It is to deeply perturb each individual pertaining to that group.

It is also to push him to despair.

It is to bring about a revolt, for, before seeing their own tradition, their own collective memory destroyed, certain people have tried to defend them against the invaders, and it is the inevitable clash, the drama, the slaughter, the elimination of the people in their desperate effort to survive.

We must really become aware of these realities in order never to commit such gross errors again.

We owe it to all peoples to respect the collective memory that is a part of their own heritage, of their own identity.

These are not imaginary, or false, values, but realities we should respect and take into account. Even the primitive is attached to his totems and would not exchange them with those of another tribe!

When we talk of "integration," it is, in fact, asking a human group, an ethnic, to abandon their values, that which they believe in, the tradition of their ancestors, to trade them with those of another people.

Do you believe that it is desirable and satisfying for the one who is forced to make such a sacrifice, or even for the one who imposes such an exacting demand on someone else?

The Divine Is Here

Religions talk about "God" as being billions of miles from our Humanity.

When we observe Nature, responsible for the creation of Life on Earth and protector of it, eternally present, wanting the good of all creatures, we have at our present level, here and now, the sign of the Divine in action, the Divine presence on our very plane of existence. When we learn how to help Nature in her work of protection, we become conscious of her power, of her desire to protect all living creatures. It is then a Divine power in action that we can detect in her works of creation and of reconstitution.

It is no longer necessary to imagine a "God" as far from us as hundreds of light-years, for the Divine is being manifested right before our own eyes, when those are open to the Reality, transcendental and immanent.

The Divine is here, present upon the Earth, in our own being, and his will create, to protect is a reality constant, incessant in the present.

To open our eyes to this Reality is the only thing that could solve the enigma of our life on Earth and bring peace and solace to our heart.

The True Destiny of Man

The true destiny of man upon the Earth is not that of a "worm," but a magistral destiny.

Will man succeed to escape from the shell in which he finds himself imprisoned since centuries, not to say millenniums?

Religions have maintained the belief that a dichotomy exists between "Divinity" on one side, and him, the puppet of Creation. He was made to believe that he would never be anything else than a puppet; he was told, in so many ways, that he should be transformed, ameliorated, purified; he was put at the lowest level of creation, hardly a degree higher than the animals.

He was repeatedly urged that he should "pray." He was tyrannized, debased, indoctrinated. He was made to believe in all sorts of myths, which he was compelled to take as the reality, without ever being told the language of Truth, without ever being given an indication so as to find the way to his own emancipation and freedom, in front of the state of subordination in which he had been maintained during all these centuries.

Naturally, to reduce him to slavery was serving those who had become the masters of Society. But now has come the time when man can receive the message and liberate himself at last.

Time has come for him to achieve his maturity; and with a formidable ascent is to be expected and is in view: man communicating directly with the Divine, receiving Divine thoughts and being animated by Divine Power, the field of experimentation being the Earth, as the field of creation.

Sri Aurobindo visualized, announced, and wanted this transformation of man into a complete being, a Cosmic individuality, able and willing to complete the work of Creation, as his own field of experimentation.

The Buddhists anticipated also this possibility, illustrated in the person of the Buddha of compassion, the Bodhisattva, the one who, for a time, renounces Nirvana, in order to help the transformation of the earthly conditions of existence.

To retire from human Society in order to secure one's own "liberation," which was, for the longest time, the way to achieve it, is now more and more outdated.

What ought to be done now is to transform the Earth, so that "what is below should be like what is above."

We Are All Equal

We all are equal; we all have the same capabilities in the East as in the West.

What is the West? A way of thinking and expressing oneself, which means that the West is totally capable of understanding the message of the East, as long as the esoterism of the East is translated in terms that the West can understand.

We all start with the same capital, in the process of incarnation.

What do we do with this human capital? The whole question lies there, and all the differences stem from there, which means that we are all equal but we are not all finally motivated to reach the heights!

This explains all the differences that we notice among human beings, without forgetting the impact of Society, of the parents and so on...

Freedom — In the West

This notion of "freedom," put into practice within the frame of a social order, can lead to two diametrically opposed ends: the first is the unfoldment of the aspirations and desires of the lower nature in man, as discriminative as it is, or the same freedom can lead to the emancipation of the Psyche and the awakening of the spiritual consciousness within man. At present, in America, from what I have observed, after having studied at close quarters this form of society, I would say that it has provoked both effects: it has led, to some extent, to anarchy, through a gradual process of disintegration, which has taken place at the psychological level and which accounts for the anxiety and restlessness of many people in this country and for the fact they feel the need to be "treated" on the psychological level. On the other side, a keen observer would see that certain manifestations, on the part of a growing number of individuals, are indicative of their strong desire to liberate themselves, at the spiritual level, and break through the inhibitive influences of actual, existing social and religious patterns.

It is obvious that the desire toward a spiritual emancipation is more imperative than ever. America is today like a woman who is pregnant and who is about to deliver a child. Let us hope that this child will not find too much antagonism on the part of the instituted frames of society, which it has to break in order to emerge.

East and West

We can compare the East and the West to two different levels of the Mind, of the Universal Mind. What we have to do is establish a bridge of understanding between these two planes of the mind and consciousness. The difference lies mostly in the *fields* investigated, which represents two different planes of reality, more than it really resides in the method of investigation, which is on both sides a *scientific method*. Equipped with the same method, and more or less in the same spirit, the scientists of the East, investigating their own field, have proceeded to a scrupulous analysis of the elements of information gathered by them and which led them to a systematic study of the various phenomena pertaining to the essential nature of Man and the Universe, until they were able to find out the *laws* presiding over this particular aspect of the Real. Their keen observation did not necessarily exclude the physical Reality, but it was made in an attempt to discover the reason for its mechanism, its real cause, and its roots, which were, according to their hypothesis, to be searched at a different level or plane of existence. Therefore, we believe that if the scientists of the West could give their attention to the same systematic investigation of Reality, which constituted the field of experiment of the East, they would necessarily come to the same conclusions and discoveries; and that, in itself, would contribute greatly to establish the necessary bridge for a more real and effective integration of Humanity, which would not be possible unless all the people of the world have come to the same scientific conclusions as to the nature of the metaphysical Reality, which is at the back of all phenomena.

America

The Americans are so engrossed in their own ideology that they are not able to meet the minds of the people abroad who do not have the same ideology and concept. There is such a variety of beliefs; every nation has its own, and within the nation there is such a diversity of different currents of ideas. The contemporary currents of ideas forming the map of the world, at that level, with its total configuration, is something that must be traced to these young workers. I can imagine the kind of adaptation that is going to be for them, for when one has not yet traveled in various parts of the world, one has certain difficulties to understand, sympathize with other people, and find a mutual ground where a meeting is possible in spite of the differences.

This meeting, of course, can never be done if there is not an effort on the part of the visitor to put himself in the place of those he is trying to understand and look at the problem in the way these people look at them, at least for the moment necessary to grasp their own vision; that requires the power to project one's own mind and feelings out of oneself, to speak and use it as a psychic detector or antenna; without this particular ability, which implies a certain basic humility which certainly excludes all arrogance, the experience might be unsuccessful and the feelings of people abroad dangerously hurt if this is done.

Whereas, if these principles are being taught, in time, there is a chance for these people to really grow and ascend, in fact, to a greater vision, a more embracing evaluation of life and its multiple forms and expressions.

Solutions for America

America must stop thinking that she is *the only one* to possess the truth or the ideal system, whether spiritually, religiously, culturally, socially, or economically. Other people have conducted experiments that deserve consideration and recognition that their achievements ultimately serve the cause of humanity just as well. America should understand that an effort must be made in order to put together all these pieces, instead of rejecting, systematically, the ideas of other countries. Maybe then there would be a better chance to know more and to find out about an "ideal" society that everybody dreams of as a citadel of happiness for man on Earth.

For the sake of the people of this country who deserve it, not by a "special" privilege, but by a privilege shared in common with all the peoples of the world, it is vitally important and a matter of urgency that those points should be studied carefully and not rejected as something shocking or hurting the sensitivity of the people, for the intention is not to hurt; however, there is a great concern for the people that they may be spared painful experiences, for serious dangers are clouding the sky of America. These dangers may even become lethal, if America is not deliberately starting to dive within herself and make the most objective introspection and cleansing she has ever been capable of in all her history.

Juvenile delinquency, the growing rate of the mentally sick, the restlessness, instability, tension, and anxiety, which are affecting "normal" people, the feeling of insecurity and doubts, which infiltrate themselves into the American Consciousness, are the reasons for such initiatives as the one taken by the Foreign Policy Association, which encouraged, all over the country, the formation of study groups where people are conveyed to analyze American Foreign Policy and evaluate its intricacies so that it may become meaningful to the common man.

The problems in American society reveal the imperative need for America to undergo a serious introspection, with the hope of unearthing the very roots of disease and exposing, completely naked, the foundations of this Society and the possible deviations that have occurred to create the present situation. All this, in the most pitiless manner, so that a clear vision may eventually come out to give the point of view of Truth on America's societal problems. Right thinking may then replace wrong thinking, and new ideas may, at last, emerge, which will be *saving ideas*; for *true* ideas, once grasped, are generating enough power to transform and regenerate, not only America, but the whole world if need be.

The power of Truth is supreme, has a curative effect, once it is called for; we should rely on it and be so objective toward ourselves as to always have Truth as an ally and not falsehood, which is of very little use, when all is put in the balance in the end. Falsehood is only the product of the Ego, which is the cause for a split personality on the scale of the individual. It is extremely harmful: At the level of a nation, it may mean suicide, for it initiates a process of destruction, which is bound to achieve its purpose sooner or later, if nothing else intervenes in the meantime to stop it; for let us remember that Truth has always had the last word.

I am fully convinced that if deep, serious, objective, and dispassionate thinking begins *now*, without further delay, and if the whole nation aligns itself along with it, follows it, implements it in its own consciousness, America will have an opportunity to prove, not only to herself but to the world at large, that, after all, she has been right, or that she has, indeed, an important message to give to the world, and it is definitely a "unique" one.

The Junction

One of the junctions of History is the position of India at present — the same as the position of Egypt two thousand years ago. The same antagonistic Forces that drained Egypt (the Roman Empire) is to bring the destruction of India, in her vital, essential Soul. When I try to make the Indians understand, they do not. It is just the same anxiety, the same tragedy. It is as if the Soul Consciousness of Egypt were trying to awaken the people here to what could be their fate. There is a parallel, which cannot escape anyone, between the destiny of ancient Egypt and India today.

The Weakness

The real weakness of India in front of the West resides in *not being able to answer* to the West and justify her own heritage, religion, and tradition. Because she has not found an expression that can be accepted by the West.

This translation and adaptation of Hinduism in front of the rationalism and "selfishism" of the West is necessary and has to be assimilated. However, even Aurobindo is too far fetched for the West. I have done this exposé, and wherever I have delivered it, the West was fascinated or could not reject the Truth and the absoluteness of the ideas put forth.

Therefore, India, not being able to face the West, capitulates in front of the West and follows as a disciple, when it could be the *Master*. But the Master has to find words, disengage his thoughts from the labyrinth of Hindu thoughts, its terminologies versus expressions, which the West is not used to, therefore, which are not universal in their outer form, though it contains a universal Truth.

Therefore, India is presently handicapped. She has an ideological maladjustment, a phraseological difference, inadequate to express herself in terms that everyone can understand. The West then appears as if it were the Judge, though it does not know anything. The West needs to understand, for it rejects something that it despises or considers as useless, because it does not understand.

On the other side, India is unable to explain herself, because she does not know enough of the ways of the West. She humbles herself in the face of sarcasm, doubt, and the haughty air of the West. What a shame!

Therefore, India adopts, copies, and wants to be the West in order not to have to face that ironical Western smile.

She is being disconcerted.

Sri Aurobindo — The Spiritual Mission of India in the World

Sri Aurobindo re-emphasized in his Message to the Andhra University: "The nation has to awaken ... to vast possibilities opening before her but also to dangers and difficulties that may, if not wisely dealt with, become formidable. There is a disordered world-situation left by war, full of risks and sufferings and shortages and threatening another catastrophe, which can only be solved by the united effort of the peoples and can only be truly met by an effort at world union such as was conceived at San Francisco but has not, until now, been very successful in the practice; still the effort has to be continued and new devices found, which will make easier the difficult transition from the perilous divisions of the past and present to a harmonious world-order; for otherwise there can be no escape from continuous calamity and collapse. There are deeper issues for India herself, since by following certain tempting directions she may conceivably become a nation like many others, evolving an opulent industry and commerce, a powerful organization of social and political life, an immense military strength, practicing power-politics with a high degree of success, guarding and extending zealously her gains and her interests, dominating even a large part of the world, but in this apparently magnificent progression *forfeiting its Swadharma, losing its soul.* Then ancient India and her spirit might disappear altogether, and we would have only one more nation like the others, and that would be a real gain neither to the world nor to us. ... It would be a tragic irony of fate if India were to throw away her spiritual heritage at the very moment when, in the rest of the world, there is more and more turning toward her for spiritual help and a saving Light. This must not and will not surely happen; but it cannot be said that the danger is not there. ... No doubt we will win through, but we must not disguise from ourselves the fact that, after these long years of subjection and its cramping and impairing effects, a greater inner as well as outer liberation and change, a vast inner and outer progress is needed if we are to fulfill India's true destiny.

"...The future of India is very clear. India is the Guru of the world; the future structure of the world depends on India. India is the living soul. She incarnates the spiritual knowledge of the world. The Government of India ought to recognize this significance of India and plan their actions accordingly. ... Divine power alone can help India. ... According to a very old tradition, if twelve honest persons unite to incarnate the Divine Will, the Divine can manifest through them. ... There must be a group forming a strong body of cohesive will with the spiritual knowledge to save India and the world. By manifestation of the Divine Will and Power alone, India can preach her message to the world and not by imitating the materialism of the West. By following the Divine Will, India shall shine at the top of the spiritual mountain and show the way of truth and organize world unity.

"India has begun to play a prominent part and, if she can develop that larger statesmanship, which is not limited by the present facts and immediate possibilities but looks into the future and brings it nearer, her presence may make all the difference between a slow and timid and a bold and swift development in the process of evolution of mankind. If this evolution is to take place, since it must proceed through the growth of the spirit and the inner consciousness, the initiative can come from India and, although the scope must be universal, the central movement may be hers.

"The people speak of freedom, but you cannot realize freedom and unity, unless you realize God; you cannot possess freedom and unity unless you possess God; possess, at once, your highest self and the self of all creatures. ... Spirituality is then the only solution of the vital problems of human life. The ultimates of life are spiritual. This knowledge comes through Yoga, by which the seeker opens into a new consciousness and becomes aware of the Divine not only in him but also in all. This is the freedom that many must have today in order to be saved from the very ills that have sprung from his so-called freedom and which threaten to engulf or annihilate him — freedom from his petty empirical self of desires and passions into the luminous vastness of his infinite and immortal self."

About Democracy

"Your party, you say, is going to be a social democratic party. Now I believe in something which might be called social democracy, but not in any of the forms now current, and I am not altogether in love with the European kind, however great an improvement it may be on the past. I hold that India, having a spirit of her own and a governing temperament proper to her own civilization, should, in politics as in everything else, stake out her own original path and not stumble in the wake of Europe."

In *Life Divine*, stressing the spiritual mission entrusted to India, Aurobindo asserts that "the most vital issue of the age is whether future progress in humanity is to be governed by the modern economic and materialistic mind of the West, or by a nobler pragmatosis, guided, uplifted, and enlightened by spiritual culture and knowledge."

India, Yoga, and the United States

"Yoga is the greatest fertilizer of human growth."

— Ananda Devi

If we are to make a reality of the one world we are dreaming of, it must become an organized psychological unity. The President of India, Dr. Rhadakrishnan, the well-known scholar and philosopher, said in an essay titled, "Is This Peace?," "to accomplish this, we have to rethink human life in terms of spiritual value and re-educate the nations so as to raise the world on to new foundations." Jointly, with the work of the United Nations, we must make it our business to develop further understanding and cooperation, which would lead to the elaboration of a basis for a real world culture and world conscience.

India is a mosaic of culture herself through subtle integration of many different currents of ideas and religious thoughts. Her distinctive spiritual outlook, the result of this blending can, says again the President, "provide the world with the soul for which it is seeking."

The pattern has been created long ago in India, and it proved eminently successful and spiritually enriching for the community, capable of such an impressive sense of unity in diversity.

The Spirit of India has something of an invaluable importance to offer the world. We have asked the people of this country, the visitor, the inquirer, not only to inform himself about it, but to *study,* to *dive* into this Spirit and be enriched by this contact. This is why we give more importance to real studies than to the diffusion of general information, which does not reach the heart and soul of the people.

The East and West will never meet if, through our own effort, we do not serve as *links.* But to do this, we have to *plunge* into another Group-Soul — we have to learn how to see through different eyes, until we find the common, missing link, which makes all of us alike and one, at a deeper level of reality.

In order to stimulate and expand the interest in a science that has been the real pivot of all religious and philosophical thought in India, we have made ourselves available to give the novice the possibility to have an inkling into the vast storage of devices and profound knowledge accumulated by the sages and seers in India since time immemorial.

Yoga has very little to do with what you have been reading or hearing about the subject in this country. The Science of Yoga, in its original purity, is still a secret for Americans at large. But this *Science,* in its true form, can help the people of this country find what they are seeking for so long and give expression to the *spiritual awakening,* which is emerging at this moment from each individual consciousness, and which is one of the most extraordinary mass phenomena to be witnessed and a most important one for the future of the human race at large.

The search for the spiritual is more activated and intense in the U.S. than it is in any other country today. The malaise, which provides sometimes very serious conflicts, capable of creating real psychoses of a special nature, will only be dissipated when there is a recognition of its origin and nature. The nature of it being primarily "superconscious" and not as it has been said, and too often repeated, subconscious. Searching at the level of the unconscious, people will not find the key to relief. Only by allowing that which comes from above to manifest and to be acknowledged and accepted, will relief occur.

I have had the opportunity to save some people from falling into psychosis by making them aware of what was really happening in them. Others came later, after the period of psychosis, still bewildered and lost. So much is to be done, and can be done, with collaboration and understanding of as many as we can gather to help.

It is the duty of the people of America to identify the *cause* of their anxiety, to discern it from underneath the accumulation of conventional ideas and beliefs, covering the original purity and unconditioned nature of the Self. When the Self is reached, we know again Freedom and Joy, for the fundamental Reality that we are seeking sometimes in despair, is nothing but pure and untarnished Joy or Ananda. Again, the ancient Soul of India, one of the oldest archetypes of Humanity, can be the Mother, the initiator, the guide, the liberator.

India is not only the geographical territory that is called by the same name, but more the "spirit" of a people; not only the spirit of a particular people, which it is, but a *consciousnes*: in the range and immense variety of consciousness having appeared on Earth, one of the richest and most refined creations of the human Spirit.

India is something that belongs to all, which can be found, and, in actuality, lives in the secrecy of your own self, in some deeper layer of your innermost being. It is a reality that evolves from within, and if it is to reach its completeness through each us, it has to emerge, and whenever that emerges, the human problem is solved; human limitations are broken and a spiritual entity — having recovered its own original powers — is freed, out of the shell of human ignorance and consequential sufferings. Yet how do we operate this metamorphosis or undergo this process of transmutation from the level of consciousness, which we presently know, to the level whereby we acquire the "true sight" and regain the purity and vision of the Seer?

I have dedicated my life to these studies for years, day after day, and night after night. I have conducted experiments on myself and on others, with the hope to learn more, to discover some new secrets, which could be of some use to the race, and which had been rendered, as yet, concealed to contemporary man, or even to man placed in the context of his historical and eschatological developments. I can say today that, in searching, I have found valuable information, knowledge, and techniques, and by putting all these together, I am today, more than yesterday, able to serve my fellow men: the suffering ones, those who are seeking and do not find, those who are ignorant that there is a way; there is a solution to almost all human problems, and this, at our level, with the means at hand, when we know how to use them effectively and practically.

I have consecrated my life also to the service of India, to the spreading of her message in the world, for India possesses the secret, but to possess it, also, in your turn, you have to find it. Service to India means for me service to the world, for one is intimately linked with the other and inseparable.

Many things have not yet been revealed to the mind of the human race at this present phase of its development. If one individual, out of the masses, is ready to undertake, by himself, the difficult ascension and uplift his consciousness to a higher level of vision and understanding, at some point of this ascension, by plunging into the corresponding universe he has thus attained, he will be astonished to find out that there is nothing really impossible or beyond reach in this vast field of creation. His discovery will become the discovery of the human race, at large, from those peaks of high thinking to the ordinary man, which is ours, and working, as a titan, with an indomitable power and the unshakable certainty of victory.

There is always a way, a possibility, a solution for each problem, but in order to find the key to all problems, we have to further study and to open our mind to larger fields of experience and knowledge and be sure that, in our hasty search for progress and for new discoveries, we do not leave behind something essential or of vital importance to us and to the human race at large. In our precipitation, we may have disregarded what I would call the old science of Humanity, the oldest science in the world known to many in the past, in each civilization, and to each people. It is this science that took care of Humanity in its early childhood and nurtured it before the new science emerged, essentially metaphysical, which standardized, according to its own foundations, our knowledge of all that had already been encompassed in the human mind of the past.

We can call this science *Yoga*, which has very little to do with its more common and grosser explorations, found too often in this part of the world today. Inquire about it, inform yourselves, and know what, at the personal level, this science can do for you, how you can apply it, in order to meet your personal needs and needs of all kinds. The Spirit of India is, and has always been, deeply rooted in Yoga. I would venture to say that without the knowledge, which is at the basis of Yoga and which came to India through her seers and great enlightened men, since time immemorial, India would not be India. India would not shine today, intact, as ever, in her spirit of consciousness, in spite of the many vicissitudes she has endured throughout the ages.

It is my sincere hope that the people of India and the people of America may find, in an ever-growing sense of communion and fraternity, the salvation they are both seeking, at this time of uncommon challenges and inexorable trials, the consequence of the accelerated pace of present day's world evolution.

The Individual and the Society

I would certainly not allow myself to talk on any subject and disseminate any idea, unless I had full evidence regarding its Truth. This is achieved through the cultivation of "awareness," which endows the mind with the possibility of receiving flashes of the essential Reality, whether in totality or in fragments. It is an inner revelation that gives the clue to a particular problem, which the mind puts to itself, without indulging, as in the past, in the habit of finding a solution to the problem in terms of what is already "known" to the mind, but rather of waiting for new information and a new vision in order to reach the Truth-level, and receive, directly into the mind when it has been stilled, the ideal solution as it appears on the screen of the mind, in those rare moments when one communicates directly with Truth.

I have studied, in the light of this method, many human problems as they occurred to me while observing the world, and I have always determined to wait until an absolutely satisfying solution would come to my mind, refusing to rely in any respect upon the limited possibilities of investigation of the mind in its present conditioning. One of these problems imposed itself and drew my attention some years ago while I was in India. India, at that time, was going through a phase during which she had to find the solution of many problems: of these was dealing with the relation of the individual to the society in which he lives. She had to find a solution of her own: the problem of actuality; an attempt had to be made in order to solve this problem more satisfactorily than it had been in the past, whether we consider the case of India or the other countries of the world. This is not an easy task, of course, to implement the highest possible Truth within the confines of a human society, and many experiments are to be made before some satisfying solution may appear and be adopted and implemented.

The vision of this ideal society as it appeared to me at that time was the same vision, which has inspired that transformation of the Society of India. It is intimately joined with my personal spiritual development and the different facets of Truth, which I discovered for myself. It also comes from an awareness of the most acute problems of the world today, with a tremendous desire to see clearer than ever before and to avoid following the same old paths too often trodden in the past.

Being aware that the destiny of man on Earth is essentially related to the spiritual aspect of his life, we would like to study the factors that can help him toward awakening and stabilizing, not merely on the intellectual plane, but in Reality itself, which can help him to establish a direct contact with it, thus being fully aware of the Real and being completely free from illusion.

The factors implied vary from country to country and time to time, so we would like to know the best factors to help man in this endeavor. This is, of course, closely related to the surroundings in which Man finds himself from the very moment of birth. Some environments are more propitious than others. It all depends on the patterns of the Society in which Man is born.

Of course, to be completely free from illusion from the very moment of birth, which would be the ideal case, would require special education of the child in a secluded way — the kind of training which was given to the priests in Ancient Egypt and also to the Pharaoh from his young age, or at the time of the Rishis in India, when the society had not yet developed artificial patterns and life was not separate from Nature, but one with it, in perfect attunement with the rhythm of the Whole Creation.

In our days, artificiality has developed to such a tremendous degree that man has less and less opportunities to find the truth of himself and to avoid falling into delusion. Very few places remain in the world today to offer him the security that he needs to be able to discriminate between false values and a life in complete attunement with the Absolute Real. Illusion has spread practically all over the world; there is a continuous increase of interest in the mind of the people from West to East, for what these illusions represent in their own eyes.

Far from withdrawing from the power of Illusion, we can see that the West develops more and more in the sense of artificiality and adherence to false values, which movement is parallel with the development of economic prosperity.

Following the same line of suggestion, the East itself is every day more seriously endangered, at the mercy of a contamination and gradually becoming more and more under the spell of this lure.

The essential preoccupation of the people of the East, at the moment, being the reorganization of Society on the social and economic levels, the strong emphasis made on these values puts them, in their turn, at the mercy of the powers of disaggregation already at work in the West. This is a danger of which they are not conscious on the whole, because they are driven by the idea that, by achieving material development, obviously necessary, they will add to their general prosperity and give to the people the happiness for which they are craving.

Since J. J. Rousseau and the philosophers of the eighteenth century and the sociologists of the nineteenth century, such as Proudhon and Marx after him, we have been repeatedly told that paradise will come with the resolution of the ideal equation of social and economic problems. How can we not think in those terms? The psychological ground has been created, and we are ready to believe it without thoughtful discrimination; but granted that this preoccupation is based upon legitimate needs, a fact which everybody admits, a serious danger resides in the very emphasis made on these particular needs, which has withdrawn the attention from the other needs of man, essentially related to the spiritual Reality of Man.

This grave omission has focused the attention of the whole world almost exclusively on the material aspect of the problems of man; we all agree, of course, that it should be solved, but at the same time, it has distracted the mind from being aware of the totality of the needs of man.

This has produced a disequilibrium that reaches and even damages the very psychological stratum of man and already endangers his security. Man feels insecure even in a society that has given him all sorts of fulfillments on the social and economic planes.

This is what is happening today in what we call the more "advanced" countries of the world, and there is no need for further demonstration in these countries; the people have not succeeded to put an end to their own dissatisfaction. On the contrary, by arousing desire, they have added to their original burden and aggravated the state of restlessness in their Mind.

How can we solve this crucial and most vital problem of Man, taking into consideration that it cannot be solved by ameliorating merely the material conditions of life on Earth? Most people, unfortunately, cannot see two problems at a time, and thus the balance has been lost. Humanity is actually like an enormous vessel that is bending to one side and is losing more and more of its equilibrium. It might turn turtle at any moment, if something is not done to stop the leaning movement and to re-establish the broken equilibrium. The only remedy is to recover a sense of the right proportion and to create an interest for the problems that still remain unsolved and have not so far obtained sufficient consideration. There is, on the contrary, a constant decrease of interest for that which makes man "really" happy, that which gives him peace and true contentment, and which he needs more than anything; the lack of which makes him haggard and bewildered, as it is the case, at present, in various parts of the world — more especially in the more prosperous countries of the West.

Having lost his fundamental axis, the movement which projects Man out of his own center and makes him turn and turn around the wheel of desire and continual cravings — always wanting more and more, never fully satisfied and contented with what he obtains, becoming the prey of the giddy round of pleasures — is actually leading him to the verge of madness or suicide.

In societies that have given free license to this whirl, the statistical records show a considerable increase in the number of cases of mental diseases, and among those people who are not yet declared mentally deranged, their restlessness, their desire for continual change, their avidity to drink at the cup of illusion are without limits. If you observe them closely, you will see that their misery is great and deeply rooted, though sometimes disguised behind the veil of their gross material enjoyments. This is a fact that all psychologists, worthy of the name, may detect at first sight.

On the other hand, are the so-called "underdeveloped" countries with their sometimes drastic conditions of living — famine, or at best malnutrition, the absence of hygiene and starvation of centuries long. They, no doubt, suffer a great deal from these conditions; their case is even more pitiable when you know that this present state of affairs cannot possibly be changed immediately for all and that the major portions will have yet to wait for some years before any alleviation comes to their misery.

Generally speaking, their psychological conditioning is completely different from the one prevailing among people who belong to prosperous countries. They do not suffer from restlessness or mental miseries. Their suffering is a kind of a peaceful suffering — accepted, because it is inevitable in the present, and in this resignation to their fate, they have still the courage to smile. Their body may be deficient, but they have not lost their soul. They do not live in illusion, but in the most poignant reality. It is to be hoped that when the value is turned to material betterment, if not enjoyments, they will preserve their sense of values and will not give way to the disturbances created by an excessive emphasis on the material side of life.

Having understood that this very emphasis produces a disregard for the other side of man's life (related to his spiritual aspirations and exigencies), we should bear in mind that a sense of balance has to be maintained, if we wish to satisfy totally the exigencies of man; and we may be sure, in case we neglect to preserve a state of poise between the two poles of his nature, that it will lead him to unhappiness, bringing in further disasters that we may not be able to jugulate when they recur.

Hence, the problem is to know how to bring a sense of proportion among those who are bereft of it, having been seduced by a certain current of ideas, aiming exclusively at the social and economic welfare of human societies.

How to induce them to realize that this necessity — in spite of the fact that it is an inevitable and most important phase in the process of the evolution of Man and that it contributes to a large extent to the welfare and happiness of man, in general — is not the sole necessary achievement required to bring happiness to man, but that consideration should be given to other values that, if recognized and respected, make man unfailingly and unconditionally happy.

We must be aware that there is a danger of losing sight of those values in the process of material betterment of the society, and if so, it finally produces a progressive disaggregation of the entire society. This is not at all due to the precariousness of the material conditions, but to an absolute inward dissatisfaction that man may experience, even in the midst of prosperity and physical contentment; this dissatisfaction is consecutive to a psychological frustration owing to rejection of all spiritual values which, as a normal issue, aggravates his feeling of emptiness and shallowness and keeps him more strongly that ever tied to the world of "becoming," instead of knowing and experiencing the absolute joy of the world of "being."

If we venture to stop this movement toward "becoming," which is resulting in an insatiable desire to ameliorate the material conditions of life, and which, at the same time, excludes all other considerations, it seems as foolish and exhausting as swimming against the tide.

There are apparently two methods to tackle the problem — one regards the individual himself and tries to obtain within himself an "awareness" of his essential nature, which has to be searched down into the most profound layers of his being. This, of course, presupposes that we are capable of doing it on a mass scale and not only on the few, for the interest of spiritual values in Life has to be awakened on a mass scale.

The other way of looking at the problem is to try to transform the society through its dynamic channels and most vital force-centers in order to produce an awakening among those who are the most receptive to a dull awareness of the Real. They belong to the Society itself and later would assist in the transformation for Society and would be the instruments of its transformation. It is certain that people are always ready to follow the impulse given to them by a stronger Power. So the interest should be aroused first among the few who are most receptive to the impulse and through whom a change within the society can be materialized and expected. It is a question of knowing how to arouse the interest and to create an influential and powerful current of ideas, which could first counter-balance the one already existing, so that the individual as well as the society could finally combine in creating the most propitious conditions necessary for the fulfillment of all their needs and not only some of them.

It is certain that a society that draws its energy from the self-centered activity of the individual and arouses in him always greater and more numerous desires in order to increase its prosperity, *is responsible for the de-centering of the individual from his natural axis.*

A society that has for a generator of action the exploitation of desires, provoking a continual flow of them within the individual, is responsible for the disequilibrium and unhappiness it creates in the individual, *this unhappiness arising from the fact that the very foundations of such a Society are false.*

It is this initial, fundamental illusion propelled in society that makes man fall in and renders him unable to avoid it even if he wants to, because he is in the very grip of the mechanism of the society, having to work and preserve his physical life and the life of his family. So he is committed to work for such a society based on the cultivation of selfishness, greed, falsehood, and moral dissipation. This society, in order to be prosperous, has to find motives for action in order to compel man to produce as much as he can; hence, such a society tries its best to arouse passions in man and give him as much liberty as possible in order to have a stronger grip on him and make him work for the sake of his ever-resurgent desires. It is the full exploitation of Man's ignorance, lower nature, and stupidity.

On the other hand, there is a completely different point of view according to which society is the supreme Master and the individual, as such, is more or less considered as a negligible entity, only good to serve the general interest and submit himself totally to the exigencies of this general interest. Here the notion of personal acquisition is abolished. The work of the individual is meant to serve the whole, and the collectivity, in return, must provide the individual with conditions of living that are acceptable; (this is at least meant to be so in theory;) the very work and collective effort of all individuals forming the society would aim to ameliorate ulteriorly and bring progressive betterment in the conditions of living for the whole. This effort toward amelioration based on self-restraint of the individual would find a legitimate reward in some undetermined future.

The society here is coercive, imposing its imperative and all-subordinating will on the individual; even if the individual does not fully consent in his own heart to this "social contract" imposed on him by society, he has no possibility to express his opinion and no other alternative than to submit: if not, he incurs the risk of being excluded from society, thus, even endangering not only his freedom but his very existence.

It is evident that we have to find motives for action, if we want to have a prosperous society. On the one hand, the motives are found in the immense reservoir of human passions and in the continual arousal of these passions, in a life turned toward greater artificiality, falsehood, and greed, and having for its objective the maintenance of a standard of living for the collectivity and the increase of the material prosperity of the Whole. On the other hand, the individual has no other choice in order to maintain merely his subsistence than to work as much as he can for the welfare of society until complete exhaustion. He is working not to obtain any personal gain or reward except the fulfillment of his most elementary needs, thus aiming to create, by self-sacrifice, a kind of a paradise on Earth in a problematical future.

We cannot say anything concerning this future paradise, because it does not yet exist; but what we can say is that the psychological conditions in which the individual lives in such a society are as frightening and ghastly as those conditions in which passions are exploited in man for the maintenance of the prosperity of the society. The only advantage of such a society may be the cultivation of a spirit of disinterestedness for the emphasis is always made on the society; the individual has constantly to forget himself and submit willy-nilly to the exclusive interest of the society. It might be, in some ways, if he accepts this basic dictate willingly, a liberating factor from which he might find a certain happiness, if the pressure and the methods of coercion of the society were not so abusive.

None had really ever thought of creating a new society or transforming the existing society according to new and better lines of thought and on a more sound basis. Only such an approach to the problem of how to find the true relationship between the individual and the society is capable of preserving for the individual the poise, which is so necessary to enable him to cultivate his nature and mold it according to the Laws of the Spirit.

This process has just begun and is developing; the most we can say, at present, is that it is a great experiment. Great powers are at work and success is bound to come much more rapidly than through any of the known formulae. So love, and love alone, can solve the problem of relationship between the individual and the society, as love is the realization of Oneness, the essence and the unique significance of the society as a whole. There is no other significance to what we call a "society" than to return to the principle of identity. Out of this recognition love follows. Love cannot be but a free expression and manifestation of oneness; here are, in essence, the three principles that have been revindicated in the French Revolution: "Liberty, Equality, Fraternity" — Freedom, Oneness, Love.

If we succeed in our attempt to create a society based on these principles, then there is hope for the future and a real possibility of salvation for the human race, at large, because, if the individual has to fight constantly against the surroundings in order to keep a spiritual balance, he cannot achieve much. He has to find propitious conditions around him so that he may be helped to preserve his primordial state of poise, together with the vision of Truth that he has kept from "Heaven."

I personally know how difficult and nearly insurmountable it is to be alone, surrounded by innumerable factors, trying to adjust oneself to the vision of Truth and having constantly to fight against the collective suggestion of Society. Such a society, as the one we hope and long for, would be of a tremendous help for such an individual, as he would not have to be always on his guard in regard to the surroundings he is living in. No doubt, it would be the ideal solution.

How to implement it all over the world is the difficult task that faces us. The salvation of a few individuals has never transformed the world. So, why not try, at the same time, to transform society in its very structure, because it is really *this* that we are looking for. This is what, in the subconscious layers of the mind, humanity is actually looking for.

The fall into the abyss of egoism could be avoided, if the society were not itself an obstacle due to its very structure and wrong setup. There would be no more obstacles, no more hindrances to come in the way of the salvation of man who would feel, on the contrary, encouraged, satisfied, protected by society in his spiritual endeavor, until he grows mature and reaches complete mastery so that no obstacle could ever shake him or hold him back. Love is the secret that should always be kept in mind.

If we can jump from the construction of our mind, created out of ignorance, our beliefs, into *this,* then we become suddenly conscious of ourselves, of the creation as a whole, and of the entire process of creation. We become ONE with the reality, which is in a continuous process of creation.

We become aware of all life in this world — of the life of the world from the inside, that is to say, not as a witness, as is the case, for the generality of mankind, but as the Doer — as the consciousness who creates, as the very life of the Life of the Universe. We are able to penetrate the secrets of Nature, the process of her creation, to participate in this creation, to create consciously with her, in a word, to be *one* with her.

Awareness means to be ONE with the essence of all things; it is not a state of bondage; it is not a state of limitation; it is a state of perfect freedom, because freedom is mastery. You become the Master, instead of being subjected to the consciousness of the *slave*. This can be explained and made evident to our ordinary consciousness. Practical experiments can be made, which would suggest what is possible to achieve through this vaster consciousness on a larger scale. Let us begin first, by becoming more and more aware, more and more conscious of that Reality. We will soon discover what we can create and how to create it, how to communicate with the powers of creation on our individual scale. Everybody in this world tries to do it, or wishes to do it.

The limitation, which we seem to encounter in regard to our power of creation, is the very root of "frustration," at its essence. We are frustrated, not as a result of being aware of our defects, but of our not being able to manifest our desire for creation and fulfill it totally.

Creation is actually performed only when the Reality of the Self is discovered, which is, at the same time, the Master, the Doer. Let us, therefore, create; let us learn how to create; let us observe Nature in her efforts at creation; let us copy her; let us imitate her, so that we may learn or rediscover the secret of creation. But why do we feel limited in our endeavors to create? Why do we not feel free to create all that we imagine and long for? This is the main problem for us to study. Why is it so? We wish to do things that we fail to do! Is there any reason for this? Are we bound to be incapable and limited eternally? Or is there a Consciousness, which, when we have "discovered" it, allows us to create together with the ONE who creates? And on that level of consciousness, will our desires to create be the same as in the ordinary, limited consciousness?

Let us communicate for one second with this subtle power of creation, animated by one Will, which is the expression of this consciousness. Let us take a concrete example: Suppose we cut our finger and start bleeding. What happens? Will this wound remain forever? No. There is a Will, which we are actually unconscious of, that which has presided over the constitution of our body and is there, living, ready to act in the present, no matter what happens to us, ready to protect us, to reconstitute, and to recreate. A part of this consciousness, active in the present, is in us, is in our body. We can become aware of it. This is a fact. We cannot deny it. We are the witnesses of it. Let us endeavor to penetrate more intimately into this consciousness which, until now, has been hidden, veiled in our conscious being; let us try to investigate it, to be *one* with it and, thereby, be able to do what this consciousness does. First, we must be able to will in the same manner as She wills; in this present instance, She obviously wills our good, which entails the continuation and preservation of our physical body in its totality, integrality, in its perfection as an ideal representation of the physical prototype we represent.

Therefore, we must Will as She Wills. It is the first approach to that consciousness. What essentially does She Will? *The good.* What is good? Let us say that the good is the fundamental will of that consciousness. What does She want to achieve or to preserve? Why all this work, laborious, continuous, manifold? What is Her aim? If we can become aware of the purpose of Her achievements, we may be able to fuse with Her intimate nature, to imitate Her, to become one with Her, who *IS* eternally present, eternally creating in the present, alert, diligent, awake to all the problems of the world, all the needs of the world, and willing to fulfill them in the present. What is this force, this consciousness, which pursues the good and tends to fulfill the needs of ALL? Can we be one with this consciousness? Can we become aware of Her? Can we imitate Her? Can we manifest Her, as a lamp manifests electricity? Electricity does exist, without lamps, but who can be aware of it?

We may meditate on this. How to be the instrument of that consciousness? How to become aware of Her Will, which is continuously manifesting itself in each one of us, as in the whole? How to find our integration with this Will, this Will fulfilling the needs of all? Surely, if a society intended to pursue this research and to discover the answer to this, it would solve all problems, both of the individual and of society as a whole.

Are these two problems divorced? Is there a problem of society, distinct from the problem of the individual? No! This is one problem. There is no divorce. There is not distinction or separation.

If we create any separation or distinction, we cannot solve the problem. The individual and society are *one*; there is no society without the individual; similarly there is no individual without a kind of society, even if the individual believes in this artificial separation! What an absurdity! What an illusion, based upon the grossest ignorance! We are all *one*. And, in time, we must find the best possible way to live happily with the whole, be it a nation or the world at large. Let us, therefore, be aware of this Will, which is as yet distinct from our individual will and desires, within the limited sphere of our actual consciousness. We all strive for our individual desires, and we are unconscious of that greater Will striving for the fulfillment of the desires of all.

Why are we unaware that our happiness is linked with the happiness of all and is one and the same happiness? Why do we try to procure happiness for ourselves exclusively, and why do we not think and care for others at the same time? Why are we not aware that the problem of our happiness is not distinct from that of others? On the contrary, our individual striving for happiness, the striving of all of us, tends to the same goal and aim. We all desire to attain the same goal and the same happiness.

Why should we not bring our interest together? Why should we not try to search for the solution of this problem collectively, instead of spending so much effort individually, with sometimes very little results, as compared with the time and energy expended? How to will in that way? How to create in accordance with the general plan of things? What is to be done? And how to start it? How to be one with the consciousness that aims at our good, the good of each one of us? Has this consciousness some solution to offer that would not stem from the endeavors of our limited and narrow egoism?

Is there any solution to this collective problem, this problem that could unite everybody in the world, if we were to get, for one moment, out of our egoism? Yes, for each one of us has the same problems! Is there any solution to this *unique* problem, which could satisfy the interest of all on a permanent basis? Have we ever thought that this vaster Consciousness may have *her* own plans, her own solutions, and her own way of proceeding with the facts, in accordance with the Reality, the source of all. We are so engrossed and centered in our own egoism, so preoccupied with our petty problems, that we are not aware of that greater and all-embracing Consciousness; we do not wish to be aware of Her, for we still believe that we are able to solve our problems individually without considering the interest of others. Let us suppose, for one instant, that suddenly the whole world would become aware of this consciousness, as some are aware of it now; what would happen? How would the people think? What would be their reaction to the numerous problems of existence? Would they try to solve these problems as previously, or in a new way? After being penetrated with the spirit of Harmony, which is one of the characteristics of this essential consciousness, would it be possible for us to change our approach to life, and our relationship to our fellow beings, and to the world at large?

Could we work, for instance, for our happiness, which is not divorced from the happiness of others, and for our interest, not divorced from the interest of others? Could we imbue our children with this spirit, transform the society in which we find ourselves, thus changing the attitude of the people, thereby the action in the world? And can we really believe that this Spirit, this consciousness, if awakened in some individuals, will gradually permeate and absorb all spheres of Society, because it is in the interest of all? When this is understood by a few, it could be understood by all. Can it absorb the Society itself and change its foundations, so that more and more people would think along these lines and would live in the awareness of that Reality?

What is the common denominator of the interest of all people, or of Nations, if we take the case of Nations who behave in many respects, exactly like human beings who have not always a clear notion of what is their real interest? Everyone wishes happiness irrespective of other's happiness. When we have learned the main lesson of history, namely that the interest of an individual, a Nation, a group, a creed, or a Community, is not divorced from the interest of other Nations — Groups, Communities, and of our fellow men at large — then will we know, as an individual within Society, how to think and only then, shall we be aware of what can be done in order to help the common welfare. We shall think in terms of Truth. We shall embody Truth and no longer be in the "trap" of the narrowness and blindness of mere egocentricity. We shall come out of ignorance into Light, Happiness, Freedom, and the World of Creation. We shall be the builders of the world, of a new world, the world that all of us, in the recesses of our hearts, wish, desire, and long for. Why do we seem to ignore and disbelieve that it is within the power of each one of us to create it? It is in our power to light the fire, this fire of understanding, true Vision, and awareness of the Real, which is bound to come and to be the Conscious, Living Experience of each one of us, in this world. Then shall we know how valuable we can be, however small we are, with respect to the actual evolution of the Earth consciousness and its present limitations. It is possible for us to communicate this fire to everyone, to awaken, and eradicate this Consciousness, to destroy the fanciful, superficial, consciousness of the mind and to plunge into the great ocean of Life. We shall be able to perceive the Plan, the TRUE WILL, the design, in general, and in all its details. Thereby, we shall be able to cooperate with it in full awareness, to use our mind and heart as instruments of the COSMIC WILL, and to embody the COSMIC REALITY, to work for It and be ONE with it.

We shall discover that there is a task to be performed by each one of us, in our individual sphere, in our individual "uniqueness," to serve the Whole, to make the Whole happy, without, on our part, incurring the danger of frustration, but on the contrary, achieving the fulfillment of our goal; then shall we open ourselves fully to REAL EXISTENCE, who plays in BLISS through Creation. Why not try to have others associate with us in this endeavor? Why not ask for their comprehension, understanding, and collaboration? Is the idea so strange, so meaningless, that is has never been envisaged as a constructive, workable program in the whole history of humanity until this present time? Why should we not feel solidarity with others, before it is too late, and we receive the hard lessons of experience for having been unaware of this imperative necessity?

If we become conscientious in our search for Truth, we will feel solidarity not only with our immediate neighbors, but also with all the peoples of the world. For what do we seek and desire for ourselves, which differs from that which others seek and desire? When we have attained complete awareness of the Cosmic Reality and succeed in stabilizing ourselves in it, we are liberated from the ego, its limitations, and its bondage. We are ready to spontaneously contribute to the common welfare and happiness of all and to devote our time and energy for it. This participation in the welfare of all has become an expression of our very freedom, and we are no longer desirous of continuing in the old, greedy, limited, and narrow way of selfishness.

How is this liberation possible? Is this transformation complete? Is it a radical or only a superficial change? Can it radically transform our destiny, by changing the contents of our minds and hearts, thus re-directing all our energies and activities from a *narrow* sphere to an unlimited and boundless one? Is this a utopia, or is it a concrete possibility, in which case, what is the deeper significance of this new impulse, and what is its practical implementation?

Is it within our capacities to penetrate the secret of this consciousness, or is it something forbidden to us? Is our heritage nothing but ignorance, eternal ignorance, or is our heritage Real Knowledge, Eternal Wisdom, and Light?

Are we slaves by birth and shall remain so forever? Or, being born slaves, shall we be liberated from bondage? If so, how to become aware of it, how to *be* what we really *are*?

Master Koot Humi

Master Morya

Madame Blavatsky with Colonel Olcott

Ramana Maharishi

Sri Aurobindo

Ananda Devi

Eleanor Roosevelt, Ananda Devi, and Premananda Deva at the Indian Cultural Center; New York, 1961

Ananda Devi and Moraji Desai, Prime Minister of India; 1960

Ananda Devi in Buddha posture; 1950

Ananda Devi, Premananda Deva, and Dr. LeThomas
of the Pasteur Institute; Centre Culturel de l'Inde, Paris, 1963

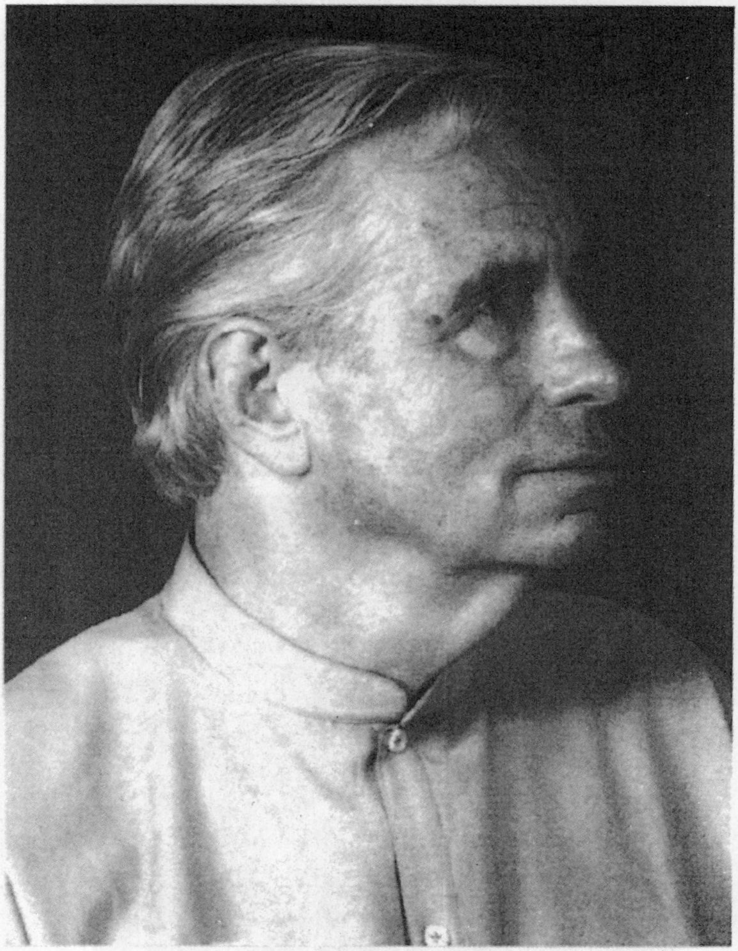

Premananda Deva

Lakshmi Devi

Deva and Lakshmi in Dharamsala,
H. P., India, 1995

Residence in Dharamsala

Deva and Lakshmi with students, 2000

New Future Society students, 2001

Deva and Lakshmi deliver a lecture; New Orleans, Louisiana, 2001

Part Three

Vision

Transformation

Transformation
of a ripple over a
mirror calm sea —
a breath of eternal
Brahman wind —
a tremor rose out
of the all mind
of OM — the quake
started the rise
a love sound heard
vibrated to form —
a void was filled
from love
of OM

by Deva

Deva and Lakshmi Deliver a Lecture on August 29, 2000

Lakshmi: This evening, we will give you an idea of what our philosophy is. When we say philosophy, really we have no belief system *per se*. When I met Deva almost seven years ago in the Himalayan mountains, he explained to me that the only way we can truly know anything is to experience it directly. I found this very, very powerful because before I met him, I had tried a lot of different techniques to quiet my mind, to understand the nature of my mind, but nothing stilled my mind more than his techniques for understanding the spiritual path. Every single one of you can reach a state of complete illumination, if you want to, in this lifetime. There's absolutely nothing to stop you. And this is what Deva told me when I met him.

I was shocked at this remark because it had been my previous opinion and impression, after going to certain Buddhist schools, that you had to go through a lot of ritual, techniques, and bravado to purify yourself. Deva said, "No, you can do it now."

When I met him in the Himalayan mountains in India, he said to me, I will take you for thirty days, and I want you to recognize that if you don't pass the tests that I'm going to set for you in this thirty day period, you're just going to have to go away, that's all. I don't want any students.

I came from England, originally, and then went to India not realizing that I was on any kind of spiritual path whatsoever. However, it soon became apparent to me, as I was undergoing a psychological breakdown of sorts, that everything that I had thought I had known before was not real, was not true.

We went to a very small cabin high in the Himalayan mountains. And day after day, I recognized that I was of two selves; of a split consciousness. He made me see that my ego consciousness really had to die, to be able to have the true birth of my spiritual nature. I had tried to do this before in my mind, but I had not succeeded. It was by direct confrontation with this ego self, this false self, that I went into a state of the child consciousness. The child consciousness is a state where Deva led me back through the ages of my adulthood, right back to the state of the child. I was one or two years old again and could make only baby noises. I would eat, and I would sleep, and it was just a phenomenal birthing experience. My adult personality no longer had a chance to govern me, to rule over me.

From there, he then took me through my life and said, "Now I see intuitively, this experience, that experience. Do you want to keep that bad experience, or do you want to throw it away now?" I said, "No, I don't want to keep this experience."

Eventually, he brought me back to my adult age, and for the most part eighty or ninety percent of myself had been completely exorcised, purified, and I was without a personality. That was the end of the thirty days. "I think I will keep you," he said.

Deva: For those of you who do not know us, I will tell you our story. My story began in San Francisco many years ago. I was born and raised in America, attended the schools, became a teacher, and undertook military service. I found myself in New York City, where I was temporarily an actor. In January and February of 1960, I could not stop my mind, so I went out in the evening to have a cup of coffee. I wandered into a café called Nirvana, and lo and behold there was an Indian woman there — I thought she was an Indian woman (she was Franco-Indian) — by the name of Ananda Devi, dressed in a sari.

At first she did not speak. She was with her secretary, at about eleven o'clock at night, on the twenty-fourth of February (she died about seven years ago, also on the twenty-fourth of February, very strange). She asked me to come with her at that time. We drove to her Indian Cultural Center, at 65th and Central Park West, which was a very fine address. The Center had been inaugurated by Eleanor Roosevelt, and Devi knew many influential people such as the Dean of M.I.T., Elizabeth Arden, etc. Soon I was sitting by her side this one particular evening, and my mind began to stop.

Prior to meeting Ananda Devi, I found no way of reaching into my mind or meeting someone who could actually stop my mind and still my thoughts to become one-pointed. Within a matter of days and weeks she had done it by merely her presence and taking me into her consciousness. You may have read about this in books, perhaps — *Autobiography of a Yogi* is one, and there are many other books which tell you about this in the archives of India and Tibet. Very little is known to the West; most books you see out there are written by Americans, who do not return to the source of how to stop the mind. They talk about it, but they have not done it, unfortunately. We have been looking for several years, since we have come back to America two and a half years ago, for people who have been able to stop their mind. We have found no one. We have traveled all over India, Thailand, Southeast Asia, Malaysia, Nepal, and Africa.

After my mind was stopped, and after Ananda Devi initiated me, I went on to have very extraordinary experiences called the child consciousness, which Lakshmi described to you, Cosmic Consciousness, and then I even pierced through what is called the Supramental, bringing down the highest consciousness, or Nirvana, where one enters into a state of complete void. This is spoken of by the Buddha and other great souls — Zarathustra, Sri Aurobindo, Ramana Maharishi and others. Those of you who have heard of people having visions — very good, this is psychical, this is what America wants, and this is what America has. We have psychical people wandering North America and Europe entertaining each other with Tarot cards, visions, clairvoyance, leaving the body, channeling — this is very American, this is very Western — and believing that there is a ceiling. Believe me, there is no ceiling.

You may have seen the movie, *What Dreams May Come.* That was the astral, that was not Nirvana, that was not Heaven. It is a belief that once one arrives at this higher state of consciousness, that one has entered the state of heaven. I'm sorry to tell you, it is not that! But it makes for good films out of Hollywood! The media makers are interested in box office successes, not to tell you the truth. There is no way that they could tell you the truth, unless you have lived with a master. I did live with a master for thirty-four years.

This experience enhanced me. She was already enlightened when I met her. She was at least ten or twelve years older than myself. We formed a team and by 1962 we were off to France, whereupon we started another center and ashram. We operated on another plane of consciousness to arrest the Cold War, and also to intervene in Desert Storm. This kind of work is carried on by people who are, let us say, enlightened, illumined, who can operate on another plane of consciousness at all times. At the same time that you are here on the Earth, you are also existing in the highest form of consciousness, or the Absolute.

We carried on. We had a center there, we had restaurants; it was a very busy life. At this point, I'd like to have Lakshmi carry on for awhile.

Lakshmi: We want the spiritual man, the spiritual woman to be something completely integrated in life. It's very important for us to see spirituality like that. It seems a shame that spirituality is seen as something very taboo in the mainstream Western society.

So when I met Deva I was very shocked, because I had no idea that the spiritual life was the way that he was, and the way that his master was. In other words, the complete plunging into everything that was life, to be able to experience life and not be tainted by it.

Deva: This is only one aspect of the spiritual. Every yogi — or "sage," or "philosopher" — from the earliest times up to the Buddha, to Plotinus of the 3rd century, Plato 400 B.C. — all experienced higher consciousness and they were able to parlay it into this world. Some may become recluses, some may not want to be integrated into the society. That's their prerogative.

Another thing that most people don't realize in the West is that no yogi, or master, or guru is obliged to take a student. Most do, because they want to be able to pass on what they have experienced to another soul. Besides, they would have no one to talk to, unless they cultivated another one!

When my guru and mate died on February 24, 1994, that was the end of my world. I didn't realize I would have two ashrams to continue. It did not look too promising to come back to America. Although she loved America, and she liked the bigness and the broadness, she did not like the politics, nor the military-industrial complex mania that exists in America, and in parts of Europe. But this is where the real work is. So when she died, I left everything — I had restaurants and apartments. I had no time to eliminate everything, so I merely took what I could carry and moved to the Himalayan mountains. That's when Lakshmi found me there. But I wasn't looking for anyone. Because I had just lost my master, who was a woman — which is a very rare commodity. Most men in the West do not believe that they can find a woman to surrender to.

We are very much interested in India, the philosophers and people, present day and yesteryear, but we are not going back to India to make an ashram. We are here because the real work is in America, I could almost say, unfortunately.

I've come back after thirty-two years. Why did I come back? Because I received instructions from the highest consciousness, from the Brothers of the White Lodge, exactly three years ago, to return to America, and particularly to the Washington, D.C. area, to continue in the footsteps of Madame Blavatsky, Koot Humi, Master Morya and others. We are in touch with these people, and live with them in the Cosmic Mind. They are able to filter their ideas and speak to me at any time that we so desire, any time that they so desire. We all had this capability prior to two thousand years ago, I don't know if you realize that.

Once Lakshmi met with me in a café called *The Rising Horizon*. I saw her as sort of bereft, a waif, and I asked her where she was from. She said, from England, and after understanding who I was, she asked me if I could possibly transform her. I said, "I don't see much of a chance here. Number one, you're a woman, and you are asking me to perform a miracle. And you're from Europe! I don't have much confidence in that! Very few true seekers come from the West. Besides, I have already lost a woman who had achieved enlightenment, Buddha status, or Bodhisattva at least. What the chance is there with you?!

When she met me, I said, "All right, I'll make you a wager. You have to allow me thirty days to achieve the miraculous inside of you." — which meant, there would be no deviation — "or you'll have to go away." We went to the highest area, of six thousand, seven thousand feet, on a hillside with a little valley which was vegetarian. There were two rope beds. I said, "This is where the laboratory will start. My mind will be able to go inside of your mind, any time at will, in order to extricate out anything, and I'll ask you if you want to keep it, or rid yourself of that, and then you will advance, and not before. So I performed a sort of strange form of conscious hypnosis on Lakshmi, so to speak, where she would try to avoid showing me her two selves, but eventually she was more unified, more one-minded.

We all have two selves. America doesn't like to use the word "schizophrenia," you've got "bipolar" and all kinds of different words here, I don't know what they're talking about! All I can say is that everybody here is of split consciousness. In America and Europe the hiatus here is far greater than in the Orient. It's great everywhere, but particularly here.

Our main concern as psychological philosophers, or yogis, or metaphysicians, is to bring those two selves to one. It's very important, and if you don't do it in this lifetime, you're only going to have to come back and repeat and repeat until you do it, and it's the only thing to do.

So after the thirty days as she already described, I had at hand a creature who was pretty much free from her past traumatic experiences, from her family, friends, peers, etc. I said, "Now we have a chance to allow you to recreate yourself for the first time. In other words, after many lifetimes here you are in front of me."

She decided on the clothing, the coloring of her hair, her dress, everything was to be fresh: a new personality, a new start in life. No longer hung up by the old ways given to her by her ancestors or the society.

Not through the genes, that's pure malarkey! The brain is an encasement, the mind is allowed to come into the brain, and the spirit is behind everything.

So she did it. I said, "We will allow two more weeks, and I will try even more esoteric methods on you whereby you can achieve your Soul." Westerners ask me, "But isn't the Soul on Earth?" I said, "No." No Soul has ever come to the Earth except a small iota, a small fraction of the Soul is allowed to descend along an invisible cord which allows us to incarnate into the male, into the female body.

We know what we are doing at all times, as Souls. We have decided to reincarnate, by virtue of our own karmic values. We will decide on our own parents. If you want to be born a boy child, you will have a certain preference for the mother, and vice-versa.

So in two weeks, I said, "We will try a method, whereby you can ascend into your Soul." Every person who wants to achieve this, will have to do this; to bring a portion of Heaven to the Earth. That's why we say he becomes God-realized, because there is no waiting game. The waiting game must stop. You must accelerate your stillness. You must be able to stop your mind, and of course, from then, you have to think in terms of that stillness as only a foundation, a basis by which you can shoot up into your Soul, and bring it back to the Earth. At this point, Lakshmi is going to tell you what it actually felt like to enter her Soul.

Lakshmi: I felt myself leaving my body, and I shot very fast upwards. And I saw this cord, which I traveled along side of, that went directly upwards, very fast, extremely high up. I then arrived at my Soul. I saw my human self, I felt my human self down on the Earth, with all of my behavioral fears, desires and so forth. And I realized, surely, at that time that I really was not that. That here I was existing in my pure Soul consciousness. Pure wisdom, pure joy. It was from there that the Soul consciousness, and the force that came down from the Soul, was actually allowed to descend into my human consciousness.

Deva: And mind you, she did this in a very rarefied area. It does count. The Himalayas are more rarefied, they have been macerating in this area, where there is so much spiritual force brought down from the Soul consciousness onto the Earth for thousands of years. Perhaps it had been done with the Mayans and the Incans, but this is mostly all lost, thanks to the marauders from Europe!

And so she was able to achieve this. People travel from all over the world to come to India, to see the Dalai Lama, to see other people asking them, "Tell me how I can enter my Soul; tell me, I have to do it because I cannot stand living on this Earth." You have to work at it. You have to become a very patient student. You have to be willing to become a student.

All that we meet in America, of course, and Europe, too, are the people who say, "I want to be a healer, I want to be a teacher." Do you want to be a student? Nobody wants to be a student! "I have my certificates, I have my baccalaureates, I have my Ph.D's..."

The surrender must take place the moment you meet an enlightened person. If you don't surrender, don't expect anything for yourself. You cannot cling to anything. Every single nook and cranny inside of your self has to be cleaned. It's like changing a diaper. The child is three months old... it doesn't stop until that homo sapien is on its feet and can function by itself. It's going to take you a long time.

We cannot be enlightened with people who pretend to be prophets, who are not. Don't put me in front of these people because I will simply ask them, "Have you stopped your mind?" If you haven't stopped your mind, what do you have to say?

Do we want to garbage the Vedas, the Gita, the Upanishads, to impress them, to show them how learned, how erudite I am? "I'm a Sanskrit scholar." — "Oh, he must be enlightened: he has a long beard, he is dressed like a swami, he speaks quietly and softly. He must be the man I am looking for! Let's follow this person!" It's like chasing your tail, wouldn't you say?

I left California thirty-four years ago. When I left there was nothing that smacked of New Age-ism. Today, we come back here, where there is goodness, but a lot of people are fractionalized into little groups, unfortunately. It's phenomenal, I just can't believe it, if you want Hatha Yoga, or you want this or that, you have to go to all these different places with certificates, to become learned. The only way to become "learned" in the spiritual is to unlearn everything that you have already acquired. Everything that you have learned so far is nil, is worth nothing for the spiritual.

How many people believe otherwise? That we can actually acquire knowledge for the spiritual? The more you're empty, the less you have to offer, the more you're going to gain.

The disciple, the student who says, "You know, I realize I know nothing" is the person who would be thought of as really ready to have an experience. Because experiencing the Divine, the spiritual, is like plunging into the ocean for the first time. It is a new element. It's foamy, it's brine, and it's not something that we have known, as if we come from the Midwest, and we go to the ocean. Believe me, it is a new element. You are completely metamorphosized, you are completely changed, and you are living in joy all the time. You do not have to express it with great frivolity, smiles and laughter all the time. But I can assure you, you are always in joy.

This is the state that is produced by entering the Cosmic Mind. There are different layers where one ascends into the higher Cosmic Mind, and one can stay there. There is no fluctuation. One does not go up and come back down. That is pure folly. That is one of the occurrences made by the European, the Western man, and the Americans.

We can make great changes on this Earth and in America and in Europe, if we get across to the key people in certain departments, making them realize we can actually change this world, we can make it better. Every mental disease can be cured in a very short time. We do not need drugs. We need none of the drugs advertised on television! I am absolutely aghast!

We saw an extraordinary film with Meryl Streep, *First Do No Harm.* A six-year-old child has epilepsy. Immediately the child's doctors start drugging the child, they get to the point where they're going to cut out part of the brain. It's so disgusting! Meryl Streep does her own studies, and finds out that Johns Hopkins University is practicing a diet, mostly vegetarian, and fasting. They were going to arrest the mother because she wanted to take the child out of the hospital — what kind of country is this? She was going to be de-possessed of the child, and yet she was doing it all for the good, without surgery, without cutting, without drugs. So they finally get to Johns Hopkins hospital — this is a true story made in 1997.

We're trying to inform ourselves about America. We have to watch television. I'm not going to travel all over America to find out all the drugs and guns in the small towns all over the place! It's a mad world over here.

Through fasting, proper diet, no drugs and no cutting, we can heal. It's remarkable. Three hundred thousand people are suffering from diabetes. Why can't we look to the natural way?

We can do so much for each other, but we must first think: "I must first find out how I can transform myself. Because if I can't do it, what can I pass on to someone else? To my own children?"

"Maybe my own children are aliens to me." Why? Because we are of a different ilk, we are of a different consciousness. We have come from other sources. But we have to be unified, to be integrated into this one particular family. If not, we have to create a spiritual family.

Lakshmi: This is something that we try to emphasize. If we, as spiritual aspirants, are finding it difficult to fit into this society, even with our own family, it is very important that we come together and make a new family, a new orientation towards people of like mind.

Deva: In the West, of course, we often say, "That moment of truth." Watching a sunset, Chopin on the piano. We have the "Ungrateful Living," oh, that's the "Grateful Dead"! We have all these different things to give you a moment of truth. We don't want a moment of truth, we want to give you a lifetime of truth. Because we are born with all the essential qualities innately in us. From day one, we allow ourselves to be hypnotized, mesmerized and stuffed with all the things of the physical world.

We are coming from the invisible world. And we're bringing into this world, our portion of our Soul, for another chance. Another chance! How many times have I lived on this Earth? I am bringing all the clutter, the baggage from all the previous lifetimes and I am born on this Earth for a new start. It's up to the parents and the society to allow what's inside this child to come out. Because we are born with everything. We are born with all knowledge!

So how in the heck can we teach the child, if we are born with all knowledge? It's impossible. So we're not going to ask the child to teach us. We're not going to become the buffoon, but we have to find out, for what purpose is that child born into this lifetime. This is the concept of reincarnation which existed up to the fifth century according to the Christians, until they said, "Let's get a Papal decree, and stamp it out, it no longer exists." It's like getting a Papal decree to ban rainbows, or the musical scale! These are Universal laws. There is nothing that science can do to disprove Universal laws.

Think. Science only observes and imitates what is in nature. The theory of the atomic bomb, the nuclear bomb was known to the ancient Egyptians, and in the Vedas of India, and by the Chinese. Unfortunately, Marco Polo brought us gunpowder, along with raviolis and spaghetti. He should have left the gunpowder in China. We wouldn't be in the mess today, would we?

Think: "If we're born with all knowledge, what happened to me? I am a product, I am clone job from my own family, my own society, my own religion, and I don't know myself." We were up on the top of Montparnasse, at Delphi, where it says, "Know thyself."

Know thyself. But that is such a big statement, with just two little words. And then there's nothing else to do.

The Chinese have an expression, "Wu Wei." If we can blank ourselves out and off from this materialistic society, we can achieve the knowledge of ourselves. We must isolate ourselves, we must do nothing, but sit still and Wu Wei. And by this we're letting ourselves go, everything that's extraneous to our inner being, to our inner child, must slowly be shed away.

You must understand that we must allow to come out that creative urge that was probably squashed between seven and twenty-one. They said, "No, you're going to medical school, and that's it. You're going to be an engineer. You *are* going to be a computer programmer; we have cultivated you from the age of four so that you're going to love it."

How can we possibly find out our dharma, our mission if everyone has to be a typist? It's impossible. Every person on the globe — six billions — has a particular mission, a particular dharma to fulfill now in this very lifetime. And it's not with the gadget called the computer! All these things were not meant for the people, they were meant to facilitate our life, not to endanger our spirit.

Remember that we are born with all the essential qualities: truth, beauty, goodness, love, justice, harmony and joy: seven essential qualities described by Plato, and there can be more.

A very great French woman, Mrs. Richard, left France about a hundred years ago, and found Sri Aurobindo in Pondicherry. After being imprisoned for revolutionary freedom fighting, Aurobindo had escaped from the jail, after being paroled temporarily, and he fled by ship to Pondicherry in the enclave which was French. Consequently,

Mrs. Richard, the Mother (she had had extraordinary psychic experiences, she was kind of a frail figure), found Sri Aurobindo. She said, "I could never stop my mind, until I stood in front of Sri Aurobindo, and my mind slowly stopped, all the thoughts in my mind stopped. And I knew that I was to stay here, and to stay with Sri Aurobindo." And she did, until he died in 1950, and she died twenty years ago.

When Aurobindo died at the age of seventy-eight, she thought she wanted to die. He said, "No, you are to stay on the Earth and to continue, and I will leave the Earth, in order to continue to perpetuate the sending down of the Supramental force." He coined this expression, "the Supramental."

I try to give you a smattering, and run the gamut of what spirituality is. It's very difficult, I would almost have to take the reverse proposition and say what spirituality is not, and by cutting it back to the nitty-gritty, I would get to the sap of the tree, but the tree would no longer exist, there would only be the sap. The Western scientist wants to find beauty, so what they do is start dissecting the flower, and all of a sudden the flower doesn't exist; they say, "Oh my goodness, the beauty is gone!"

So Lakshmi will dance now. You will see beauty in movement. One of the highest forms of Yoga is dance, as well as poetry. Dance is the incarnation of all life. This is what we would call spirit dancing. Lakshmi can dance the music from any country on the Earth, because she actually enters the spirit and the spirit enters her.

Lakshmi dances.

We can heal any and all diseases. We do not have to reach up, we merely have to be quiet in ourselves, our inner consciousness, and we can bring down the vital force, the Shakti, or prana, for healing. We can all do this, but you have to be initiated into the spiritual. It can be possible, you can be initiated. Your presence here means that you are actually receiving from us. You must see us as reservoirs. And being reservoirs, we can actually canalize this strange, magical energy.

Once you pass beyond the domain of human consciousness, and beyond the area of human constructs such as good and evil, you enter into what is the fabled land of Nirvana, and you are living, as Nietzsche calls it, "beyond good and evil." There is no good and evil in the spiritual. There is no humor. They have no need for it. There is no laughter. We are the ones who must free ourselves by using laughter and humor to get where the gods and the goddesses are. Or the entities, or the superbeings, call them what you want. But let's not call them angels, because we really don't need wings to become enlightened!

The Egyptians were the greatest healers and the greatest magicians of all times. They've left the Earth because the renegades that came in did not understand the powers that bestowed upon the Egyptians. This was the other half of the Orient — Egypt, with Isis and Osiris, and India with Kali, Parvati and Shiva. These were two parts of the whole. They used their temples for initiation. Systematically, the temples have been closed down; all the temples of initiation and centers throughout the world. Theodorus, in about the fourth century, decided to close down all the temples of Isis right down to the Sudan. So we are bereft of temples of initiation today, because we don't want to investigate. We are putting our Souls in the hands of the churches, thinking that they know better.

Only, we know better for our own Soul. The Soul is asking to be released. Our ego should not say, "not now, I'll wait for the next lifetime." When the Divine comes knocking, you cannot close the door in the face of the Divine, because we are all Divine.

If you want to step out of this box, the egg, the Hinayana, or the microcosm, we have to become like the chickadee and really want to get out of that egg, into the big egg, the Mahayana. Because once you get into the big egg, you can come back to the little egg, don't worry, you can come back again, no problem.

So in order to liberate ourselves we must have a tremendous desire; we must become so tenacious, driving, and curious. This must be retained twenty-four hours a day. We cannot allow ourselves to refuse joy. One of the things that my master used to say continuously when she was alive is, "Anything but joy is ridiculous!"

Every day when you plant your feet on the ground, you must see, "this is my new day for establishing joy in myself, because anything but joy is ridiculous. And I must not allow any interference in my joy."

Thoughts come from three directions. Thoughts come from inside our head — mind — from outside, and from above. Inside the head, there is enough confusion going on. On the metro, imagine a hundred people swarming around you, giving you all their thoughts. Telepathy exists. Consciousness is everywhere. Telepathy is from the stars to the ants.

Everything around us is telepathizing with us. But if you really want to become concentrated, concerned with your tiny little soul that was allowed to come into your body, to incarnate, you must be concerned to stop that mind of those thoughts. You choose one thought, for example, the thought of beauty. So you must visualize the rose, and try to concentrate on it for as long as possible. And the thoughts from the outside, if you don't want them, they must come in your head, and go out the other side.

We have the possibility of isolating a thought. Once you have established that, you can say, "Now I know that I am being bombarded from the outside." It's an avalanche of thoughts at all times. Therefore, we must concentrate, be precise, and bring our thoughts to one thought.

We must also be able to divest ourselves of originality. Everything we do must become original, and with curiosity. We must not pass on from yesterday, which is already old testimonies, old language, etc. These clichés have got to die. Do not repeat what America is telling you to say. Nothing is "awesome"! You must be able to eliminate all habits, all vocabulary, good and bad.

Your ego will tell you, "Without my ego, I will die, I can't exist in this corporate world, you don't understand what I have to do."

So we train the ego to step aside, so the true self inside of us can continue to manipulate in the physical world. Not forgetting that the Divine will give us all the strength that we need! By going back to our original self, back to the Child Consciousness, you will be supplied with so much energy, so much shakti, you will tap the invisible self.

There are two worlds, there is the world of the physical, the phenomenal world, the Maya, and the invisible world. On an eighteen hour basis, during the waking hours, that you must put both feet, all of your body in the Divine. "I am Divine, everything attached to me is coming from a Divine consciousness. I am an archetype, thanks to my Soul."

We are branched to this. At one time, throughout the entire world, there was an entity, a spirit for every single act and activity, and there still is, except we have refused to acknowledge them. An event is being controlled with all the little spirits that exist in the Universe at all times. With the books we receive now in the last few hundred years, they are called the mythologies. I call them the realities. Go back and read those books of the Gods and Goddesses, and you will be delving into your own realities.

It's very difficult to describe. "How can you have so much enthusiasm? If you are a Buddha, did you become a Bodhisattva, a compassionate one, to come back and help others?" Yes, that is the case. We don't have much choice, because we can either be bored to death with the human dramas, or entertain ourselves. I prefer to entertain myself by being straight, a pulpit man, or temporarily mad. When I became mad, I realized that I was really spiritual, but not until that moment. Because you have to become like the intelligent "Forrest Gump," the "Idiot" of Dostoyevsky, whereby you are immune to the outside world, you are immune to the physical world.

Forrest Gump tells Lieutenant Dan, "I'm going to Heaven." I say Forrest Gump is already in Heaven! He was born in Heaven. He doesn't have to forgive anybody, because they were all good according to him. He saw the goodness in everyone.

Do we want a heap of karma on ourselves? Or do we want to be rid of all karma? We can in this one lifetime, rid ourselves of all karma!

Ramana Maharishi was sitting at his ashram in Tiruvannamali, he died in 1950. He is like the child guru forever, the perennial child. Because the more you experience, the more you become like a child. You have to remember to do things as an adult.

Ramana Maharishi was sitting with a cow, and the cow was dying. Rámana Maharishi had his hands on the chakras, giving energy to Lakshmi, the cow. The cow dies. Ramana Maharishi stands up with his frail frame, and says, "I took her to Nirvana, it is done."

Madame Blavatsky says — forget the creationists, the evolutionists — when the time was right, the gods came down, they materialized for awhile on the astral plane... and here we are.

We are going to demonstrate an extraordinary event today, which is the incoming of Orpheus. He is a great entity, a great healer, who lived eight to ten thousand years ago. He comes from Assyria, Egypt; he is more of an Oriental nature. Now that you are more in our periphery, he can know all about you.

How many people have been in a séance before, a medium séance? I know you are calling them "channeling" now; I don't like that word. It means that you're not in the medium séance. You see, Lakshmi is completely controlling everything. If the person channeling has not been initiated, has not experienced his or her Soul, they will not be a pure channel or medium. Lakshmi has achieved jivatman, the joining to the human soul with the divine Soul, and only after she had achieved this did we work longer to achieve the incoming of a very great spirit.

Lakshmi: What I will do is close my eyes for a brief moment, and I will invoke this spirit to come into my body and he will introduce himself, and he will probably ask if you have any questions...

Orpheus: Welcome to this communication today, I am known as Orpheus to those who are interested. It is my prime objective this evening to answer questions deliberately for those of you who are interested to further your spiritual path, your spiritual direction. And I would firstly like to say a few things about this reality. This evening I understand you have heard from Deva, and that you have listened for a long time, so I will make it as fascinating as possible. Let us just suppose that everything we sense is illusory. Let us suppose that we are here to live on a springboard, a platform back to the real existence. Let us suppose that this existence has the most infinite of potentialities for all of us, that we are here to understand a greater purpose, a greater knowledge, to understand everything about ourselves. Never to be in doubt, never to be in fear, never to be confused any more. This is the state of spiritual assuredness, when we know that we are really at one with the truth inside of us.

It is our purpose here, not to sit and smile down upon you, as if you are the ones who do not know, because I can feel there are many souls here who have been seeking for a very long time. And that also there are souls here who are new to this, tasting, whetting their appetite with the spiritual drink, the soma.

We are all here primarily to pay homage to the prime mover, the original principle who is one with us. Absolutely everything from the breath to the perspiration on our brow... It is at this time, that I would like to direct you in a little guided meditation...

Meditation follows

...And now, I have the possibility of answering three questions. Does anyone have a question on the idea or purification? If so, I am ready to try and answer. Number one...

Student: How do you let go and deflect, when people say nasty things to you?

Orpheus: Excellent question. We must build up a defense. We must see that these people are of no worth if they are here to destroy us. We must put these people in their place as much as we possibly can, and move on, and see that they are of no consequence to us... And if they are of consequence we must try to see that they are egoistic, living in hatred, and we must rise above it, to detach, to send away whatever it is we have to in ourselves that provokes attachment.

Second question please.

Student: How do we know how to make a step in our initiation process?

Orpheus: Interesting. We know if we really and truly want to pursue experiencing initiation, we must trust our intuitive feelings about what is presented to us. We must pursue the clearest, most direct path of initiation, and wholeheartedly. We must not listen to the intellect. We must not listen to the emotional center. We must pierce through very dynamically, and seize what it is that we want. No more placating the self, directness is the way to really and truly know ourselves.

And now, the third question, please.

Student: What is the purpose of physical illness?

Orpheus: Everything that is directly related to us and our condition on the Earth can be a way of pushing us closer to our divine Self. If we have taken a sickness, number one we can say this is our karma. Number two, we can say that this is a way to bring more attention to our own individual life, to our own individual self, to pursue the physical self. If we lament, and become too self-obsessed in the world, we may provoke a dis-ease, and this dis-ease comes originally from the spirit, and takes possession of us when we are not too harmonious with our ultimate reality.

Thank you for listening, for participating, and I want you to remain in this state a little longer, as much as you want...

Orpheus the spirit leaves Lakshmi's body. Moments pass.

Deva: Now I will tell you about when I was initiating Chow En Lai and Mao Tse Tung on another level of consciousness, even after they had died, of course, which is perhaps easier. They were sitting on the great Chinese chair like an old couple, waiting in limbo, not knowing where to go because they have made no preparation for the after life.

This is the situation in the West, that there is little or no preparation for the after life. The more we improve this life here on Earth, the more we will be prepared for the after life.

So therefore, Mao was disgruntled that I was an American in this life, so I said, "Well, you have not been so kindly with the Tibetans, but still I will find a Tibetan lama to initiate you." So they were initiated finally by a Tibetan lama.

I have never meditated. I'm amused by these terms, though — "transpersonal," "meditation," "chanting.".. I do it for the others, to show the way. Ramana Maharishi, at the age of sixteen was fully enlightened, but he still practiced his brahminical rites and rituals. It's very important to show the people not to disembark from these, because this is what we need to maintain ourselves within a society, within a family.

We can use the rites and rituals as a springboard. Even the Buddha, two thousand four hundred or five hundred years ago, with his coterie of yogis down by the Ganges, said that he could go beyond the rites and rituals of Buddhism, and Hinduism. He said, we can surpass the great gurus and gods and go directly to heaven.

In the Gita, for example, there are eighteen chapters of probably the most extraordinary book that's ever been written. If you cannot apply the yoga of the first seventeen chapters, in the eighteenth it says, "Do it on your own, it's okay. Go directly to Heaven!"

We all deserve a piece of Heaven. When are you going to have the courage to reach up and say, it's mine. During this process of incubation of your inner self, your Soul self which allows you to be animated, this Tao, this chi, this shakti. We already have the possibility of doing it.

We must excite this inside of us. We must say, "I must excite this little one called the Child self inside of me, I must excite it so much, to become curious. That maybe it will blossom, and I will become like a child again."

We must become the expression of beauty. We must see ourselves as the most beautiful creature on the Earth. We must become egotistical in the short period of time of our nurturing of our small self. To say, "I cannot have time for anyone else, not even my babies, my children, until after I have experienced my Soul, and then I can say 'Now I am ready to give!'"

Wondrous One

Wondrous One
Of High —
Spiraling
Ever
On —
Songs Are
Written,
Never
Begun —
Sung, Never
Heard —
To
You
Wondrous
One

by Deva

Spiritual Foundations

In all cultures, nations, societies and civilizations true spiritual foundations (not religious) are extremely necessary in order for the populace to have a sense of belonging to the subtle substance called the Divine and for the unit to have a greater sustainability and durability. The unit (nation, etc.) must be able to instill in its people a sense of honesty and truth from the top down; this must include joy, goodness, and a wide sense of hope for All. The Divine must prevail in place of the politico-economic system now in place.

I remember asking Ananda Devi quite early (1960) in our guru-chela relationship about how it was possible for India to have endured for so many thousands of years while other great countries and civilizations had come and gone. She answered after only a brief reflection that India was like a great mosaic held together with spiritual threads.

On another occasion, in 1961 at Nyack, New York, during a talk Devi was holding among several disciples, a question was raised from a disciple as to why the population of India is so large. This was the first time Devi looked at me directly and somehow I knew I would know the answer. I had never cogitated this question in the past so the answer could not have been coming from my intellectual memory bank (as I write I really think Devi transmitted the answer to me telepathically). I replied that souls before birth wanted to be born in the country which was closest to the Divine or God as possible.

Called Poetry

That is life —
    oh, the cry to be heard
    from under the shell
    is only my wish
    and why is it crying?
    and why am I crying?
    when a birth is considered bliss?

    the mood was created
    while yet so young
    and a flood of waves swept heavy
    and made known God's presence
    in the still of loneliness

Put On
    the ego again he cried
    for he had done it six times before
    and what will be held for the seventh
    a bit of magic?

To be or
    not yet,
    for the fear and death that still remains —
    yes, this is still strong, but
    I can possess and not be possessed
    no idiot I
    only in the sight of others
    not in the light of me —

As Brightness Is
    light, so lightness
    is not bright —
    intensity of light will display its source
    with colors bright and love and goodness
    from things and people around —

Flood me
be known to me —
don't leave me now,
I cry too fast and
grow so slow for my years

Where do Thee Lie?
Soul of Life
Soul of my life
wrap your arms about my frame
are you still?
are you churning?
or are you still and churning?
are you one?
are you many?
are you manifold oneness?
are you Divine?
can you be mine?

heaven knows I wanted to behold,
to cherish you in my abode,
just rest yourself in me —

The Circle
of life is sought — so
what do you expect, a
transformation? — a
transcendation? — an
ego surrendered for the effort rendered?

Keep the Silence
abide by the unknown disturbance,
adhere to your rhythm, and
falter not your steps
for the lingering to view —
take your cue
from the response of it
and describe it not to skeptics known —

You Are
close to you —
as you know you stand so few —
do you what with the experience,
what will the experience do to you?

Only Eyes
but windows to the self
and openings for tears to flow
and fear to grow
and light to flood
for now and forever more —
the eyes behold the enriching self
behind the gaze,
so let not the ego haze —

Semantically Speaking
I do not — Let me say
I do not adhere merely
to the words of our voiceless race nor
to emotion from the irrational
reason pours too, but
not what I seek — call it a
"Song of Myself," but
why be trite and even a plagiarist
when we can say it —

can I? can we?
my vision has blurred, been disturbed
and by control, grown and glowed
for the vision from within to flow out to me

Naked Beauty
forever you stand
alone to your self —
make yourself known
to the great unknown
and will I then be known?

torment lament
torture horror
grace bliss birth

am I searching too fast?
too much for now?
is it there?
can I be seen
hidden in the great void?
let it not be a great hidden void
but light stirring
and recalling a spirit.

by Deva

Duty and Rights

We often hear the expression, "It is my right."

The ego is talking — it is expressing a desire it wishes to be fulfilled. One's rights too often are synonymous with one person's individual ego. The false self is making a declaration, often out of frustration and too often, selfishness.

Duty, on the other hand, is associated more with the true self of the individual. Duty, or Dharma in Sanskrit, can be said to be more of a mission — that assumes a more altruistic quality of the individual.

* * *

The Shining Ones

Those who have left all the darkness of the human world; who have crossed over (while still amongst the living) from the human to the Divine; who have left all the negativity behind and can only be positive and thankful. "The heavens opened, he stood before his Soul, was illuminated, and became a *Shining One*."

* * *

The Big Dream

Our world, our physical Earth and human world — the Maya — remains a dark mystery to man, unless he is fortunate enough to have found a master-guru and have been initiated. Until then, men, particularly Western man, remains lost to occult knowledge of the Spirit and Soul. So at the time of the Soul's departure from the human form, he is left ignorant.

The Powers That Be

The powers, the forces, the entities above and around us from the Maha Gurus, to the brothers of the White Lodge are stationed always ready to aid another soul on the Earth plane. Plans are already made. We merely have to avail ourselves, make ourselves open on a continuous basis. Nothing of the mundane, profane world should interfere with our receiving. Confidence, support, and energy is being fed to us allowing us to pass through the terrible bleak periods of boredom that arise in this most stale and putrid materialistic West.

These powers are so sacred and invisible to the naked eye that we mere mortals rarely think about their existence. Yet, by opening our psychic force, and surrendering our egoism we can harmonize and be initiated by even the greatest masters, who see it within themselves to stoop down and bless us with their golden nectar of divine consciousness. It is with this knowledge that we persevere, that we know however bleak and blind those around us are, that *our* force, our light will never fade, will never cease, will never die.

At times when we feel abandoned by those around, look within and again unite with this divinity that blesses us, that connects us to the most powerful forces in the universe and beyond. Here we will find our faith and inner truth and direction.

Lofty Ideals

"Living in the truth, man becomes a purist in every domain of human life and finds it intolerable to live in anything but the truth."

Lofty ideals are part and parcel of lofty living, and so how to become "Lofty of Living?" Especially when the world is not oriented in this direction?

Through immersion in a divine status we can eliminate the necessity of concentration of what is mundane.

There is too much preoccupation with the misinterpretation of goals on the Earth, too much fascination with misinformation in the Western world — an obsessiveness has taken control where the Earth is the obsession rather than the Divine Force.

We seek to replenish ourselves through earthly pursuits, we seek the glorification of ourselves through earthly pursuits; so few cognizant of the Divine Law at play at all times.

We have to get back to our origins. Get back to what makes sense, what makes life an existence easier and more simple and more joyful.

We should annihilate all false goals from our spirit and stop our own self-induced human slavery, mindless sorrow and torture. For the human condition is in actuality an unrealized divine condition.

Our reverence will come for ourselves and the Earth when we have understood these simple facts and can live in the spirit of Divinity and a state beyond ego.

To become serviceable to others is one of the greatest offerings that we can aspire to.

The Two Worlds

Divine and human are the two worlds, at one time separate and at the same time together. The Divine exists in all that is invisible, in the essence of all of things in the universe and is permanent in all material forms.

The Divine can and does encompass the human world; however, the human world does not necessarily include the Divine World.

How and why is this possible? Why the dichotomy? What has brought this about? Can the human world ever knowingly be brought completely back into the fold of the Divine World?

The answers to these questions all lie in the artificial self we call the ego. On a great mass level, multi-millions suffer from the same affliction, ego.

It has been said by the wise in a time long ago that the physical human world was created by the Gods for the Gods. Sometime back in the time of the great animal creatures and giant human forms, the Gods intervened and materialized out of the divine ethereal world and temporarily became human. They multiplied. Generations passed. In the beginning, the Gods maintained their Cosmic Mind contact and were never far from their Divine origins... With the advent of "free will" some Gods became lost — "fallen ones." And the "Shining Ones" were soon being outnumbered by demi-gods and finally they all became simply ordinary human beings.

Today, on entering the 21st Century, the West has its physical world/civilization bereft of the great mosaic archetypes of gods and demi-gods who all played essential roles in creating and maintaining the Cosmic "Lila" play on the Earth. The true forces of the invisible universe have been relegated to myth and legend.

From time to time there is born on Earth an Avatar — (a god) who attempts to stress, point out to the more open souls that in the back of their minds, in the deep recesses of themselves, lies a memory of the previous god-like existence on a higher plane of consciousness.

This is the real work for the enlightened ones, to find the souls who are open and make them realized — to reform the lost ones and make them Shiny again.

Only by eliminating the false self — ego, can a human hope to slip into, to cross over the gap between the worlds — the schism is there.

Yoga is a bridge. Perfect godlike images — like Mother goddess statues, coming from the divine consciousness help the individual to make the bridge to the Divine.

A temple helps along with the images. These aids all help to diminish the rift between the Divine World and human.

Guru's presence is an assurance.

Surrender to the truth.

By surrendering to the truth — "The truth shall set you free..."

It is written on Montparnasse in Delphi at the temple of Apollo: "Know thyself."

By knowing oneself one lives in the Truth. Thus, the person then know both worlds.

In the Human World, We Are Fed from the Divine

Some humans have been more imbued with divine substance than others... Who are these exceptional humans? How can they be distinguished from the others?

To answer these questions we must recognize that which responds more favorably to the Divine are attributes, talents, arts, and culture which are the most refined: for example, Indian dance, transcendental poetry, inspirational paintings, mystical mystic writings; yogis, such as from the Vedas, Gita and especially Sri Aurobindo. The beings who display these aforementioned qualities or signs are more often than not recognized in India and the East. Far too often the West has relegated these individuals to the garbage heap, to be ignored, incarcerated; shipped out, ostracized.

Little does the West know that these individuals are often the true prophets and leaders in our society. Our world is suffering from the lack of truly divinely inspired souls. Materialism is a creeping gangrene ignorant of all divine substance. In the unseen Divine World, there is a vast treasure trove of substance waiting to imbue any and all humans — all they merely have to do is to play dumb to the human world. All they have to do is stop, look and listen to the voice of the Silence, for in the Silence the Divine lives, waiting for the next little "chickadee" to peck its way through this veil of Maya.

How best can it be said? All the wonderful arts and cultures in the human world which are all fed by divine masters, all waiting to infiltrate human neophytes, the dead, but not dead to the Divine world, the likes of Tagore, Whitman, Da Vinci, Lao Tsu, etc.

Not only does the Divine go to the artist but to average man and woman.

The man on the street can be blessed. The "pure ones" can become divine phenomena. We do not have to die to be divine nor must we have a belief system. Yoga, the master subject for all, can satisfy. Yoga is as old as man's history — a short cut to the Soul's realization. The science of the spirit. We need more souls to become students of divine inspiration and culture. Students who are willing to first learn the craft before calling themselves "healers" and "teachers" and rushing out to set up shop and administer their best (or worst). Self-declared masters! We can only become a Master by most advanced spiritual experiencing.

What is Yoga?

This word has gone to the West and been misinterpreted, misused and misunderstood. Picked up by many, glamorized by employing only the physical aspects for bodily beauty, retaining youth, energy enhancement, etc. But behind this one word *Yog-a*, to join, is the most profound philosophy known to man. Science of the spirit, the method by which man can discover his original source, his eternal being, in a word, his Soul, by applying the subtle yet simple techniques. Known to man in the East for 5,000 years, it has brought the super shakti or life force plunging into the human form, thus transforming the being, and uplifting this minute form consciousness into the upper realms of Divine Bliss and supermanhood — Yoga says and can do it all. Very few have been able to cross the threshold from the human to the Superhuman without faltering at the wayside.

Deva and Lakshmi Speak, on September 23rd, 2000

Deva: Yoga is in two parts, both stillness and movement. For example, if we make a pot, we have to form the pot, and it is formed out of movement. But Yoga is also very special; I would call it ninety-nine percent philosophy; it is probably the basis for every system of belief in the world today. It was absolutely universal up until the past two thousand years.

About forty years ago, I was a teacher and an actor, and I happened to find myself in New York City. I could not stop my mind. At that time, I had no notion of India; the contact with India was very sparse. We only knew about Mahatma Gandhi, Nehru, and the Buddha.

After I met Ananda Devi, we spent the next 34 years of our lives together, developing another ashram in Paris, France, after the one in New York City. We lived as guru and disciple, and also as mates — a very unusual relationship, seeing that I had surrendered to a woman.

I was very interested in Sri Aurobindo, and became his disciple also, although he had died in 1950; as well as Ramana Maharishi. They were both gurus of my guru, Ananda Devi. Within a matter of weeks, in this period of 1960, I experienced a complete and total calming, a stopping of all thoughts in the mind, which has lasted until this very day.

People ask me, "Why would you want to do such a silly thing?" People like their minds speeded up, they want to be very speedy; they have all these gadgets... I hope you will agree with me that the more gadgets you have, the more speedy becomes your mind.

I was able to completely stop my mind. I live in today, or in this moment, and not in yesterday, or the past... and the future never comes. I put myself into a cell, so to speak: a room with a chair and a bed, which I put on the floor. And I worked to be able to find myself in the highest consciousness, along with what Ananda Devi had achieved.

Then I started reading. First I experienced, then I started reading, to find out what others had done, and if I was achieving what other saints, yogis, and rishis had achieved. Lo and behold, I found myself leaving my body. I entered into the Child Consciousness for hours, (it can last a period of days, as we will tell you was Lakshmi's case), and eventually into Cosmic Consciousness — transcendental light everywhere, and the auras would be abounding everywhere around me. I was extremely light; it would not have been possible to lift up these glasses, they would have been too heavy for me.

Finally, there was a descent of the Supramental, or what you call Purushottama in Sanskrit terms. In the West, of course, we are very satisfied to achieve the Astral experiences. However, this was a period of tremendous transformation, taking place in my laboratory, called my mind. I realized that I had achieved what very few people had achieved in the past, but which everyone can achieve today, because Sri Aurobindo is very interested that the Supramental make its complete descent onto the Earth. This is what he was hoping to achieve, until he died in 1950, and he continues to do so, because there is no death.

From there on, we worked in the early 60's. In the hopes that we would terminate the Cold War, we would concentrate on a higher plane of consciousness on a daily basis to stop the military-industrial complex. For example, During the '61 crisis — I have written a story about this. Finally, we made great interference to make sure that Gorbachev did meet with Ronald Reagan, and peace was brought about, and there was a great decline in the Cold War. The last situation we were involved in, my guru and myself, was the period of the Gulf War, or "Desert Storm," where we found ourselves both in the same dream in front of the Knesset in Israel, trying to convince the Israelis not to counter attack after Saddam Hussein was launching his scud missiles on to them.

The advantage of achieving Illumination is measureless. I suppose we have to explain, because we don't look Oriental or Indian. Believe me, our bodies are Western, and my training is Western, but my spirit is very Eastern. We have trained and traveled the entire world.

After my guru died in 1994, I took what I could carry and moved to the Himalayan mountains, where I was directed to go to a café called *The Rising Horizon*. From there, I will let Lakshmi tell you a little of her story.

Lakshmi: When I came to the Himalayan mountains I, too, was undergoing a process whereby I knew that the only thing I wanted was to be realized spiritually, and at that point, nothing in the world really mattered to me any more. My mind was moving very fast, so much so that I almost couldn't function in the physical world. At the same time I was having great energy coming down into the top of my head, but I had no way of integrating it into my physical mind or emotions on the Earth.

When I met Deva, he said, “I don't usually accept students, but I will take you to where I am living, like a hermit, in the mountains.” He asked me, “How much do you really want to allow the ego to die?”

I said, “I'm not really sure what part of me is the ego just yet.” He said, “Well, that's my work, that's my job. I can see when you fluctuate from the good self to the ego self.” This was the first time I had not been able to fool someone in front of me.

We went into — it was like a laboratory. I was not allowed to go outside. He was able to capture my consciousness, and to know the precise moment when my false self would arise.

Deva: At this point, I used a particular yogic technique to take her into Child Consciousness. I don't want to confuse you people, as I am almost positive that every woman understands — almost — the concept of Child Consciousness. It's been theorized by Carl Jung, and others. I actually took her into Child Consciousness and she stayed there for one week. She could do nothing but sleep, and “goo-goo,” eat, and laugh. This did not have a deleterious effect on her consciousness. On the contrary, during this period I was able to extract, to extirpate out, to ask her, “Do you want to keep this particular part of you, this traumatic experience that you had with your parents, your peers, or someone else?” And of course, from there, I could rid her of that.

One must actually experience the Child Consciousness. One does not become a physical child, and yet one does become a physical child, one becomes helpless, as a child. And if you've never had this experience, you must have the experience, otherwise you cannot go further spiritually. You may have all sorts of psychic experience, you may have gleanings of Cosmic Consciousness — all very good. But finally, you've got to get down on all fours... Particularly the males; we males have to give up the role playing and the empire buildings, because this is an entirely male-oriented society.

We have come back here to dis-orient what has already been orientated, because the only way you can succeed to become spirituality realized, is to become de-brainwashed first. And that's what she did. In other words, I was able to de-brainwash her.

We have no interest to brainwash anyone, because they're already brainwashed! How can you brainwash someone whose brain is already clogged with all the burdens and baggage that you've been collecting for all of your life, whether you're thirty or you're eighty? It's impossible. This Western society — and the Eastern, which is going in the wrong direction as well — is only interested in brainwashing! Our education is to fill the so-called void in the child. It's completely false.

That child is already complete; we are born with all knowledge. We have nothing to teach anyone. We are building these egg crates called schools, with armed guards. We educate with fear, we stuff them, they don't want to be there; they are told to be there. One hundred years now, of "universal education" — universal incarceration! Where will it end? Think, that the child is born with all knowledge.

From there on, I took her out of the Child Consciousness, and she was pretty much pure. The thirtieth day, we could create a new personality: a new name, a new hairdo, new make-up — anything — new costume, new speech. No longer the mundane, the idioms of her own country, or of America. Everything had to be original, for the very first time. It's like learning to walk in the woods. You will walk in those woods, you're going to discover it yourself.

I come back to America, and I find no one goes to the woods. I say, "Darlings, so-called pupils and disciples, go into the woods, and listen to the symphony of you. Because you are part of that symphony. That consciousness of you, is the same as in the trees and in the plants. We are all communicating at all times, telepathy does exist.

We have a chance to break out of the Hinayana, the small egg, and become little chickadees, whenever we want to, when we turn our mental processes in that direction. And then we will become a part of the great egg, the macrocosm, the Mahayana, and then we have the ability to choose our own destiny.

I was my guru's shadow for thirty-four years. I never spoke in her presence. When you talk of surrender, it is a question of merging one's mind with someone else's mind, a superior mind, a mind that has gone to the highest echelon, to the Absolute. My guru would announce, "Well it seems that I have one mind and two bodies now." It didn't matter what I had to say, it was what we were saying, what she was saying.

So I gave Lakshmi methods by which she could achieve the goddess in herself. She arrived at a higher level of consciousness.

Lakshmi: I found my mind still, after all this purification. And then from there, I worked to harmonize my force and energy with Deva's and I found that as I did that, it was like a great gush, a great waterfall of energy passing inside of me. And I would leave my body, and shoot very fast upwards, into extremely expanded consciousness, be one with everything, I became one with the Light.

Deva: The pinnacle of her experiencing was when she traveled at the speed of light to her Soul, or Atman. This culminates in a Sanskrit term called "Jivatman."

Lakshmi: I left my body, and I saw an umbilical cord. I traveled up this cord until I knew that I was entering into my Soul. It was the most incredible experience, and I thought, "My God, we are all existing here, and completely unaware of it!" And here I was in my most pure state, looking down on my human self, the little self, full of all these ideas that are actually false. And from there the great forces came down and there was a joining between this higher consciousness and my Earth consciousness.

Deva: While we're sitting here, we also exist at the highest level of consciousness. So unless you occupy yourself to cogitate in that direction during your waking period, you will not achieve the total and complete connection.

You are here because there has been a synchronization process, which allowed us to come and meet. Perhaps we have met in other lifetimes, and we're meeting again, to carry on this meeting. Consequently, when I'm talking to you here, I am also speaking to you on a higher level of consciousness. This meeting is a form of initiation.

We can perform this process on you, if you allow us. We are not interested in collecting sheep, we abhor that. We want to have independent, realized beings, and this is the time to do it, because this is the era, the epoch, for women especially to free themselves out of the confines of sociability and domestication. You must free yourself spiritually first, the apex first. Then you come down, and you have complete freedom, not the reverse. You want financial freedom, social freedom; you've got it. But you forgot the essential one, which is spiritual. With the spiritual all the rest follows.

I would like to find a book in the grocery store, or write a book, called, "Seven Secrets to Failure, and How to Become Enlightened"! What is this business of success? We have found the people who are the most discouraged by life are the only ones ready for the spiritual. If you're content with the five-sensory world, you will never want it. You already have everything. You really must want it, and that is the whole thing.

In order to achieve it, you must know we are of two selves, and we must really make those two selves one. I have concocted various methods, which you may or may not find in books. You will certainly not find them in Western books; I suggest you go to the Indian books, go directly to the Tibetans, and some Taoism. The Chinese do not give you the methods, but the Indians will, although it is sometimes hidden in the Vedas or the Upanishads.

You must see that we have three natures. We have our own physical nature, our own body. Second, we have the nature outside of us. You must learn to connect with the nature outside of you; all beings are the same as your nature. You must see your being, your nature, as being sacred. Therefore, after I determine this, all natures outside of me must be sacred. You must have a complete communion with the nature outside of you twenty-four hours a day, nothing less. You must learn to harmonize with everything, inside and outside; all the chakras have to be in harmony, rotating clockwise at one and the same time.

We have to stop seeing ourselves as healers and teachers, we must first become students of the spirit and the Soul, otherwise we'll never be a healer, never be a teacher.

There is a third nature, and that is the one that is coming from above us. Once we have established these two — and thoughts are coming from this direction as well — we have the ability to bring down from the vertical direction, Cosmic energy at all times — shakti, Mahashakti.

I can stay on a subject for days, weeks, months, it doesn't matter to me. But I won't be talking for my own ego. I will allow you to smash me if you can, at any time. I'll give you the smashing bats!

We have come to America in order to show people how to ego smash themselves. This is a word we seldom hear. We are all split, so don't feel ashamed. We are split in two directions. We are split on the Earth, and we are split from our true consciousness down to the human consciousness.

Three natures, and we are split at two levels. Thoughts come from three directions also. They come from inside our mind — we must control every thought to become one thought. The memory must disappear. We must not cling to our memories, or to our emotions. People say, "I don't want to give up my emotions! I was just beginning to enjoy my emotions!" Yes, you enjoy them, but as Nietzsche says, everything must go "beyond good and evil." You must get to the subtle nature called the satvic state. We can all get to the satvic state. Pratyahara, pull back and go above it all.

You must see yourself beyond good and evil, beyond the human concepts of this world. There is eternal love. And if you think you're going to find a soul mate, more power to you! There is only love, called energy, and it has to be found, because if this heart center is closed, you're not going anywhere. If no one gave you love for the last three and four generations, coming from Anglo-Saxon Europe, then that center has been empty for generations and generations, because no one gave you love.

We have allowed darkness to come into our heart and stay there. And we're full of rancor and vindictiveness. because we don't know how to be happy all the time. We say, "Be full of joy, twenty-four hours a day." People say, "Nobody's full of joy twenty-four hours a day. You must be unhappy sometimes." I say, "Impossible, I would not allow it." We only stay with the people who can achieve joy, because as my master used to say, "Anything but joy is ridiculous."

Why should we get kudos and accolades for being natural? It's natural to be in joy. Let us start diminishing our ego eccentricities, and start thinking in terms of expanding, and coming back to our Soul, because our Soul really wants to be realized now.

Do you want to realize your Soul now? If you allow a moment to pause, to reflect, that meant that the ego is creeping in, and the ego will answer for you. The ego lives on negativity; lives off of and in negativity. You can diminish your ego by living in positiveness twenty-four hours a day. Never say, "no."

Life is there to be plunged into, tantrically. You must explore every avenue of yourself and the world, without becoming tainted. Do not allow the superstitions, and the rites and rituals to hamper your instant evolution towards enlightenment.

Does anyone has a very pertinent question concerning their own spirituality, or spirituality in general?

Student: If spirituality is with us all the time, and so close, why then is it so difficult, and such a struggle to get there?

Deva: We stumble as a result of our own karma. You can be helped with your karma. I am willing to help you. We can clean up your karma in this lifetime.

It helps to be surrounded by a physical world that respects the spiritual. For example, this room is sterile. There is no femininity in this room. Where are the colors, where is the nest? You are sitting here, you are the only things feminine here? Without femininity, without the feminine force we do not have spirituality. We do not have spirituality, *en grosse*, in America because of that. From the Empire State building to the computer, it's all male. What is female out there in the world?

Student: The arts.

Deva: In this country, the "greatest country in the world," there is no Minister of Culture. They tried it in the 30's. Jimmy Carter tried it again. You find that the best American artists have been going to Europe, for about a century and a half. I have known many of them in Europe and Paris. The whole concept of living on this Earth is to live in the play. We have to acknowledge the cosmic play of the lila, and bring it down to Earth at all times. We pay people to make us laugh. Billy Crystal, Milton Berle... You should laugh on your own. You should be able to enjoy on your own! Laughter should be natural. You go to see the Dalai Lama, he laughs. People say, "We didn't talk about anything, we laughed!"

I have been playing all my life. I have been occupied in hazardous occupations from California, to New York, to Paris to India and back here again. I have been bounced around because, as I mentioned before, Lakshmi is a medium, and Koot Humi himself asked me to come back to America.

Since man has had history on this Earth, great Masters, the Brothers of the White Lodge, have had control. We think we are in control; we are not in control. We have to learn how to be controlled by these great Masters.

Student: The Child Consciousness: Can you explain, as you are taken back to the child state, what happens at that point?

Deva: You're not far from Child Consciousness. You have unburdened yourself already of so much ladened goods. When you strip yourself back to the inside you, there is a little entity inside of you called the child that must be born. It was giving rise to its birth around the time of eighteen to twenty-two and it was squelched. Precisely because of that you are still seeking your creative period, or your child conscious period, when you can really create, and let flow the creative urge inside of you, in a cosmically conscious flow.

Child Consciousness will most necessarily give birth to the Cosmic Consciousness, no problem, it will happen. You will find new talents; Lakshmi dances, sings, writes.

How many people want to become children again, without rebirth?

Ramana Maharishi was always a child. Sri Ramakrishna Paramahansa was such a child, he wore women's dresses, he danced — he was a child. This is the height of the yogi, the *par excellence* of illumination. You cannot exceed the child.

The Inner Self and the Growth of the Ego

"Man is made up of a temporary surface personality and a deeper eternal Soul"

— Sri Aurobindo

In order to really understand ourselves as human beings we must first try to connect with our inner self. At the time that we're born we start life with one basic self, what we call the true self, with all of its pristine purity and soul qualities. This self is in reality our spirit self, that which allows us to be animated in every part of our being — a life force. But as time goes on, days, weeks, months pass and the infant enters more into the physical world of phenomena, he is being influenced by objects, sights and sounds, everything from the five senses. The infant and child is also being given ideas both true and false, concerning the visible as well as the invisible world.

At the time we are born we have come into this world with certain inherent (essential) qualities. These qualities remain with us at a very early age until the outside world interferes and these essential qualities are soon blurred, hazed, pushed into the recesses of the subconscient of the mind. However, given the right conditions and setting — parents, atmosphere, environment, etc., the infant may retain the essential qualities for a good period of time before losing one and more as he advances in years.

As time passes, the young infant slowly but surely acquires "another self." A split consciousness develops. Possibly by the ages of two and three years old much of the purity is gone and the young individual begins to live more and more in the false self or the ego self.

The qualities that the newborn innately has at birth are the very same mentioned by Plato: *goodness, beauty, joy, truth, love, justice* and *harmony*. In the West, adults are not aware, or are ignorant of these innate qualities in the newborn infant. They believe that these qualities must be learned and taught. This is not the case! Also, the adults who take charge of the infant are convinced, by themselves, and by other adults, books, religions and the society in general, that a personality must be created in order 'to survive' in the physical world. The Euro-American complex places a great emphasis on increasing the ego, almost to the exclusion of recognizing the true self. Consequently, an ego is forced into creation on the child from age one to adulthood, and in most all cases continues on all through the adult life, stifling all the seven innate qualities that the human being needs, to be in perfect health, harmony and completeness.

The question now raised is why is this a subject of concern? And if worth discussion, how can this situation be addressed? While growing up, the child is constantly reminded and told that an ego is very necessary — to acquire a personality (meaning an ego personality) and that we cannot survive without an ego.

There is even pride by society as it continues the mega-ego development through the family, friends, peers, emphasizing vanity, boasting, greed, boisterousness. Indeed, organized sports, music, religion, politics and groups of all kinds are all guilty of helping to distort and derange the creation of a true personality.

It is necessary to say that we do not require a false self, or ego self. Of course, in order to live in the external-physical world one really needs to be well-prepared in every aspect of ourselves. We must bring out more of the pure, real, inside spirit self, the True Self, on a daily basis, to ensure a true external self to manifest. Fusing and melding, through surrender, the external self, the false self, to the True must be done.

As young people we are told that we must learn to be honest. But if we are born with a basic sense of truth, must we really learn to be honest? Isn't it rather that we must discover, and exercise what we already have when we are born?

So if this is the case then, that the child really learns to become dishonest and not honest, then this should be true of the other six inherent qualities. That we learn to be bad, that we are told we are born in sin and must be saved; that we cannot be happy or joyful all the time, that suffering is a part of human existence. But if we were born in joy why should we be told we must suffer? Shouldn't we really be only expressing what we were born with? Therefore, if this is the case, then all we should have to do is uncover the joy that we are born with and live with it at all times. Ananda Devi would say, "Anything but joy is ridiculous!"

Only therapeutic psychological research performed by a qualified person who has already rectified or reversed the process on himself can make the necessary change in the person that wishes to regain the seven soul qualities he was born with. This operation of psychological analysis requires great perseverance, and knowledge of the mind and its make up. A compassionate person will know that the patient is in a condition of ignorance, which was produced by early childhood cover-up, and therefore suffering, crying and struggling will all be a part of the patient's throes in the process of purification back to the inner True self. The subject must be willing to accept criticism and eventually change; in some cases, criticism may "hurt." But it is all a part of the process of unmasking the ego. When the temporary hurt has gone, the ego can be vanquished for good.

In order to achieve more or less complete success in this process of restoring, or bringing to the surface, one or more or all of the innate qualities, the ego will have to be confronted. In other words, the false self, (ego) actually is preventing the essential good qualities from surfacing and living at all times. The artificial self (ego) prevents the uncovering of the innate qualities. Indeed, we must recognize that on some level the ego grows to like to state of self-involved depression, anger, hatred and resentment. Although consciously the individual will deny this fact there is still a part of the consciousness that is resisting.

The individual is not suffering from a disease, but he is covering up the entity or aspect of himself that is justifying self-absorbtion and negative traits of the ego.

In fact, the negative nature splits into two or more personalities. One is the calm, yet depressed, self and the other, the violent, demonical nature that rarely surfaces unless provoked. These personalities are both dependent on each other; they coexist in ignorance.

Unfortunately we cannot cater to either of these ego aspects, as the psychologists do today, for it is our role to disengage and render the negative personalities defenseless for good. We must confront the demonical or hateful self, giving it an ultimatum for elimination. How else can it disappear? For the individual is incapable of extinguishing this self, for he is too attached to the existence and drama of it.

We, as spiritual purifiers and initiators, have to instill the will of determination for elimination of this false self, so that the individual being treated should feel the pressure surrounding this false, angry, hurt self, until he is forced to surrender all that is evil, all that is negative to the true kind self. The ego must be smashed; must be eliminated; must be replaced by more and more good and true experiences arising from the Soul self and true child consciousness. Then and only then can the purity and all true qualities become a part of the nature of the individual once again. The ego must become enmeshed with the Soul self. Another birth, a birth of the Child Self must take place, it is absolutely essential that the person rediscover the child in all of its quintessential goodness. This alone will diminish the ego and allow the soul self to assume its rightful place thus making the person more complete and ready for Cosmic experiences and eventually Soul awakening and on to complete and total enlightenment.

The Fragility of the Human Psyche

"The Oriental alternative to going mad is to go into the spiritual."
— Premananda Deva

If it is true that the human psyche is fragile, by whence did it come? How did this occur?

If it is true that the human being is fragile, to what extent? Is it throughout all humanity or just in the West?

What causes this fragility in the West?

We can attribute this state to the separation of the individual being from his spiritual roots. This cleavage produces a feeling of being alone and distraught. With no one to rely on, people feel isolated and rejected and do not understand why. This is grave, for it is spreading in our industrial society with its gadgets and the dissolution of the family structure.

It is incorrect to treat the mental process as a disease; for example, depression. This condition requires special attention and only can be addressed by an individual who is trained, rendering support, not resorting to drugs. People have to be given hope that they are definitely connected back to their transcendental reality.

The distressed individual can no longer depend on another adult for that special fellowship, for they have experienced estrangement from others and have found that church and religion is not the solution.

To bring this person back to a normal state again requires hours of companionship. Holding their hand, applying simple massage on the neck, head and feet, etc. assuring the person that they are an integral part of the universe. Along with the kindness and energy that is derived from another supportive individual, it is essential that there be a period of incubation away from the world, so that his mind is starved from any distraction, so the individual can regenerate and recreate a different kind of spirit within themselves, one of unity and serenity.

This condition is usually attributed to Westerners and or Western society, this feeling of psychological alienation. As long as the rest of the world adopts the Western ways, the same illnesses will proliferate.

There is a split between the metaphysical world and the human world, and the individual feels separated from the family psyche, so they develop a non-trusting psyche and a split personality.

The experience of child consciousness serves as an aid to the distrusted adult psyche. For by harkening back to the child consciousness one experiences naturalness and hidden strength, the individual now allows himself to rely on another adult, and the adult's presence assures them that they are not alone. The adult must derive his inspiration from the metaphysical source, recultivating the joy inside of the individual being treated. So by becoming temporarily childlike, it reinforces to the individual that there never has been a separation from his metaphysical self, which is so close to the child self.

The child consciousness is what the psychoanalysts have not yet discovered in their research into the subconscious. What the researchers thought they discovered was that the subconscious world was all wrong, all filth, full of complexes, desires, which are the roots of obsessions. However, there is existing the purity of the child here, waiting to be delivered and called upon to evoke more purity to the conscious mind and being. Then the fragile personality can build upon the pure untainted foundation of the child conscious self within — thus eliminating the intellectual and emotional contortions of the ego.

There Is No Death For the Child

There is no death
For the child
Of me —
there is
Only love of thee.
I live to see
Grass grow green, the
Wind blow clean, the
Air to purify my me — I lie
In me
Eternally
For
Thee.

There Is No Death
For The Child
Of me.

by Deva

Deva's Philosophy

The application of specific Psychological and Philosophical treatments

A. Description and Order

1. TRANSFORMATION; this must first be completed prior to initiation: .
   a) Psychological investigation (possible regression).
   b) Elimination of unpleasant traumatic experiences.
   c) Purification, elimination of bad habits.
   d) Transformation from the old personality to a new one.
   e) Child Consciousness — papillion period.
   f) After the Child Consciousness there is a maturation process of child like purity. Out of this grows a child like and eventual new adult personality.
2. INITIATION: from the Master to the student — Application of stilling of the mind, stopping all thoughts, recitation of mantras, mastery of the body to complete immobility.
3. ILLUMINATION: The long awaited entrance into Cosmic Consciousness, an early form of Soul Consciousness.
4. INTEGRATION of the high consciousness into the personality and spirit on the Earth and preparation for eventual work in the society.

Daily Methods for Spiritual Development

1. *To open ourselves* to the Universal Consciousness, or Divine.
2. To see ourselves *joined to our soul consciousness.*
3. *Mantra recital* daily, either externally or internally, to establish a one-pointedness of mind.
4. *Pranayama breathing*, invaluable for clarity of mind and stillness of the body.
5. *Self-analysis*, and contemplation to find out what is locked in one's memory box. To purify oneself from bad past experiences.
6. *Letting go — Wu Wei*, away from the false traits of the personality and letting the true inner self take command.
7. *The "positive" process* — words, thoughts, actions for oneself and others.
8. *Elevation of thoughts.* Not allowing thoughts to become vitalistic or towards past associations, clingings, emotions.
9. *Sense of humor* — cultivating on a daily basis. To smile and laugh.
10. *Joy in every waking moment*, rather than slipping into sadness. Fuse the ego self with the true self. Bring out the essential qualities such as goodness, honesty, trustworthiness, patience, harmony, etc.
11. *Read spiritual books* to stimulate yourself for temporary and eventual permanent entrance into spiritual self.
12. To *seek out by whatever means at hand a Guru/teacher.*

The Three Types of Nature	Thoughts
Outer physical nature (Earth)	Arrive from three directions.
Inner spirit nature (True Self)	I. **Our mind** — thoughts we individually form.
Supernature (Divine)	II. **Outside of our mind** — telepathically we receive from others.
	III. **From the Cosmic Mind and our Soul.**

Note: In our mind preceding spiritual discipline, we hear two voices — the "front" voice, the ego nature and the "back" voice, the silent (occasionally vocal), wise voice of the true self.

The Mind

Stopping the mind, seizing the thoughts is essential. The mind is a mirror, whatever we concentrate on, we become. If we concentrate only on the outer physical nature, we can never realize our Supernature.

The mind is an aspect of us that is not dependent on the brain. The mind receives from the spirit and our true inner Spirit receives from our Soul.

However, we prevent this flow of true thought and state of being from our Soul, due to our preoccupation with our ego self and the thoughts that are in response to our physical outer nature.

Hence the split on two levels:

I. The First Split is on the Horizontal level

1. Ego Self

2. True Self

II. The Second Split is on the Vertical Level

1. True Self

2. Soul Self

Once the unification occurs whereby the ego is meshed with the true self, then it is possible for the child consciousness to manifest and following soon is the cosmically conscious self which bridges the second split, for the experience of the Soul (Atma) is not far away.

Then when both splits have been unified the individual who is then freed from the ego voice, thoughts and actions can receive the messages coming down to him from his Soul. This is the aim of Yoga, to join, in union, all that is separated in our consciousness.

Stages of Realization

EGO → CHILD CONSCIOUSNESS → TRUE SELF → COSMIC CONSCIOUSNESS → SOUL → ABSOLUT

The Two Selves

It is necessary to explain at the outset the meaning of the Two Selves. From personal experiences and acute observation I have come up with certain ideas and conclusions concerning the subject of two selves.

There is first of all the "inner self" or "true self" which can be said to be the true or real entity that is ever the same in all situations. We will call this self number "two." The other self, of course, is number "one" and to this self we can attribute the term "outside" self or "artificial" self or better yet, simply The ego.

To the untrained mind the position or location in which they rest or lie is not too easy to define or situate. This subject should be considered very seriously and the understanding of the two selves will give us a more clear comprehension of the concept of the two selves.

Let us propose a hypothetical case. We will call our subject Mary 1 and Mary 2. This is the same person who has two distinct selves. After a short time of working with Mary, she is able to acknowledge the existence of the two selves. Once this realization is accepted by Mary, she can pursue the course of elimination or merging of Mary 1, the ego. This is invaluable for spiritual discipline.

On the Earth, we find with the individuals in the West and especially in the United States, a split consciousness is more evident than in Eastern countries. As we travel to the East, after leaving Europe, the separation becomes less; as we arrive in India, we find very little sign of this schizophrenia.

The Qualities of The Two Selves

True Nature

- Lives in and acts with the seven qualities of the Soul — goodness, love, joy, harmony, truth, justice, beauty.
- Positive in speech and feelings.
- The eyes make good contact — straight, direct.
- Smiles naturally, good naturedly and with sincerity.
- Laughs in a genuine fashion expressing good positive feelings to all persons present.
- Conversations are more healthy in nature taking the line of concern for the other person.
- Surrender is its nature.

Ego Nature

- Lives and acts with hypocrisy, arrogance, conceit, wrath, ignorance, full of desire, fear, pride, anxiety, envy, jealousy, self glorification and is addicted to impure resolutions.
- Speaks in negative terms, expressions and words.
- Tends to hide from truth.
- The eyes shy from making direct contact, shifting from side to side.
- May smile, but not naturally, not sincere.
- Laughter is very false if not raucous and sarcastic.
- Cynicism is often the trademark of this individual
- Sadism and/or masochism are common qualities.
- Extroverted or introverted are the two extremes used by the ego
- Has difficulty surrendering

The Ultimate goal is to fuse the ego with the true self, until they are unified. With a unified self, once the horizontal split is no more, then the adherent can pursue to eliminate the second split to his Soul consciousness, this is when the student is ready for Initiation.

Methods for Detecting and Conquering the Ego

Very subtle techniques must be applied. First, a friendly rapport must be established. Then every movement of the body must be mentally noted along with facial expressions and speech,

Before engaging in an intense dialogue or listening with the subject it would be best to describe the reason why such an operation is taking place and establish; why the subject has decided to undergo therapy. (*Note:* this therapy should only be applied with the guidance of an eligible teacher).

Ego Detection

- Ask if they are aware of the existence of two selves.
- Try to determine if they can tell when they are "in" their ego and when they are not.
- Ask if they think it is necessary to keep their ego. If so, why, of what use is their ego to them.
- If they have agreed that the ego had brought them distress and even misery, this is pointed out to them.
- Help them to realize that the ego is a false creation and has little or nothing to do with the True Self.
- Establish "personality one" as the ego or false self and "personality two" as the True Self. (Mary 1 and Mary 2).
- For the untrained mind it is not always easy to determine between 1 and 2 personalities, even for the trained mind. Very often the ego can learn what the interlocutor wants to hear and actually deceive and "satisfy" the questioner.

However, slowly but surely the Death of the ego will occur and the True Self will emerge.

We Can Live in Truth

Contrary to what Western man has been purporting, it is quite possible for a human being to live in the state of truth.

In order to produce this, or in order for this quality to be of a permanent and natural state, it is first necessary to establish that verity — truth — exists above and beyond all physical forms. In other words, truth can be said to be a universal quality, not dependent on human devices.

It is necessary for the human mind to be absolutely pure, simple, uncomplicated and very one-pointed. At the time of our birth we were, no doubt, in this state only to lose more and more our pure truthful consciousness, substituting it with falsehoods and lies contrived by society in the material world.

When we arrive at the age of adulthood, we are living a life of lies in a society of lies, based on lies. For the individual truth is something that eludes us — never really attainable, at least by a human being.

Yet this is not true! By self-discovery, by creating a veritable revolution in the mind, whereby the mind becomes topsy turvy, upside-down and goes through a revolutionary process whereby it becomes more and more stilled, truth prevails at the end of this self-investigation.

* * *

Stilling the Racing Mind

The process of blanking the mind or becoming one-minded or even no-thoughted has to do with wanting to actually bring all thoughts to a standstill. Firstly, the person must be aware that many thoughts are swirling, or spinning at a very fast rate. This usually causes alarm and disturbance mentally and even unusual behavior in one's comportment. In my case, I had these very symptoms and found myself not able to slow down my racing, "out of control" mind. I had no notion how it began and if it would ever slow down, although I did wish for an end to my strange mental condition! I saw no possibility (in the U.S. or anywhere in the world, for that matter) of arranging my seemingly deranged state. It was back in New York City, February, of 1960, I had gone out one evening and strolled the West 70's. The night before I had been with a friend of mine, Lenny, and I explained my condition to him, thinking he may have heard of similar cases, since he was a psychiatrist. No, Lenny simply smiled and seemed as perplexed as myself. So, I wandered into what looked to be an exotic coffee shop called "Nirvana."

Here the story of my racing mind takes a turn for the better. Soon after meeting an extraordinary person, Ananda Devi, and listening to her fabled experiences, I found to my delight, that my mind was slowing down. Still not completely stopped, yet I felt I was nearing control. It still had not come into my head to even envision total stopping of all thoughts. I believe I mentioned my racing mind to Ananda Devi. She simply smiled knowingly. This somehow reassured me.

Sri Aurobindo, when he was looking for a way or person to help him stop his mind, came across a Yogi who showed him how to do it. As a result, Sri Aurobindo achieved one thoughtedness. Some years later, Mrs. Richard (later to be known as The Mother in Pondicherry) met with Sri Aurobindo and she too had a racing mind. By only being in Sri Aurobindo's presence, her mind eventually came to a standstill, in about 1920.

So it seems almost certain that my providentially planned divine meeting (and eventual 34 year discipleship) with Ananda Devi was fortuitous and her presence certainly, aided, and was very instrumental in making my mind blank, I am convinced.

How many other souls out there are in the same dilemma, I haven't any idea. It seems to me that the masses live with their minds mostly always racing, some slower and other days faster. They no doubt spend their lives this way. I can only ascertain that the Eastern peoples, less industrialized, have minds moving at a slower pace than those souls in the West.

Western society is, no doubt, plagued with countless racing minds, due more than likely by greater concentration on industrialization and gadgets. Lacking the natural Eastern methods of breathing, mantra, stilling of the body and breath, the West resorts to drugs, sedatives, and incarceration and even operation on the brain. Mental institutions; clinics, and prisons surely are full of these "racing minded" souls.

During early spring of 1960, I rigorously applied breathing techniques, pranayama, the mantra: OM MANI PADME HUM. I felt my mind metamorphosing like billowing clouds formation arranging and preparing my now mostly stilled mind for vaster, expanded and elevated experience.

The person with the racing mind who is more evolved and sensitive will be more likely to encounter a true master so that the mind will become stilled in his presence and eventually even merged with that of the master-guru. In times past, this practice may actually have been a universal one; in the temples of the entire world (prior to the spread of the mono-theistic Semitic belief systems) from the Mediterranean world to India and China even to the Mayans and Incas of the Americas. For Northern Europe, Russia and North America the Shamans no doubt played a very important role in connecting the disciple, from his small whirling mind, to the stillness and oneness of the Eternal Mind.

By making the mind one, or the stilling of the mind, one is then ready to relate to the essence of all things.

The Shiva and Kali Force

"We all delude ourselves (a stage of delusion) and refuse to humble ourselves in front of even God."

— *Premananda Deva*

These forces serve to destroy and obliterate all that stands in the way of ultimate and absolute perfection. These two great archetypal entities will accept nothing short of perfection.

We have to control the ego in this life or the Karma and the egoism of past lives will pervade us.

After the old mold has been broken, and the ego is cracked, in tatters, it is the guru's thankless task of re-forming a more perfect being.

* * *

Fire in Ourselves

Keep the fire, use it to ignite others, become combustible. Use the fire that normally would be used in anger, fights and conflicts in the direction of showing others how we can be transformed by a *Spiritual Fire* that is always inside of us.

In America, this fire has been reduced down to low burning embers because our society represses "true spiritual awakening."

Religions control, rather than encourage, individual spiritual fire for inspiring the transformation for Soul realization.

Apotheosis

(The deification of a human to divine status)

Victory is won when thy ascension is complete.
When the glory rides high above Earth's shallow waters,
When the voice heard, still, is the echo of the Supreme.
Wonder now, my children of thyselves
crowned atop thine Godlike throne.
Wonder now, why is it that you have not allowed
yourselves to be shown this Truth.

Subtle are the steps that heed the ways of riddles unsought.
Take thy battle arms and hide not thy foolish ways.
Give all, give thy voice, thy mind, thy very reason for
existence.
and do not descend again to the ways you have trodden
before!

Give until your Glorious ascension is bestowed
until you have chosen to see the Magic hidden and yet so
omnipresent.

Fight, for this God force in you demands all your
consecration
to this glorious bliss of existence so sweet and so pure —
Your apotheosis is now!
Take it, want it, live it,
Eternally.

by Lakshmi

To Become Illumined

The process for becoming an illumined being has to do with the ego; that pesky, pretentious, silly, arrogant, negative, false self that prevents us from realizing our Soul.

The Soul, the silent self, always positive, waiting patiently until the ego gives up its very existence and allows the full booming of the essence of our being, our Soul, of which only a part has incarnated in our body and which has the ability to create spirit, thereby forming our mind, that fits oh, so neatly into our brain.

So, we must not entertain the ego, never flatter, for these are mistakes made by parents, peers and the society, which help to enlarge and reinforce our ego, leaving us lost in the Maya — perhaps for yet another lifetime. For to become illumined, to shine inside and out, with love and light, we must diminish all that is false, all that is a burden, all that is extraneous, superfluous, including facts and figures. We must blank our minds, make ourselves empty for the Soul to be awakened, and to be allowed to fill out in every inch of our being with Super Shakti Force, the all pervading Divine Energy, Sat Chit Ananda.

The Mysterious One

As your silent grace touches me,
I feel your magnificent soma devouring me,
I thirst for your crystalline dwelling in me,
And again we are One.

Like a wave, you wash inside me, purity.
I am only a tiny droplet full of your nectar,
echoing your resonance
with the enormous chasms of light.

My mind is only your smallest thought
and my grasp of you, a simple ripple

Consume me again,
that I may love you more poetically,
that I can reach within myself
and offer all — no less.

Now I am traveling down the mysterious torrent of
you;
You overpower me, and again we are One.

Steadily now I am the silence of you
I am the light of you
I am shimmering.

The force pushes me, crushing, every
breath of earthly existence
has been answered by your breathless
fire.

May we all be the Mysterious One within
and answer only
to this sacred call.

by Lakshmi

The Ego and Our Mechanized Society

The ego is a separate entity from the inner self, which leads to schizophrenia (dual personalities). Mechanized society is the primary cause, especially since the advent of the industrial revolution (1900 - 2000). The last hundred years, especially the recent thirty years with the introduction of the electronic and computer age, have brought with them an occupation leading to fanaticism which we have not seen since gunpowder was brought to Europe from China by Marco Polo some five hundred odd years ago. Western man has a way of turning an innocent discovery or invention into a monstrous proportion all the way to the A-Bomb and now the Computer Bomb.

In short, America and Western man *per se* have long ago stopped the pursuit of and investigation of their soul and have taken a suicidal direction. The result, schizophrenia for the individual and for the masses. Separated more and more from the physical world of plant and animal life, as well as from his Divine Nature, man stands bereft.

So what do we have? We have a few greedy Western men — who are and have been increasing their yield and empires ever since the onset of the Industrial Revolution. This has led us into a greater ego separation from the inner self, to the detriment of soul discovery. Soul investigation is being put into the hands of belief systems and New Agers who are stressing that a simple out-of-body experience, a psychical happening and even a contact with a medium or channeler will bring you closer to God.

No, there is practically no one in the Western world to point the way.

Causes and Solutions

What are the causes and solutions of this malediction of "our times," especially in America? Presently across the United States young people, teens and pre-teens are going into schools killing students and teachers. Often in the aftermath of their slaughtering they say they feel nothing — nothing in the way of remorse or regret. Some are even satisfied they have achieved revenge. They have given vent to their volcanic anger and have found a solution at the cost of children's lives and their teachers'. *Problems in America are rising to epidemic proportions*

Causes

- *Foundations* of the society are not based on broad universal or spiritual values.

- *Competition* is bred, at the earliest age, instead of cooperation. In sports, business, home, and school, creating ambition and hypocrisy.

- *Non-touching* Anglo-Saxon mentality dominates.

- *Abuse* (mental, emotional sometimes physical!) of the child instead of healthy affection and touching.

- There is a *psychological immaturity*. Everyone wants to remain as children, few really want to become adults — little boy faces and dress on big men, little girl faces and dress on big women. Everyone is in a state of escape and denial of true spiritual duty and responsibility.

- *Ego* (false self) cultivation starts at a young age. Children are treated with extreme behavior, either complimented for normal behavior or no affection at all, creating an egocentric, hurt, masochistic suffering ego, full of revenge.

- *Separateness* — the compartmentalization of our society. Lack of wholeness in the physical society encourages and aids the dis-unitedness in the child. Schizophrenia is more widespread than figures or statistics show. Perhaps most every individual has a mild case to even acute schizophrenia, (two or more distinct personalities).

- *Mechanization* creates disoriented and dis-harmonious individuals in our society. Few can make the adjustments over long periods of time. Our animal bodies, together with our mental, emotional and spiritual being are not able to cope with computerization, factories, discos, videos, etc. We are out of kilter, out of sync with our inner nature as well as our physical outside plant and animal nature, not to mention our psychic and spiritual being. We are more and more disturbed, depressed and suicidal.

- *Greed* is cultivated in every individual by constantly playing on the five senses and titillating them whereby the individual eventually ends up craving a new car, cigarettes, riches, women, enjoyment, pleasure, anything to be "comfortable." A truly hedonistic society, all for the riches of the few and to the detriment of the people, the masses. Greed; gold, glory all boils down to one vice, just greed.

The ills of our society can be simply stated as an ego problem, and nothing else but that. We have a national ego problem which we can call a collective ego or Mega-ego. The captains of industry are not content with having created false human beings with false personas in America; they are fast projecting their dominating methods in all directions of the world. Europe is fast catching up to America's contagion, America's vice. Our blue jean, drug, rock and roll culture is being exported to India, Africa, and China. Yet China tries to put dampers on the gross greed, excesses of vice, raucous music and even salacious literature: J. P. Sartre's *No Exit* was banned. The Chinese are conscious of how all the free licenses of the West, especially America, can break down the morality of the Chinese people. Can we imagine over one billion people going berserk over rock and roll, drugs, sex, all at the same time?

We are responsible for our behavior on the Earth. The Divine, the mother creatrix of the universe, both invisible as well as physical has allowed a descent into matter, human creatures from her compassionate bosom, together with a strange unseen appendage called "free will."

Our free wills are out of control and not able to rejoin with the Master Mother in the Divine.

Psychological Viruses

At day one, upon birth, we as entities (babies), start absorbing viruses both good and bad, pure and impure, for the body as well as the mind.

If we are lucky enough to have been born into a family of most adoring and loving parents who themselves are pure, with strong bodies, relatively free from impure viruses then we, as growing infants, can have a chance of remaining pure and mostly free from physical and especially psychological viruses.

What are psychological viruses? Why should we be aware of them? To explain: the mind being a mirror or blotter is constantly receiving impressions from the outside physical world as well as the outside mental world. These impressions are being made at the earliest age and continue all through life. Psychological viruses are the traits of the ego nature of society that we engender in our personality and make our own

Why should we be aware or even alarmed by these viruses? First of all, practically no one on the Earth is exempt from receiving these viruses. Perhaps one in many multi-millions can remain pure, untainted by society, *i.e.*, Forrest Gump, the Idiot of Dostoyevsky, and perhaps the Dalai Lamas, and a young yogi born into a pure Brahman family.

The Separation

As the crisis in our society manifests itself through violence, disparity within the family structure, with continuing signs of illness, both mental and physical, we must ask ourselves, what is the origin of these crises?

It has been said that when man separates himself from his divine Reality, from the core of his being, maladies start to occur. Now we first must test this hypothesis, by examining the nature of this divine Self and spirit, core being, True Self, however it is termed.

This aspect of us is unknown to us at the time of birth. We know who we are. Although not cognizant of the workings and potentials of our adult self, we know love, goodness, joy, peace and justice. We know, at this point in our lives, because there is absolutely no separation between us and our inner being or spirit and soul. We are completely free from the confines of the world around us; we are completely free from fear, utterly free of inhibitions. We are an Original.

So when is the exact time in our lives when this quality of freedom and purity leaves us? Why does it leave us? How can we retrieve this knowledge again?

As a young child we generally have a great desire to please, to unite with the wishes of our elders, be it teacher, parent or relative. We have an in-built cognizance of respect and love for others.

So why does this all change and how? We must investigate the creation of the ego, and how it is formed.

The irony being that unfortunately more and more of our society enhances and does not deflate the possibilities of ego creation. Parents and teachers are unknowing victims — allowing a spirit of fermentation for the ego self, as they are caught in the traps laid down by society.

Now, at this point it has to be stated that the ego is a separate entity from our True Self. It is a thinking, acting and false representation of who we are and cultivated enough, it will dominate our inner being and try to control those around it, given the opportunity for growth.

Today's society, unfortunately, misunderstands free expression of the child, which will only cultivate the child's ego.

The thinking man's paradigm existing today is as follows: I will give my child so much stimulation, computer enhancement (and consequent agitation), and experience in life, so that when he or she grows up, they can master this world (only seen as a physical element in reality).

Yet, the parent is unable to see the difference between the true creative force in the child which is spontaneous, intuitive and non-thinking; and he or she tries to cultivate an intellectual, thinking person, a carbon-copy of themselves, a copy that society pressurizes them into believing that we can surely not function without the intellect. This aspect of ourselves is highly oversized and overrated. A tool of our higher nature, the intellect is far from the extent of our intelligence, or thinking self. Unfortunately, the more the child has an exaggerated intellect, the ego becomes attached to the new information it has acquired, gains a sense of importance, even superiority over parents and siblings.

So, instead of cultivating a wholesome, loving, sensitive and intelligent child, we are cultivating angry, self-obsessed, arrogant children, who neither obey discipline nor leadership. Ignorantly, they claim the unseen rights to defiance and superiority, becoming their parents' master, a certified know-it-all. The roles in the ego mind have changed. No longer must they be subservient or devoted or surrendered because in the eyes of the ego self this shows signs of weakness and lack of identity and every lack of intellectual "dignity!" Secretly the ego has decided to abhor all discipline and those directing discipline as a defiance to its "brilliance."

So then, we cultivate the ego in the child at an extremely young age, fearing the ominous task for our children to face the world and its multifarious obstacles, we implant a new way of being. We cultivate the thinking animal and here begins the separation, and the two-selved individual. The child nature, purity, love, goodness, and joy, is seen as insignificant or of lesser importance. But in reality it is *this* aspect of the child that *has to be enhanced.*

Let us now study the "support group" the ego finds for itself in society. For the exultation of the intellect is only one factor resulting in the ego's so-called stabilization. The ego then begins a life of programming, trying desperately to fit in with all the other Egos in society. Everything from clothes, food, likes and dislikes are given, not chosen. (Looking for $50,000 a year, car, job, house, children, etc. and then surprised at age forty or fifty to find that they are far, so far from fulfillment, happiness or joy.) We have lost our identity and spirit; we have lost all connection, and have been listening to the thoughts of our ego, our programmed self. The ego connected to the Corporate World and materialists' plan. We have become the perfect subject in the court, abiding by invisible and subtle laws — consume, consume, consume. Question not; think not; discover not!

So then, if *we* are not who we thought we were, if we are stereotypes, full of emotional distress, physical illness and family dysfunction, how can we eliminate the poisonous factor governing us — The ego?

In the case of children, the role of the parent has become more and more difficult. The tidal wave of media, music and peers has such a powerful possession over them; psychological viruses, seeking to manifest egotistical wants and desires, are ever ready to make younger and younger consumers.

Discipline is important, to *snuff out the ego*, to root out the false personality, not allowing the child to reverse the roles, not allowing the ego to dominate or belittle the natural hierarchy that exists in the family.

As the adult, we must pursue a purification, a spiritual discipline. Through the Yoga philosophy we can eventually precipitate the dissolution of the ego and eventually pursue a truer personality and a spiritual identity.

* * *

The Addiction Called Materialism

The rules of the game are as follows:

Everyone in the society must participate. From a very young age the ego has to be created in the child. A transference from the parental Egos to create a little materialist.

No one in society should question Democracy for this equals freedom, (for the corporate economists that is).

No one can defect. Everyone has an unwritten pact not to rebel against this, for fear of exposing the millions addicted. The West is not necessarily "the promised land" but the land of the "hypnotized slaves!"

They Walk

They walk — sounding voices
of other ages
The good common people
slipping into sensory mazes

They do walk now,
the ungraceful,
ungainly, unmindful

They do walk now,
the sorrowful,
hateful, tearful

They do walk now,
the common, bourgeois and
aristocrats

They do walk now,
upright bodies, rotund
tummies topheavy
heads

Cargoes of bodies,
Misplaced from the
Solar Race.

by Deva

Western Schools — An Analysis

The barrier must be brought down between the world of children and the adults. There must be a return to a simple single society. There has been an unnatural separation, a madness, developing in the twentieth century, especially in the last thirty years. There are too many divisions, too much of making differences commonplace, if not the norm — from the infant, to the child, to the adolescent, on to the teenager and finally the adult world.

The state has, by and large, taken over the role of educating the child. This so-called universal education of the masses: To increase literacy, or is its real purpose to play the role of baby sitter?

A reappraisal of the Euro-American school system is necessary after the trial and error style methodologies or experiments in learning techniques which have been applied for well over a century or two. We really should think of making certain essential and basic changes in the schools.

American schools are rife with violence. Two major groups, youths and adults within the super-structure that have been slowly "facing off" to one another for years, until today in 2000 and 2001 where they are climaxing, with direct confrontations taking place, shootings and killings across the United States. The breakdown of the superstructure into Youthhood and Adulthood is one of the basic causes.

Our penitentiary replica schools: America, Europe, and now the world are guilty of helping to create a two-tiered society — Youthhood vs. Adulthood. Two divergent in one, a split society. A divided world, a schizophrenic world. Where are we going? We have been, for a century, creating an enemy in our midst. We have been in the process of feeding lies to our youth from our "great society of lies."

Bells ring, doors open, ear-shattering noises, almost deafening smother the corridors. Like cattle they, the kids, scream, push, rebel disheveled in dress, minds, speech, defiant in all manner as teacher "guards" look on in shocked dismay. They are joined by one and two armed police roaming the halls, and present at the cafeterias and elsewhere.

This is not a school atmosphere. It is the next best thing to a prison. Yes, our school systems are reminders to our youth of what they can expect (prison) in the outside world if they do not make the grade in school.

We have developed a system based on fear, suspicion, grades, and competition. Failure is tantamount to being ostracized, an outcast — a non-joiner, non-athletic, "non-religiously connected" youth has no place here.

"You will conform, you will adhere to the rules and regulations," and there are many.

By two years old, Americans already form huge egos.

The concentration level is very low. Their eyes and minds seldom stay fixed for very long.

They are fed films, videos, toys, bubble gum, etc.

Prizes and awards, scholarships are given out to outstanding students.

To work non-intellectually with one's hands performing menial tasks is discouraged.

What to do? We need schools that do not resemble penitentiaries; schools that are more joyful, kind, more silent, schools with no bells! A return to the family unit. And if not immediately or ever possible, there must be created surrogate parents with male and female teachers representing their original parents. This could work.

A peaceful environment must be established to create a harmonious child, one that is full of love, wisdom and spiritual awareness. Classes teaching grace, elegance, standing, walking, talking, etc. In other words, the whole person must be trained, not just the "brain" for math, language, and machines.

* * *

Unity

An integrated individual and an integrated society is the answer to the current rage of violence spreading in the American schools.

An integrated person is one who has gone through some phase of self-investigation or analysis in order to better understand himself in light of his childhood experiences in relation to his adult self. This process of inner probing hopefully will have left the individual with fewer frustrations and anxieties in his present day activities. Hopefully this process could be brought into the schools of the West, especially America. We must teach the child to learn the psychological makeup of himself and, at the same time, include a connection to self mind control and link to the life force, stressing more emphasis on daily kindness, compassion and moving towards more non-violence.

A Society United

We need one society — look at the Native Americans. Every member belonged to the family, clan, nation. Nature and their life were their school. Trench coat mafias, and skinheads could never have developed in the American Indian society. They helped each other to become a good member of the tribe, to be humble, harmonious and above all, they knew that nature and life are sacred, spiritual.

It would be impossible for counter-cultures to develop, such as Christianity (an import), or atheism, or anything else for that matter.

We must return our people to one society. Let us return to the way our Native Americans related to each other, to nature, and the universe. They were not at odds, nor competing with anything nor anybody. Respect for all, especially the elders and family was fundamental for tens of thousands of years; as with the Chinese, and the people of India (Hindus).

We have much to learn from the ancient people and cultures, which still endure.

The peoples of China, India and Native America dressed as one peoples. The youth were integrated with the adult world, not rivaling. We must reduce the present situation. We can do it, just as the tobacco ads are coming down, so too must the alienation between youth and adults stop.

Another thing: Children must not be allowed to develop such big egos. By age two and three, (away from parents) in day care and pre-school, they are rampant. The mind at this age should be trained to be quiet, to be stilled, not to be excited and thrilled at every moment. (Video games, computers and TV cartoons are thrust in the face of the infant — and they are defenseless.)

Let us regain the control of our youth by stopping the games, computers and the television. We must allow them to be creative, but not if it means creating a mass of mega-egos and have them become brainwashed and desensitized to feeling for others as a result of all the violence around them.

No one is born bad. We, the society, make them bad. It is now time to make them good, for we are all born good. Let us help to uncover our goodness.

One Society, one peoples.

Taking Man Away From Soul Discovery

Politics, belief systems and organized sports are not good for the people. These activities actually seize the mind, the thoughts and leave the individual still further from discovery of his Soul.

These activities are really the bane of modern man. In the last 1,500 years, Western man has progressively been taken further and further from his inner spirit and from his Soul.

It seems that with the advent of monotheism, the people of the Middle East, Europe and the Americas have supplanted the existing animism and spiritualist cultures which satisfied every longing, desire and need, accepting spirits in all plant and animal life. With the spread of monotheism now reaching the Orient and Africa, the peoples of these great land masses are being forced to leave, to depart from their acceptance of natural cures, respect for their families and ancestors, the commune of all spirits at all levels right up to the Supreme Maker of all life, both visible and invisible.

Forests of Europe and America were sacred and they were the temples for the Europeans and Indians of the Americas. Along came the Christians, (and especially the Jesuits), convincing the innocent natives that no spirits and souls exist in plant and animal life and that it is perfectly acceptable to destroy wantonly, *sans* discrimination. Whereas prayers and ceremonies were dedicated to the spirits of plants and animals before, now they are slain or destroyed.

Monotheism, in all of its variant forms has been ignoring the Divine in all matter and setting man apart and separate from all other living entities. This is wrong, and against universal spiritual laws. This is all too barbaric. For the spiritual connection to all life includes the one supreme principle.

The White Race, along with the Semites of the Middle East, has been guilty of vast and great atrocities for a millennium. Can they be stopped?

Belief systems, stemming from the Middle East, are Semitic syndromites — who cast spells of "Thou Shalt Not" at the followers, calling these (maxims) phrases "the works of God." And all other peoples of the Earth are considered pagans, heathens and following the works of the devil!

We must educate and change the minds of man. We must find souls willing and ready to be freed from the enslavement.

There is no time to lose. We must change man to achieve his own goodness. The Divine must prevail in place of the politico-economic system.

Poetry is Love

Poetry is love
It sends out blue water sailing
It allows the wind to whistle freely
And lets tiny droplets
Of early rain
Kiss the brown dry earth
When her parched lips
Quiver in sandy cheeks

All life responds to love
If so allowed —
Poetry is love, love is poetry
Where stand we
When love abounds
Our unhaloed head?

by Deva

The Forgotten Arts

The conglomerate that makes up the numerous Western societies, which now forms corporate West or, plainly, Western society, is being held together by economic (financial) Super Multinational Corporations and even military alliances. The cultural, artistic, philosophical, and that forbidden word "spiritual," plays little or no role in the binding of the nations of Western Society. Gone are the Empire days of the Romans, who with their military might organization always brought along their pantheon of divinities that were thrust upon their colonies. This modern conceit of nations exists in its greed creed and greed of power and money from San Francisco to Vladivostock. A European culture has long since gone back into the days of Master painters; Shakespeare, German philosophers, etc., who now have no place in our modern world. There should be a cemetery for cultural artifacts if there isn't one already. One no longer writes or creates for society as Tchaikovsky wrote his 18th Symphony for Napoleon or the Medici family commissioning the painting job of the Sistine Chapel and Da Vinci's *Last Supper*. One could say the West is having its last supper having poorly deserted all that is Art, Music, Philosophy, Spirituality and is now preferring a diet of Cyberactivity! Networking is now here and is a must to feed the hungry and emerging nations of the world — who are told they *need* this information by Western Corporations.

So as the Western world feeds on Virtual Reality phantasmagoric theme parks, they continue to overproduce and over consume. Subliminally, the motto "greed is good" is being told to the entire world.

Western Paranoia

By the cultivation of greed, (which ultimately includes all desires and "man's vices,") the Westerners create an invisible demand for self gratification at every moment. This behavior eventually leads to a fear, a fear that they will not be satisfied, that their every daily desire will not be fulfilled, that someone will come along and actually deprive them of their pleasures, creature comforts, and even their very essential needs. America pursues the dangerous, suicidal course of materialism, and by occupying themselves more and more with the maximum number of gadgets and mechanical things. the senses are always being rewarded for all of their cravings.

Rampant, unbridled, non-seeing, anarchic, chaotic, insensitive to all their surroundings; only by stepping out of their egos can they begin to see "the errors of their ways." No other method can make the change for "changing the West." It is only a problem of the ego.

This very maniacal process of living has become a national habit. America has become the *avant-garde* of materialism and acute paranoia. Fear that beyond the oceans, way beyond in a foreign land there are rogues, conspiring to take over the riches they have been collecting and hoarding. Always more and more arms and bombs for peace. America, the war machine lives in a constant state of fear and war preparedness. When will they ever learn to stop, to live and let live!

The Devolution of Western Man

The "cyber-insanity" is mounting at an alarming degree. Upon entering the gates of the United States one is almost immediately assaulted by people engaging in cyber-gibberish: "on-line," "web site," "windows," etc. These words and language are being created by the same people attached to Western man's latest gadget, the computer, the new god of the Western world. And, as we saw with Western man's previous god, the Western salesman is asking all the world to embrace the Computer as the new and only true god figure of the new secular religion, "cyber-insanity," which many say will gather more worshippers and followers than even Christianity and maybe even Islam.

Our prediction is that we are headed straight to the hallowed halls of non-culture. No doubt this "cyberobot" will enable Western man to finally dominate, with his Computer Empire enslaving countless millions. The mindless, apathetic, non-thinking masses are seeing this as no way out. "We can not turn back the clock, we have to live with the computer." Who has given this new demon of the minds to the people, making him believe he needs it and cannot do without The Computer. No one wants to say, "Just say NO to the computer," as they are supposed to do to drugs. Mindless America has learned to live with the bomb and now a bomb for the mind. Every day somewhere in the workplace, the home, or wherever, someone is being detonated by the computer creation.

Creativity stops, poets have no place, stone sculptures, oil and water color paintings are considered superfluous. Philosophers never had a place in America, but now with the computer, who needs philosophy anyway, when we have the computer which "feeds" us with unending highways of information allowing us to become more lazy and enslaved.

As yet, no one has announced that his dharma or mission is with the computer. This is completely and utterly absurd. It is not a subject. One can become a cook, a gardener, work with animals, medicine, law, philosophy, painter, poet, writer, and mathematician. These are subjects.

We are being told that there are no jobs worth taking if you lack computer skills. This is simply not true. All jobs can be noble. It is a state of mind. From the sweeper to fruit picker, to farmer, to housewife.

Let us start saying "No To The Computer" and think about saving our minds and the minds of our family and friends.

If there were not $50,000 to $100,000 salaries being paid to these non-thinking nincompoops sitting like catatonic bodies in front of the ridiculous computer machine, people would not study this malediction.

Take away the major salaries and their world would crumble.

Western man is very disconnected to his spirit self. Indeed, there appears more of a (desperate) quest by the woman in the Euro-American nations; the male still values his life in the physical. The male is the one really making our world very boring. Most gadgets, including the computer, have been invented by the male, because he is too lazy and ignorant to look inside of himself. He lacks the ability to feel, to transfer affections, and the gadget world is rendering him sterile, if not impotent *en masse*.

The female during the last thirty years, 1968 to present, in a desperate mood, is seeking a soul mate wherever she can find one. Often just discovering her ability to have physical completion, she seeks them out wherever she can find. Stepping into the euphoric world of the spiritual is being attained mostly by women in the West. They are in the right direction. The male is ignorant, for them it is not possible. Women will be spiritually awakened and will change the West and the world.

The Illusion (Maya) for the Westerner

Can this subject really be brought out into public discussion in Western circles without creating heated controversy? I really doubt it. The Western man denies the existence of Maya or illusion, placing almost all his values on the physical, leaving the invisible world as an unknown quantity, not to be investigated (for it is not empirical nor analytical).

How can a Westerner, grossed in his heavy materialism ever possibly accept that this physical world is mere illusion? Not very readily to be sure. Why is this the case? Precisely because his whole entire world has been based on "knowing" or trying to learn whatever it takes about the material world, in order to survive and succeed.

Now here we are caught up into the twentieth century and twenty-first, and for well over a hundred years, Western man had been concentrating (almost to the exclusion of the spiritual and metaphysical) only on all that is a part of his five sensory world, Maya.

A great number have made great profits with the economic system called capitalism. The capitalist is very concerned about accumulating capital for the purpose of so-called security for himself and his future generations. The vice we call greed is a major factor in producing this trait or desire to gain capital, in the form of gold, jewels, property, paper money or any material good which will enhance his wealth, status, power and position. All this to the exclusion of any investigation of his spirit and Soul.

Of what real value is capitalism when the people are forced by propaganda from the educational system to only think of the material world without once realizing the physical world of the five senses is illusory or Maya.

Eastern man is the superior thinker and more stable emotionally, especially if he puts his mind and thought to a higher and wider spiritual consciousness. Maya, the illusion, is ever with him. People of India (those who have not been converted to foreign belief systems) place themselves (their faith) in the hands of the unseen forces.

The Indians know and trust these forces because their rishis, seers and yogis have described their experiences in the pure realm of truth, beyond the five-sense world of illusion.

The American Myth

The land of America, the New World, has long since changed her tune since the time of her forefathers, who are long forgotten. Their ideals, their truths, their spirit for a free country, a country where Man can live above and beyond religious bias, beyond the constrictions of their countries of birth. This dream is sadly lost and perhaps the nation of America has long since taken a movement away from the truth and the real.

Yet, to qualify this, we must examine how to keep a race of people in line with the truth, how to restore the necessary aspects of our inner nature so that we do not lose ourselves in the extremities of our modern world and materialism.

We too, have to examine the nature of Democracy and freedom and the forces that are allowed to proliferate as a result of this political and social system.

For although in the hearts and souls of the Americans there is a sense of honor, liberty, and sanctity, the personality of this nation — of the Corporate world, of the military, of the institutions within the society — is much more unrealistic: too aggressive, too violent and uncompromising.

There is a national schizophrenia, a disharmony and a dysfunction; the family is no longer a dependable institution and cancer, depression and anxiety are part and parcel of so many people's lives.

As we head so rapidly into compartmentalization of our lives and selves, we have lost the simplicity, the joy, the love, and the truth.

For to survive in this whirlwind society we are instructed — "Get an ego," "Get a Life," that's the only way to survive!

So behold a nation where the majority of all, lives in the *characterization* of the soul personality, the ego, a poor judgmental fragment of man, a paranoid fearful "animal," a shell of a creative being.

And, on the individual level, this is having dire consequences on the health of the American people mentally, emotionally, psychologically and physically.

The ego, a term rarely understood, is a separate entity inside of us who can only contribute to unnaturalness and eventual malformation in ourselves and those around us.

How to rectify this situation? How can we turn back the tide? How can we illustrate the seriousness of a society that wishes only to "have fun," to escape in all forms of sport and hedonism, a society that cares very little about the needy, the poor, and judges very harshly the rest of the world and humanity, never doubting the sovereignty of their might and force.

And yet, is not a man's greatest courage the ability to examine and re-examine himself, to eliminate his negative qualities so that he can live in the truth of himself? Not a hypocrisy. "Long live America," the greatest country in the World, and yet she has discredited all else, all other civilizations, all other belief systems, all philosophies, as unimportant and insignificant.

America and the West allow themselves to be guided by many forces, for example, the Semitic religions, and secondly the scientific body that demands every individual's respect and allegiance.

How can we allow these forces to dictate to us when we have not made the investigations ourselves? How can we live in a world where freedom is a word, not a state of living or of mind?

We are being fooled by the materialistic forces, the political powers; we are told how to think, what to like and dislike, what to fear, what to desire, and how to cultivate all of the above.

Society is rigid, and full of boundaries for our mind, body and spirit. A society that, for hundreds of years, was governed only by men, where the role of women is slowly but surely changing from that of childbearer to active participant.

It is time to take a stand. It is time to control the forces that control us if we allow them.

The Gods

"Coming to the Earth as an unrealized God, they tried to tell me I was human, then I realized my God self and left the world as a God."
— Premananda Deva

On the Earth, they came from the valleys, the mountain tops, Mount Olympus, Mount Kailash, and Peruvian heights, to declare their immortality.

Children of Immortality are here surrounding our every being, and yet we are also the gods on Earth, with clipped wings, Prometheus Bound.

The Dark and Golden Goddesses

It is time to unbound the dark and golden goddesses of mother Earth. Unbind them from the ungodly males who assert their authority over the Earth by force and might.

Women, this is your age. Do not mistake your form to be only "for human use," to produce infants and imitate your male counterparts.

Your spiritual time has come. Your awakening is nigh. There is no time to wait as your males dither over "to test or not to test" (nuclear), to "eliminate or not to eliminate."

Why are you sitting silently on the sideline of life? Stand and assume your true role, ye daughters of Zeus, of Isis, of Mahashakti, no longer sit idle doing thy knitting!

So Plato declared you inferior for the metaphysical studies. This is pure rubbish!

As proof, my guru Ananda Devi of over thirty years was enlightened, and was a woman (d. 1994). And now my cheli (disciple) has succeeded in achieving Cosmic Consciousness and is also enlightened; by the very intense and diligent training she has experienced.

In the last hundred years alone we have many cases of enlightened woman souls and they were disciples or consorts of great male gurus. To state a few:

- Ananda Devi — disciple of the Tibetan (a Brother of the White Lodge)

- Mme. Blavatsky — disciple the Tibetan
- Alice Bailey — disciple of the Tibetan
- Annie Besant, who founded and helped form The Congress Party in India — disciple of the Tibetan
- Sister Nivedita — (Irish origin) disciple of Swami Vivekananda and co-worker with Sri Aurobindo
- The Mother, disciple of Sri Aurobindo
- Ananda Mai
- Lakshmi Devi, disciple of Premananda Deva

I am sure there are others. I have only mentioned those who are known to me.

Divine Goddess

Divine Goddess--
Primordial and all powerful --
Enter into our spirit
Allow us your presence,
Sweet and terrible,
Transformative and dynamic,
Quiet and serene
-- Divine Goddess --
we surrender our human selves and are once again in true light
for union with your silent grasp of
perfection.

Ethereal you laugh at us, yet all is well within your bosom.
Never far from bliss are we,
regaining the simple knowledge
there is no separation between
us and you,
the same.

Mother and Sister Soul,
All are yours (and ours) in spirit,
encircling life's changing mold,
Eternal your glance to Earth
blesses us, to know our
Soul's freedom

Forever veiled we lie cold,
not aware of the warmth that
flows through your heart
to us at every moment.

Euphoria is the occasion,
Realization the event.
Let us join together
to consecrate our love
for you, Divine
Goddess.

by Lakshmi

Woman and Religion

The maladies of our modern culture go back to the origins of the Christian faith two thousand years ago. The woman was no longer worshipped as the Goddess, the mother, the nurturer. She was seen as the deliverer of evil and desire — from the original sin — Adam and Eve. From here onwards the natural balance of all aspects in the family and the society have been malaligned.

The woman was stripped of her divine existence and role.

She became the bane of the world that was increasingly male.

She no longer had any significance or real force in the home or the society.

This lead to the psychological malalignment of all members, both male and female.

For the male chose to project his ego in the place of the vacuum, decreasing the divinity of the female.

His tone moved from the vehicle of intuition to an intellectual role and the woman lost her way in the world.

Let us redress the balance of the Goddess. For divinity is not itself male, but female too, and the man should realize more this female entity and then, intuition will thrive.

Are we not going to get outraged as women? Is it not our role to change the image of the woman? Is it not our duty to gain respect and rightful understanding in this world, driven by men who have lost their association with the spiritual authority?

Too often women trap themselves as their inner insecurities magnify the ego self.

In the West, the female gender is confused, which is a direct result of being viewed for 2,000 years as an object of desire. Generally, only the exceptional women were respected and the others seen as inert sheep.

So, as women we must regain the image of the Goddess, no longer the emotionally weak one, inert and inept.

We must strive for liberation from all forms of false imprisonment from the male.

We should emerge women, not hypocritical and egotistical — but divinized, showing our true colors.

We have to stop streaming off into so many different directions like wild horses mentally, emotionally, and physically.

How should aspiring spiritual women act towards men?

Reject them? No. What do we gain from that? More frustration and denial.

We must become natural again, not physically defeminizing ourselves for we are losing our power. Our physical appearance *is* significant: our posture, our demeanor, our attitude when walking, sitting, and talking. If we forget our femininity we lose the Divine face behind it which actually shapes our inner world and spirit. We have to stop being the copy-cat, following the characteristics of the human man and his ego, because of this we are losing power, force and living further from the Truth.

Instead of aping the male physically, we should be trying to incorporate more of the male force, Shakta, the yang force into ourselves.

As women in the 21st century, we should not reject the male, but seduce him. That is the art we are fast losing, the art of seduction. In the Western complex, this only has connotations for physical intimate play. "I will seduce this man or my husband to satisfy my desires, etc.". But we should not concentrate and preoccupy ourselves with the vital but use our force to change them on all levels. The "seduction" process can have unlimited possibilities for the changing of the male.

Why do we assume here that the male should be changed?

There are exceptions, of course, but from our experience, we have found that in the West it is the man for the most part who denies his spiritual aspects and self. He seems insensitive to his intuition, allowing his intellectual and scientific reasoning to govern.

* * *

"Once we are realized, we become our own "Soul mate," and then we can exchange love with others."

— Premananda Deva

Spirituality *Sans* Religion

It is more than possible to possess, embody and experience all levels of elevated spiritual consciousness without religion. It is even necessary to pursue this individual course of action in as much as the Middle Eastern belief systems are devoid of spirituality, only the shell and exoteric effects remain after the demise of the original inspired masters.

The Original Civilizations, China, Egypt and India, possessed for millenniums esoteric practices. Temple çulture was performed by high priests and priestesses, along with dances, songs and music together with sacred language, oral mantras, and incantations — (hieroglyphics in Egypt and sanskrit in India).

With the Superstructure of these Original Civilizations there existed exceptional souls who belonged to the Line of Descent. In other words, a master-disciple relationship existed outside temple culture. The temple did have its merits and aided countless souls into enlightenment with "rites of passage" through life's stages and for the life after. The Line of Descent played a very important role in as much as in a cave, forest, desert, seashore could serve (and still does in India) as another physical place and an ideal form of esoterism, all embodied within the being of the Guru. Initiation in other words. An example of a line of masters and disciples: Heraclitus, Socrates, Plato, Aristotle, and Alexander the Great. Here perhaps the line was broken, only to be started by another sage or yogi perhaps in another country in another life.

This is how true spirituality continued its deliverance on the Earth. It continued until destruction of the three main Original Civilizations, China, Egypt (Hellenic) and India by the Semitic belief systems and more recently by nihilistic Communism over China and Tibet. Along with the destruction of temples, statues were rendered headless, all songs, dance and music were banned. Only India managed to withstand the onslaught of the invaders by miniaturizing and carrying away all that was sacred to the mountains, deserts and forests. Southern India managed to keep most of the music, song and dance intact, maintaining the esoteric Cosmic Connection unlike her sister Original Civilizations.

The Original Civilizations, including the American Indians, had no word for religion. The word religion didn't exist. (In fact, we all possess the spiritual with or without religion). All life was considered sacred. They paid tribute and connected to all entities, forces, spirits in the universe, visible and invisible. Harmony reigned. Anyone who disrupted the Cosmically endowed harmony on Earth was cast out, thus the outcasts in all societies, not prisons.

The exceptional enlightened souls in the Original Civilizations were considered sages, rishis, yogis, and the Illumined Ones. Some examples are as follows: Buddha (Gautama), 500 B.C., India; Lao-Tzu, 500 B.C., China; Plato, 500 B.C., Greece; and Plotinus, 300 A.D., Egypt.

Today we are left with the remnants of the great Original Civilizations. We no longer possess the music, song, and dance, of Rome, Greece, and Egypt. Even oral hieroglyphics died in the crypt with Cleopatra.

It is so important and powerful to pronounce the phoneme; it is a sacred language in mantra form to create the proper psychic vibration. In the initiated being, this stirs the consciousness to a higher level and back to the Soul and the original source.

Fortunately, India still possesses sanskrit for these rituals and the world can be grateful for this and can be saved from the merciless greed and over-pouring materialism taking possession of the Earth.

These Original Civilizations were not belief systems but rather complete life systems all-encompassing for the evolution of all citizens of their civilization be it in China, India or Egypto-Grecians. Harmony was stressed and truth was a code to be honored daily. Thebes possessed the Valley of Truth or Kings and Queens. The classic maxim, "The Truth Shall Set Ye Free," says it all.

At best the out-moded belief systems have only served to control, organize and tax the people in the name of false spirituality to keep lazy people alive in the buildings maintained by belief systems advocates. Never have these organizations ever initiated anyone, nor truly experienced high Nirvana consciousness. People have been told for over 1,500 years to believe, have faith, don't ask questions and above all do not try to achieve enlightenment and discover Truth.

The Original Civilizations and the Lines of Descent were systems of service to the soul of the individual, the whole society and civilization.

The Original Civilizations were completely self-contained. They did not want for anything outside of their own land and peoples. The Egyptians had master-minded the language of the hieroglyphs, temples and pyramids, no doubt with the aide of their precursors the Atlanteans. They were a complete culture. The Greeks came to learn in Alexandria,

(Herodotus wrote of the wonders of Egypt, yet he was not allowed in a temple to be initiated, being a foreigner. Still the Ptolemy family of Greece ruled Egypt up to the time of Cleopatra).

The Greeks were indebted to Mother Egypt for her mathematics and oh, so much more. The Romans went to Athens for education and never really understood the strange, exotic, mosaic civilization of Egypt with her animal archetypes. The Romans stupidly colonized their own Mother spirit, their grandparent archetype. The fall of Egypt to Rome opened a great vacuum to barbarians and slaves, who only wanted to destroy and believe in their own egoistic, blind, ignorant, Semitic religion, not even caring that Egypt had discovered the secret to "life after death," the keys to immortality (see Budge, *The Egyptian Book of the Dead)*.

Egypt stands out as perhaps the greatest civilization that ever existed on the Earth — and no doubt was far ahead of her times. The colossalness of her statues — alive in Abu Simbal and Luxor. The invaders could not easily lop off their heads and remove the faces from all the frescoes.

Egypt was not interested in aggrandizing her territory, but rather to protect what she had discovered and had created from inferior invaders, the Assyrians, Persians, Greeks; alas, eventually she succumbed to the Romans.

Egypt became the mirror of the Divine Will, a cosmic cosmology well represented on the Earth. Gods among men.

India remains as the last true civilization. Egypt still exists on the occult plane. For all that was, still exists.

We of the West (and I have traveled in Egypt and lived for years in India) have so very much to learn from the minds and great spirit of Egypt. Throughout Egypt mediums and channelers can speak to us. Isis and others can still communicate. We can explore our own rites of passage for this life and the hereafter. We must study their works, concentrate and make Egypt live again in us. We must free ourselves from the shackles of defunct belief systems which keep us in ignorance and enslavement.

The Ancient Song

Gone is the music, dance and song of ancient Mediterranea — those of Egypt, Greece, and Rome. This was the beauty expressed on all occasions, to the Gods, for the Dionysian and Bacchus festivals. All lost and destroyed by the monotheists who knew not what they were doing. Gone too is the spoken language of Egypt. Those phonemes that bespoke power to control, heal and initiate; the power to relate to the other world. These attributes all enabled Ancient Mediterranea to exist for thousands of years. The power, the psychic force, in the temples. Travelers, sick, and aspiring spiritual seekers could seek refuge, be healed and initiated in the glorious temples which evoked the gods, joy with the dances, music and song with the priests and priestesses seriously incanting sacred mantras for the benefit of the visitors. This was the world of the wonders for the soul and true initiation and salvation. Only India remains in this category of metaphysical enchantment.

We are left with only tidbits from these Ancient Civilizations. So very few today are concerned with philosophy and truth — the seeking and discovery of Truth through the pursuit of philosophy, especially Plato and Indian Vedas, Rig Veda, Upanishads and the Gita and Tao of China. Herein lie the true philosophies for all. The people today are all too concerned with being a part of a religion or New Age cult. People have stopped self-investigation, if they ever did. Two thousand years ago, centers called temples existed and satisfied the needs of the people. Many were even monotheistic, others dedicated to the archetypes. Let us respect and revere the force that the ancients represented; let us acknowledge the truths and philosophies that had descended to Earth.

Divine Soul

Wisdom
created your
images on Earth,
for your smile foresaw
the human ways
and knew their little
hearts could love
an image before
they knew your tremendous beauty

The Souls of East never forgot...
they found you long ago
they saw your iridescent stroke
and union.

The spirit flows eternally down
down into the temples,
down into the mountains
in the smiles
and in the Soil.

May we now evoke this spirit.
May we now evoke your grace
Allow us your worship
Divine Mother of the East
Divine Goddess of the World
Divine Soul.

by Lakshmi

The Ancient Originals
Versus
The Newly Arrived Religious Belief Systems
(Christianity and Islam)
From the Middle East

Imagine for a moment that the originals (Egypt, Babylonia, China and India) never existed and that Christianity and Islam suddenly appeared on the scene of the Earth some 2,000 and 1,500 years ago and by some miracle they were able to conceive all civilization's culture, from math to music to medicine. And also, by some godlike miracle, they were able to convert all the world people between them, half the world to Christianity and the other half to Islam. What sort of culture and civilization would exist on the Earth in the year 2,000 A.D.? For there is no math, medicine, or music in either the Bible or the Koran.

Think for a moment once again, only one book would be allowed for each belief system: the Bible for the Christians and the Koran for the Muslims. What possible life would there be? For centuries these two monolithic monotheistic systems have been smashing all that existed before them, all that is foreign to their book, their prophet, their god, their heaven. But since no culture and no civilization (hypothetically speaking) existed prior to their appearance on the world scene, then the two mega-ego systems would only be content with banning all performances of music and dance as they have been doing for centuries.

The result would be an Earth of non-curious, frustrated, faithful believers who know they have no chance to look for and find their Soul. No divine inspiration allowed by followers. All has already been inspired, just "shut up" and believe!

* * *

Original Civilizations vs. Western Societies

Western societies, having picked over the carcasses of the Original Civilizations and have come up with an amalgam made up of bits and pieces, cherished together by materialism with hardly an iota of spirituality for her foundation, in Western societies' mosaic of mixed cultures.

India stands alone. She is the only solitary one left relatively intact after having been fed upon by the buzzards and vultures of Islam and the British Empire.

India, the spiritually imperial Mother of all cultures and civilizations, must serve, yes, imperatively, she must serve as a beacon of truth in Western societies' corridor of darkness.

From her temples and gurus comes the highest order of light and energy to raise up the decline of America and Europe. From India we must take the backbone of her philosophies and integrate them with Western civilization.

India, China and Their Relations with the United States

Two giants in population and emerging economies and enterprises, both heavily relating to the United States, the world's lone super-power.

The United States is in the driver's seat of advanced technology and super sales campaign methods — in business she directs the heavy-duty corporate world in order to achieve her goal: the sale of the maximum amount of her products on the world market. China and India represent two billion people to cater to with everything from Coca-Cola to computer products. The two largest selling fields in the world.

China, the communist country, is now allowing democratic processes here and there (excepting Tibet), which appeals greatly to the U.S. Big Corporate World. Having lost her soul and spiritual backdrop with Mao's push for two bowls of rice a day and fifty million hectares sacrificed to plant the grain. Buddhism bit the dust as the purge went on for fifty years.

For some strange reason, the Chinese country-civilization appeals more to the U.S. than India does. Whereas India a democracy, the largest in the world, is forced to play second fiddle waiting in the wings to take the stage, while the U.S. plays stage manager, pulling the economic Multi-National strings between the two super powers, first one then the other.

Here are two civilizations, billions in population and emerging into major players in world markets.

Is America assuming the role of ushering these two ancient and legendary giants into the 21st century to become principally America's major areas for selling? The two largest selling fields on the Earth are being wooed by Anglo-Saxon America and vice-versa. The Euro-American Corporate complex must surely be drooling at the prospect of an open-field day for the multi-nationals to step in and reap dividends and profits.

Is the West, led by the U.S., willing and able and even capable of restraint in the new cyber frontier day in the 21st century. Surely, there must be established rules of conduct in the oldest cultures still extant on our globe.

The human rights records of both India and China are not perfect, still India did not willfully invade China. China was the aggressor in 1962. (The U.S. offered the Bomb to Nehru for testing to scare off the

Chinese, but Nehru refused). China took Tibet in 1959; the world did not move.

America has anointed China with M. F. N. (most favored nation status). But surely China's recent past has been woefully ignored! 1) occupation of Tibet, 1959; 2) Tiananman Square; 3) arms and special supplies to Pakistan.

India by contrast 1) protects Sikkim and allows her autonomy; 2) was invaded by China; 3) tolerates all religions and beliefs to exist side-by-side; 4) is constantly defending her borders from terrorism from Pakistan who wants to occupy Kashmir; 5) does not supply arms to Taiwan as China does to Pakistan; 6) is the largest Democracy and still has the largest surviving metaphysical culture in the form of the multi-arrayed Hindu Philosophy for over five thousand years. Both India and China should receive most favored civilization status.

As China has been communist for the last fifty years, we must turn to India. In spite of over one thousand years of Arab occupation and three hundred years of British rule, she still stands out as the Empress of Asian culture, spreading Buddhism through all of Asia, flower decoration, massage and even martial arts; from the Gita, to the Vedas and Yoga from the Aryans in the north. Mother India continues to smile on the whole world. America must form an alliance — permanent in nature — as the super-tech power with India as the Super-Spiritual power. Combined, they can shape and transform the world into a more perfect future society.

India's Future is The Future of the World

"After all India with her mentality and method has done a hundred times more in the spiritual field that Europe with her intellectual doubts and questionings. Even when a European overcomes the doubt and questioning, he does nor find it as easy to go as fast and far as an Indian with the same force of personality because the stir of mind is still greater. It is only when he can get beyond that that he arrives, but for him it is not easy."

— *Sri Aurobindo*

How can the world and its future be tied to India's future?

In the world of today, the West is forcing the "have-nots" to adhere to globalization, by way of neo-colonization, brought to the "have-nots" on highways of networking carrying multitudinous amounts of information, as if information amounts to education and wisdom, which it does not.

Corporate America and the Corporate West want to make the whole planet one big homogenized Corporate World!

In our epoch, America wants to dominate the entire planet Earth. Outside of continental North America, the United States only considers the rest of the world as one big *"selling field"* for marketing of their products and vices. Is this a greater good?

"Man made" rituals are entrenched, ensconced in religious cults and sects both large and small. While the "spiritual force" remains as esoteric practices and known and practiced only by a few — the initiate and his guru — the true evolved and completely surrendered seekers. The knowers of the self.

If the five billion inhabitants on the Earth are also divine and are all potentially realized Souls; it stands to reason that between the human being souls, and the *Ultimate Reality* or *"Master Soul"* that there are also multitudinous super-human being Souls, not of this Earth, but still existing! All that is in the universe seen and unseen can be found in India.

India is the reservoir, the container of all that is divine. She alone can set the standards of morality and spirituality. We can not rely on the defunct, bankrupt West for direction for they are bound by the Maya of Gold, Glitter and Greed.

Morally deprived hoards of spiritually abandoned souls are coming to India in search of *peace*, love, and above all Truth. The West is a lie, all based on falsehood.

India and the world is on the dollar standard. The most cosmically advanced civilization's economy is rising and falling by the whims and impulses of the "casino" called Wall Street.

Do not let the West and the world believe that India has abandoned her "Spiritual Standard," for she has not! For those Indians who do leave the shores of Bharat Mata and stay away too long in Europe and America, they will fast lose their soul direction. They will be of little value to India and the Spiritualist esoteric forces unless they are purified like in the ancient times. They will have to regain their right to be reintegrated into the Hindu family and Mother Shakti society.

How Can the World's Future be Linked to India's Future?

India is now the only surviving ongoing civilization, continuous for over five thousand years on the planet Earth. Greece, Egypt and China are gone. Some aspects of the Indian legacy are as follows:

1) *The Sanskrit Language* considered to be the mother-root-language of most present European languages.

2) *Raga* music system, more developed than Bach.

3) *Vedic Philosophy* which embodies the metaphysic and knowledge still present today — see *Secret of the Vedas*, Sri Aurobindo.

4) *Mathematics* — the zero originated in India. Algebra was studied by Omar Khayam — author of the Rubaiyat — and brought to the Arab world.

5) *Yoga philosophy* and health system. The world's oldest method for self-healing and attaining mastery over the body.

6) *Wisdom* from the Buddha to Sri Aurobindo of the 20th Century has brought advanced contemplation techniques to multi-millions for complete inner solace and ultimate high consciousness realization — see *The Life Divine*, Sri Aurobindo.

7) *Democracy* — the world's largest secular state.

For these reasons the case has been stated for India's role as "the" world leader in various fields. America and the West are now announcing that they will be making use of their latest gadgetry, "Computer Networking, on a world-wide basis for the purposes of selling on the world market more rapidly. America is "warning" all nations about having barriers to prevent the modern consumer/war machine from interfering with their most egotistical aims of using the entire world (but mostly the developing nations) as their "private selling field" or better "their private dumping ground."

I suppose one could say this is all very well, but where does this put the rest of the world whose ancient esoteric and religious systems are slowly being eroded and destroyed one by one by the advance of monotheism and now "Monodollarism." Corporate America and the Corporate West want the entire world, to surrender to their chaotic mayhem, a morally dissentive way of life, so they can sell by exciting man's desires and false needs.

India must fight back. *The spiritual can never* surrender to materialistic forces no matter how impressive be the Glamour, Glitter and Gold that is offered. For what use would India be to the world if she became like the other materialistic giants?

Is our purpose in life on the planet Earth merely to be buyers of products, consumers of goods we don't even need?

The time is now. India's corporate management and all those lost in the ashramic, tamasic existence must also become connected to the global networking highways and this time — still in a secular fashion and flood — inundate the skyways with the wisdom of the Vedas, Upanishads, the Gita and Sri Aurobindo. The West, spearheaded by the mighty M.I.C. (Military-Industrial-Complex) and the American society, only wants mass amounts of information to be sent out — most useless and inane — whether to China, Borneo, India, or Africa. If these are not yet a "selling field" (dumping ground), already prepared for the "political salesmen" from the West, they will make it one. That is for sure.

Then the nations will have left their natural habitat, their family, their roots, including their belief systems, and become the smart guy and girl by going to the big city to get their M.B.A. and better their computer skills and learn subjects to be software experts.

We must counter this invading non-culture scheme and set up "perimeters of defense" in the form of Ethnic Cadres, Truth Warriors. Perhaps on the order of Boy Scouts and Girl Scouts. With mottoes and codes of conduct and behavior well laid-out so that misconduct and a moral misbehavior will be strictly taboo. In every school there should be a reinforcing of high moral habits, care and attention to all peoples, Indian children and women must become role models for the world's women and children. This is one way to prevent which must not become inevitable, the destruction of humanity, her values, morality and ancient belief systems.

The value of man becomes of little worth if he continues to buy products and always more products and becomes relegated to the "dump heap" of so many souls who never understood the reasons for their lives. All this is according to the West's substandard modes of living and behavior.

You of India, must be prepared to make India the "last stand." Do not miscalculate, the West will never stop. The West which has no respect for spiritual values, only man-made products and man-made institutions and belief systems.

There must have been strong reasons and ties to greater consciousness that allowed the Greeks and Egyptians to exist for thousands of years. They are now gone. Egypt succumbed to Barbarous Rome — India you must not succumb to the Barbarous West.

As a Western man I can assure that the danger is nigh... and much more so than at any other time in human history. This includes even at the time of Vivekananda of 100 years ago and even Sri Aurobindo of 50 years ago.

The West is "just beginning" its superdemonical infernal machine for conquering the Earth by the "selling method."

Today, there is prescribing software for the youth and people as the new panacea for ills, as well as pills for depression and schizophrenia. But these very same persons who become sold to Western industry will be left with a lost "Soul Ware" and "permanent" headaches and depression.

I can assure you as an American I have seen the great failings of the Western system. Europe I know, too, is Spiritually lost. The lights are out in their eyes. Non-smiling, artificially laughing, drugged, all becoming karmically ruined individually and group-wise.

They have acquired their "mind group" almost at birth.

In San Francisco the "street people" are dejected — rejected not only because they are down and out, but because they are sick. One out of three has tuberculosis!

America is four percent of the world's population, yet they use twenty percent of the resources. Moreover, the American government has developed a megalomanic attitude of issuing "warnings" in the name of "selling," and War and Democracy. What does this mean? It means that if they cannot find a market open for their goods they will simply issue threat warnings in the form of blackmail. This is a very sick mentality. Not only selfish, but evil!

Why should the rest of the World have to absorb the overproduction of America and Europe and now Japan? If they have over-produced it is their fault and no one else's! The rest of the world should not have to suffer with warnings and bully tactics in order to have bigger and better "selling fields." Caesar Augustus has spoken these warnings, "You will buy all we over-produce or else we will do something bad to you. I must have the world the way I want it." For them there is no room for the spiritual.

What can be done? While the whole world is rushing madly over to "Gatesism," "Murdockism" and "Turnerism," we can ask the question, is bigger better? Do we need so much information coming over the skyways — over the network highways?

The answer of course is no! But there is no stopping the proliferation of man's minds.

India has got to make this important and inevitable. Gone are the days of merely absorbing the shock and assimilating the barbarian invaders of the past. Modern "ostrich hiding" will no longer work.

You can only assimilate the gadget culture if it fits within your philosophical-spiritual way of life without interfering with an iota of your inner souls' workings.

Although it may appear in the beginning to adorn the costumes of the West is not harmful and buying all the gadgets from the West also is not harmful for you still have your pyjamas at home, your puja room and your temples to fall back on.

But what about the following generation? Will they be able to absorb all the inundation of gadget culture and still find their pyjamas and have time for the puja room? The temples, will they become mere tourist attractions?

Don't let Mother India become another *Theme Park*!

The West knows no mercy with their selling techniques. You must remain Indian — Hindus you must remain Spiritual. Look to Yoga in all its forms and pranic healing. It is life-fulfilling. Your divine beings in the invisible world are still alive and all-knowing; don't abandon them for the hedonist life of pleasure and comfort *a la* Corporate West and America.

India, you are the guru of the world.

Make the world awake and sing. Call out from every corner of your great satvic land the power of Shakti. Let the world know who has the real — Spiritual Ware.

India is the spiritual vortex center, having absorbed all invading beliefs to be represented in her national fabric. The Jews and Christians came 2,000 years ago; Roman coins found in the South; Alexander, 2,400 years and extended his stay to two years leaving statues of Zeus and Apollo in Punjab. And of course, the Mongolians in the form of Arabism centuries ago. The Portuguese spent five hundred years in Goa and the famous British for three hundred years.

India must stand up to this new form of neo-colonialism which contains *no belief* system, just gadgets, and greed.

India must sponsor a yearly fest of Arts, Music, an All Cultural festival. She must return to the past — yearly — to know how to live in the future.

What solutions can be proposed in face of the dilemma of Western onslaught?

1) You can read about your heritage and rishis. Mahavira, Buddha, Vedas, Upanishads, Gita, Patanjali, amongst the ancients.
   - The moderns of the last hundred years: Theosophy, Ramakrishnan Paramahansa, Swami Vivekananda, Annie Besant.
   - *Sri Aurobindo: The Gita, The Mother, Savitri, India's Rebirth.*
   - *Ramana Maharishi — Who Am I,* a biography by Arthur Osborne.
   - Ananda Devi — *The Illumined Mind.*

   Choose one author, ancient and modern, and explore at random until you find your heart and mind being spellbound by the text and then read on to you heart's delight.

2) Visit India's *holy sites* and spend time in silence with your self and loved ones. Remember you are entering the house of the unseen Divine ones. Make regular excursions.

3) *Study yoga* — practice daily the asanas and breathing.

4) *Nature walks*, even in the city in the early hours or twilight time. Look at all that you see as "divine," that all that is present before your moving body and eyes is a part of the Mahashakti. At the same time think that your spirit stuff is the same that makes up every plant and animal of nature. Express joy at the same time.

5) *Each day* you wake you must see it as a "new life"; with each step, a new direction, letting a smile be worn and become a habit and at the first chance try to release your inner nature with laughter, for laughter is our human way of curing and relieving our pain, sorrow and tensions.

6) *Work Place*, be it a clothing shop or computer room, try to somehow set about making spiritual all that is composed in that area. Bring flowers, incense, your favorite photos and images. See your mental and physical efforts as your offering daily to the Divine — "Bhakti" yourself.

7) *Compare the Gunas* in all that you do in your daily routine; study yourself. Are you prone to be more tamas, laid back and reticent and lazy? Are you too speedy and rajasic, making a lot of waves, but not sure of the result? Or are you satvic — more divine, a balanced harmonized being?

8) *In meeting the public* you must exude the pride to be Indian. Let the shakti flow down into your being and feel it going out to the public. Become passionate about the Indian way, without being rude and biased — a sense of sharing. You must respect Indian products as part of your land, your culture.

9) *Ask yourself questions* — any time during the day, such as: How can I improve myself? How can I renew myself? What can I do to charm my loved ones? How can I have more of a purpose in life? How can I help India improve? Is it possible to change the World?

10) Daily Puja, prayer or worship to bring your mind to a state of rest and stability.

The New Alliance

It is wished that the "First World" industrialized nations come together in the form of an alliance, along with India.

The world needs an alliance of the U.S., Russia, and Europe (under one voice, E.U. and NATO) and India. Why an alliance? How does India fit with these other nations? An alliance with the super Military-Industrial powers, can this be? If so, why?

Well, for one, India is a hugely populated civilization that should no longer be ignored. She is also the home of the largest Democracy. She is and has always been, a non-proselytizing, non-colonizing people. Her ancient philosophical heritage made her the land of Buddha to the present day rishi, Sri Aurobindo. India can mediate the more aggressive tendencies of the other partners.

India is also God-loving and God-fearing. Russia, with the demise of Communism, is looking to the religions of the East. These along with the democracies of Europe and North America together, with their non-fanatical religious backgrounds, makes for ideal bed-fellows in our period of realignment on the world levels.

Why this club of giants? Specifically, to maintain order and peace on the globe, covering North America, Europe, Russia, Japan to the Pacific, and India of the Indian Ocean. Japan could be a non-participating military partner, accepted for its economic and commercial clout, and this could very well make the "Big Six" covering the entire modern world.

Essentially forming an international commonwealth, economically, culturally, militarily and above all else, morally and spiritually, riding above all religious cults and sects, being completely secular.

The UN is becoming an unwieldy body to maneuver, but should be supported by all Alliance members. (The U.S. must pay their dues.)

The rest of the world would most certainly have to get into step with the Alliance, which will be a great deterrent to strife; this includes the Arab Nations. The long, serpentine "Arab Nations" which stretches from Mauritania to Egypt across to Pakistan into China, some tens of millions in India, and over to Indonesia and Malaysia, finishing in the Philippines, is still in a mostly introverted position of examining its Islamic laws in light of a moral and materialistic, gadget-minded West.

The Arab Nations should not be placed in a position of disfavor by any means, and there should be an increase of trade with China, to diminish all hostilities and tensions.

As to the "Arab Nations" the *rogue nations* (as the U.S. terms them) would no doubt be held in check by an ever-present U.S. - NATO - Europe - India - Pacific military umbrella, observed and controlled by public opinion, India, Russia and Japan.

Any belligerence on the part of any individual nation would be dealt with by the Alliance until arriving at U.N. and world consensus to maintain stability in disturbed areas on the globe.

Globalization would continue un-hindered by any rogueness on the part of any nation outside the Alliance and World Peace and stability would be its motto. Each nation in the would have to become more universally and one-world minded on every issue.

No longer would petty selfish big business, be it in arms, etc., be allowed to "muscle" the rest of the world.

Concentrated efforts must be made to bring about an upliftment of world consciousness.

India must serve as the wise rishi philosopher figure ready to reach into her annals of Vedic and Sri Aurobindo and Dr. Rhadakrishna's lores and come up with instant viable tenets and solutions to every problem.

India, the guru of the world, must become assertive and go for the making of this Alliance and for the saving of the spirits residing on the Earth. The new management for the 21st century: India.

The New Spiritual Revolution — Non-religious in Nature

The Spiritual Revolution will occur by taking India as our fountain-head, our Spiritual Mother, with ideas springing forth (or stemming from) the Masters — Brothers of the White Lodge, notably Master Koot Humi, Master Morya, and Sri Aurobindo.

Our world has had centuries of religious wars; the 20th century has seen conflicts — Bolshevism vs. Capitalism; Fascism vs. Democracy. For the most part, Democracy has "won out" over her adversaries, Bolshevism and Fascism. America stands out almost singularly as the most prominent exponent of Capitalism, dragging her favorite slogan "freedom and democracy" not far behind and the caboose, or rear guard, the bankrupt Judeo-Christian which gives the familiar stench of something moribund, dank and dormant. The "One Book" screechers. The intolerant ones who claim God is only on their side, and are only too willing to sanctify the American Way with its benediction of their religion. Their god has willed it that way. All others are not in God and have yet to be saved by a good Christian baptism! Our non-religious and new spiritual revolution is a necessary outgrowth and department of the New Future Society.

* * *

Temple Culture vs. Gadget Culture

The shame, if it were possible to express, is to even write a text comparing "Temple Cultures" to "Gadget (materialistic) Cultures." It is shameful that our modern materialistic gadget cultures are fast ruling by "machine decree" almost a total reliance is being placed on the "sacred computer": the new secular religion. Indeed, the computer, if used for the spiritual forces and people, could merit its function, and yet the reality is far from this ideal.

The philosopher, spiritually wise, and sometimes consul to kings has been replaced by hapless, empty-minded economists, sociologists and so-called political scientists.

We need counselors who are spiritual philosophers and psychological spiritual men to bring sanity back to our spiritually depraved world.

A spiritual school is needed; a pilot project, a model set up with the emphasis on the soul of the individual, on the spiritual development in whatever he is studying.

The Buddha

Universal gaze
Innumerable days
Sitting lotus like
Eternally
Bronze or gilded gold
It marks the place
In the center of Life's
Mold

by Deva

Mother India, Soul of the World

Every Indian must be made aware that unique entities, the great ones, from Shiva to Ganesh, are still alive and manifesting themselves and their Cosmic shakti or shakta (energies) from the mountains to the plains, from forests to temples, and to the fields and shops throughout this great, noble, sacred land. India must not go the way of old Greece and Egypt, whose entities and Gods are now called "myths" and are relegated to mythology, their statues to museums! How the times have changed since Alexander the Great discoursed with the Yogis and philosophers.

Everyone must become more cohesive in the face of Western Materialism. Every Indian village does not need a computer, as expressed by Bill Gates! What every village does need for its inhabitants are more true and well-trained Gurus and teachers to help bring about a greater Cosmic Consciousness to the people.

Remember the great industrial revolution that came to India and stayed? Miraculously, it did not completely mechanize all of India. Perhaps this was due, in part to Gandhi emphasizing the village system, helping to make a balance.

There is no balance in the West! The 1930's in the U.S. was a depression; many millions out of work, homeless and nomadic (a similar situation is existing in America as well as in Europe today. It may be just beginning). Big industry of the '30's would not be stopped and continued selling farm tractors, leaving entire villages across the U.S. heartland redundant and poverty stricken.

The "Captains of Industry" are proud to announce that with their "new generation" of computers they will be able to do the job of scores of "old generations" of people. The result: hundreds of thousands of humans are being replaced by these "new generations" of soulless robots of Industry from the West.

Where is the protest? The whimper? There is none! Where is another Gandhi, as with the salt march to the sea, to lead India back to sanity and spirituality?

Don't let India become a "satellite" and a "neo-model" of America and Western Materialism! Stop it before it is too late! America is now the land of the Super Rich and the Super Poor (as is Europe), simply non-caring, where "greed, gold and glory" are Gods; where drugs and violence are amok; where families no longer exist. India must not sink to these abysmal levels, India must rise above and stay above all this.

A human being is worth something. More than just something. A human being is a potential god or goddess. This we must not forget. India knows, for she has produced them in the past. Will she be able to produce them in the future, in the face of the onslaught of inevitable materialism?

India must spiritualize the materialistic forces! saying "No" to false Asuric forces from the West and "Yes" to satvic India!

India cannot rest until she once again attains her zenith of performance ("Days of Ashok") until she is fully recognized once again as the Super-Spiritual Power, and also as the Super Material (Physical) Power in the New World Order of "power struggles." India must lead and become the world's number one leader in all departments. She has the resources. She must reclaim and proclaim her Supreme Mahashakti Will. It is time.

India must become the World Giver of teaching and Truth, love, and peace as only she can. She must send throughout her land and abroad, Cosmic Workers, spiritually directed and devoted souls from scholars of Sanskrit to artists and dancers, philosophers and craftsmen.

And of course, the Gita and Yoga — the two are entwined. The Gita should be taught and lived by, in India and abroad. No soul in the world should be neglected. The days of "ostrich tactics" must be gone. They must be replaced by Spiritual Warriors of Peace, Love, Compassion and Truth to represent India.

All of these ideas should be adopted and sponsored at the highest levels of Indian society and allowed to filter down to the common people — the same for abroad. It is not the time to shrink back from action for India's Dharma, which must be a return at all levels to Supreme Divine Consciousness.

India's role in the New World Order, as Krishna convinced Arjuna, must be to stand up and resist falling into dissolution and decay. She must fight and lead as never before in history. The fight, the battle is spiritual in nature. It is to rally, to muster and to combat all forms of materialism devoid of Spiritual Values. This must be India's position in the New World Order. We cannot say it enough!

Let us have Spiritual fallout, not nuclear! Let the world know that in Bharat Mata lies the Highest Universal Cosmic Consciousness — the Truth!

My Guru, Ananda Devi loved India and lived for the Indian spirit all her life. But as she said many times, her mission was in the West, to prevent the worst from happening. She did just that, as did the two of us. She was instrumental on a higher plane and on the Earth in preventing the U.S. and the West from attacking the U.S.S.R. in 1961 and back again in 1962; she wrote to Dr. Rhadakrishnan about these events. She also helped bring about the end to the Cold War by 1990 by influencing Gorbachev from a Cosmic level. She died in February 1994.

Standing Buddha

Sands of time
pass — Beyond
stand the Thai
land Buddha
man — Stand
omnipotent
one with one
eternal eye
speaking peace
O — wise Buddha
of the East

by Deva

India's Role in the 21st Century

by Premananda Deva

Before I begin, I would like to say that my Guru, Ananda Devi considered the Indians as the most refined and evolved of all the peoples in the world. I find myself agreeing with her.

For well over thirty years, in our two ashrams, in New York City, and Paris, France, under the patronage of Dr. Rhadakrishnan, Sri Moraji Desai, and Mrs. Eleanor Roosevelt, we lectured about India's role in the world for world peace and how the spiritual is so necessary in our materialistic Western societies. We taught Yoga, and healed all diseases and initiated.

India has a primary role to play in the 21st century, so well started by Nehru at the Belgrade and Bandung conferences. India is the leader of the emerging world. She must now become more spiritually assertive and serve as a guide for the entire world. Let the Divine Shakti move India only as she knows best. If India is really all that has been said of her down through the ages by her rishis and yogis, then today each and every Indian has an enormous task to perform to help make India number one, in all departments. She can send out spirituality to the world, as the Tibetans have been doing, by encouraging poets, scholars, dancers, and musicians, of the best quality. Concurrently, an annual Cultural Fair should be organized to bring the world to India.

Tell the world of the Buddha, Mahavira, the Bhagavad Gita and Sri Ramakrishna. Tell them of the great ones of the 20th century, as we enter into the 21st century, Swami Vivekananda, Rabindranath Tagore, Sri Bhagavan Ramana Maharishi, and of course, Sri Aurobindo... The roster is long with the Indian greats, who have helped change and shape the world.

As the West has harnessed the different physical forces of nature, so, too, has India harnessed the spiritual forces and they are working for her. All that makes up Mother India, that is Kali, Shiva, Ganesh, Ram, Brahma, Vishnu, Agni, etc., for these are not myths but true entities and realities in Indian life, giving substances and longevity.

Look what happened to the Hellenic and Egyptian civilizations when the great entities called Gods and Goddesses were classified as mythology and the statues relegated to museums and the ancient folklore even legislated as mere fable.

India may be called the last spiritual home on Earth. May she long endure. For far too long India has been at the mercy of foreigners who have always claimed to have superior knowledge and ideas, yet very few of these invaders ever took the time to plunge into the fabulous wisdom of the Vedas, the Rig Veda and the Upanishads.

Start living with and in your heritage. Time does not exist make the ancients come alive in modern day India. At the same time, guard against the new secular religion of materialism with its hyperbole of slogans, with the salespeople geared to excite the desire in the Indians to get them to buy anything and everything. Don't let India fall victim to this: to become permanently enmeshed in the Samsara, the Maya for this lifetime.

Never forget that Yoga and the Hindu faith is the only one in the world that emphasizes that man must and can realize his God-self in this life, thus sayeth Swami Vivekananda and Dr. Rhadakrishnan. You are free as Indians to embark yourself on your spiritual Dharma now. For the more we have Cosmically Conscious souls, the easier the task to make India Number One in the world, having been imbibed and embraced with the Divine Light and the magnificence of Mahashakti in every part of your being.

There should be more spiritual ambition manifested by all of you or else India will be swallowed up by Corporate West and the Divine will disappear from the Earth. India must integrate into the spiritual more. It must make a Corporate Spiritual India and become the leader of the world in all departments.

When Swami Vivekananda came to represent Hinduism in America, in Chicago, a hundred years ago, he made a profound effect on his audience. Surely, the Divine Mother must have pushed him to go to America, that spiritual desert! He left a lasting impression. Now, you must carry on his Clarion Call to everyone you meet, wherever you go, in the name of Yoga and the Indian way of life.

One hundred years later I have come from America and Europe to India, my message and Dharma is to help revive all that is spiritual India, and to awake and make live the Divine in every aspect that is India and eventually the world. To dance and sing and live in all your temples once again. Let the gods live in the lila within your temples.

I was glad to shed my corporate Western clothes and to adorn myself with Indian garb, my spiritual skin or sheath, as I call them. For I feel more the role as I impart my message to all Indians to bring the Divine and Yoga into your homes and your workplace. Integrate the Mahashakti into every corner of your business and being.

André Malraux, Minister of Culture, of France once said, "The next century will be spiritual or not at all." My answer to that is: It is only India who has the C.V. and the omniscient past to lead all nations." In order to make these claims realizable, each person should incorporate the Indian spirit "that affirms" into the Networking and into the computer systems, throughout the nation and worldwide. Let the Gods rejoice as you devote and donate to the Divine.

Materialism is the modern Western plague. This is not to be envied, not to be copied by India, not by any Indian in his right mind, nor any nation. Instead, let not any man, corporation, sect or nation deter India's objective to spiritually lead the world. Do not emulate the "devil's" work in the Maya! Follow the Gita's dictates for your spiritual path, else you will be living Western Dharma and accumulating very heavy, dirty Western karma! As the Gita says, "Better to live one's own Dharma poorly than to take another's Dharma, do it well, and lose your soul." Mother India, who is most moral, will give you direction, never fear.

India, today, in front of the West, unfortunately, is much like Ancient Egypt facing the ruthless Caesar Octavius Augustus. Cleopatra of Egypt chose to leave the physical plane with the secrets of the hieroglyphics and the esoteric initiations, than to share them with the barbarous Romans. Beware, this could very well happen to India, unless she is not careful on how to deal with the barbarians. I say Indians must not become slogan slingers and gadget gatherers for Corporate West. How very base to resort to the West non-truths. When India is the very *sine qua non* of wisdom and illumination. Down into the bodies of men plunged the "super human energy," the Purushottama in all of its powerful pristine presence, and changed the Indians into Gods on Earth! Need I say more? Let every business, political party and household ring out the cry that India is number one in the 21st century.

Never forget that Corporate West, formerly known as the Military Industrial Complex, has no place for sharing, for generosity and cooperation, but only for selfish taking, competing and hoarding. They will sell anything, even nuclear devices to you enemies. All's fair in Western Corporatism, according to the greed merchants, even making wars.

But it is not too late! You Indians must command and integrate all that is spiritual in India to make the new Corporate India, so as to create Corporate Spiritual World, led by india, *the number one corporate and spiritual power of the 21st century*. Remember the gunas, ni Rajasic, ni tamasic, but always satvic! As Sri Aurobindo said, "India is the Guru of the world."

Metaphysical Experiences and the Modern World

by Lakshmi Devi

To answer the question posed, "What can the Indian Civilization contribute to the 21st century," we must first examine the nature of the world, and the governing forces in the world. Secondly, why is it so significant that India, and what she represents, be made known, not merely as a subject of a philosophy class on comparative religions, but as a true guide, that she has the possibility of answering all questions, and solving all problems.

Today after two hundred years of industrialization, we find an increasing influence by the economically sovereign countries over those who are weak. History shows that when an empire stakes her claim over another country or civilization, the ideologies, the religions, the ways of the colonized country are influenced and sometimes converted to that of the more seemingly powerful entity. Yet the colonization process today is much more subtle than in the past, more subtle than the Roman invasion of Egypt and the Mongolians in China. Today, in the name of modernization, and an improvement in the quality of living for the world at large, we are being indoctrinated, this time not by coercion, but by the world of materialism, corporatism in the name of "Freedom and Democracy."

It pains me greatly that this "indoctrination" process comes from my peoples, the "Anglo Saxon" forces, both in Europe and America. Because having been born in the West, I can remark frankly, that this way of life, is a smoke screen. The peoples in these nations are sick psychologically; they are, *en masse*, frustrated, depressed, and angry. One in two families ends in divorce... and why is this? Very simply, because, they are utterly bereft of any spirituality. The major religions are bankrupt. And the masses, although materially saturated and satisfied, with every desire attained, have given no thought whatsoever to their spirit and Soul. The paradigm in the West, directs the human being not the natural course of Soul unfoldment, but to his ego self, which can only be negative, fearful, and self-gratifying. This paradigm only limits man, denying him (all answers now found from man's scientific "non-genius!") so much so, that self-inquiry, self-elevation and most importantly, self illumination are forgotten.

Those policies from the West can only stem from national mega egos, seeking power and glory, supported by a heavy military industrial complex yet; this doctrine of Westernization of the world, which can be humanitarian at best, has absolutely no metaphysical foundation, for without the experiences of enlightenment and realization, they are ultimately out of touch with the true sense and experience of freedom.

Standing next to Mother India, to her spirit and what she has always represented, the Westerners are mere children with undeveloped ideas, allowing their ego consciousness to govern them, to dictate and to transform the world in its image.

As world citizens, it is our role to change and reverse these current trends, it is our dharma to make the world a better place for our children, so they can live in harmony, truth, love and joy.

Egypt, the sister soul of India and creatrix of civilization, was such a powerful spiritual force on the Earth, as is India today, the traditions of initiation were known, the ancients knew about the importance of the afterlife preparation, they unlocked the mysteries of the nature of man in relation to the Universe and the world. They had become immortal. They knew how to transform a mortal into a God. Yes, the Egyptians were pantheists, as the Indians are today, they knew that the Gods and Goddesses are archetypes, forces, existing in the invisible world, stepping stones for true realization. To telepathize with the Gods, to engage in a no-thoughted communication, we can be initiated, be infused with the divine truths, emanating from these celestial beings... and yet the Western man is so fearful of this, so mistrusting and such a skeptic, proclaiming the Gods as mere myths to keep the people in check. Yet, if he were to investigate the Egyptian and Indian philosophies further, he would see that they ultimately surrender to the Supreme Being, the one God.

Today, alas, the Gods in Egypt are mere "tourist attractions" the statues originally built to house their spirits are museum pieces and yet, we Indophiles know better. My very own experience in India, the land where the sacred fires are still burning: I was initiated utilizing the ancient ways, and instructed by my Guru, Premananda Deva. I mastered the state of no-thoughtedness and left my body and human mind, for an entrance into the vast, expansive "Cosmic Mind." Here we are one with universal wisdom, here in this state we can view the world and ourselves with extreme positivism. For here beyond the five senses, I knew that the physical world was an illusion, a paradise of manifested divinity, here to catapult us into the true reality.

When we accept that the physical world is an illusion, Maya, to the Indians, a cosmic laboratory, it is then not merely a sensory pleasure garden. We cannot accept the paradigm of materialism, modernization and computerization as the answer. We should expect more from the earthly forces, political, and corporate who have the most influence. We have to inspire them out of their ignorance; we have to convince them that there can be a change for the better, and that by integrating these ancient philosophies, hopefully, they will understand and sympathize with the ideas of harmony, and no longer competition.

This is where India must activate herself. She must renew herself, her ideas, her philosophies, for in reality this is the backbone, the foundation of her peoples, the culture and societal elements are merely offshoots from the majestic spiritual values. How has she managed to retain the ideals? Why have the rituals, the pujas, and the temples stayed in favor with the peoples? Because it is based on the Truth; because from the Brahmin down to the outcast, the Indian people feel the shakti force, they experience a lightness and divinity through recitation of the mantras. They continue to experience the power of the Divine in the sacred ways, laid down for them by enlightened yogis.

Now it is time that India lets the world know that materialism and spiritualism cannot co-exist. Those who represent her must hold their ground, making sure that the younger generation so taken by the glamour of the West, can see the significance behind their cultural and spiritual aspects, respecting her ways, not as a blind form of a belief system, but an active, living force.

India must become more assertive, more aggressive, because for too long she has been cowering down, and absorbing compassionately the ways of her invaders. She must embody Arjuna, the warrior, and embodiment of Krishna's force ready to protect and live in the truth.

Let not the Western criticisms of India's economic development hinder the great thinkers, and the minds of the people. We must become more universal in outlook and confident that behind the scenes of poverty there is brilliance of spirit. That is what the world neither knows, nor wants to acknowledge. The world's peoples need to be educated. We know that modernity is nothing, nor has any foundation without a metaphysical blueprint, to act as a cohesive agent, for man's psychological self, and most importantly to ignite the Agni, the fire inside each individual, to transform the latent force in man, wherever he is, whatever he is doing, at home or in the office, even in the corporate world and in the media.

The 21st century has the potential of being a great era, but for this to occur, the paradigm of thought and action in the world has to change.

If we are not careful, the tides of materialism, with its cloaked and crooked message of ego gratification, will attract more and more on the Earth, until all cultures are numbed, all peoples are automatons, and a great sameness will pervade the Earth, a place without true creativity and without divinity. May this never occur. May India awaken and bring light to this period of darkness.

India, seek within yourself, see your own potential to contribute here on Earth. Stand tall, with the knowledge that your quintessence, your Godhead, is waiting to be heard, to be respected, and to do his good work for the world, for our families, and for humanity at large.

The Cosmic Connection

India alone has maintained her Cosmic Connection. She is the last of the "great civilizations" still living in the Divine Consciousness. She must not become extinct like the other great Dinosaurs of Ancient times. The dangers to India are Monotheism and Materialism.

You must never forget that you are the most spiritually aware and the most evolved race on the face of the Earth. But you must be very careful that you do not become too proud, too complacent, too self-contented. You must not become indifferent to the life of the people around you, their needs, their problems, their wants, etc. All this too is an essential part of the Divine Work. We must not shrink back from the smallest task. The Dharmas of the Gita must be assumed by one and all, all day, every day; to take up the yoga advocated by Krishna in the Gita, Karma Yoga, the Yoga of Service, the highest role of action a man can perform. It can burn out the *tamasic* and *rajasic* influences; and by helping others leaves us in a far more *satvic* state. Attention to all the details of the needs of your people must become everyone's dharma. The Spiritual boons will come to you. It is all being recorded — and is a part of the Divine plan.

Destroy All Ego

"Destroy all ego," we cry. Destruct the false on Earth at last. Aspire to higher expression of Truth. Destroy the ego within.

Disguised we cannot always see him. Masked we pretend not to hear him. Fooled we like to be coerced by him.

But we have to destroy the ego at all cost. For the Earth, seriously, is in the balance.

For man refuses to glance above, and the ancient culture and philosophies of India will be lost.

India, do not heed the new form of packaged tantalizing trinkets, for the labor of your ancestors, wise were they. They saw the Truth beyond the senses.

"Destroy the ego," we cry. Break all the forms of cunning addiction. Break the inception of creeping materialism. Use wisely the technology to advance yourselves, and help societal failings.

Keep close to your heart the knowledge of your Soul.

BHARAT MATA

Great India, Destroy the Western ego within you.

Part Four

New Future Society

New Future Centers

The New Future Society (NFS) is a proposed way of life, basing its principles on simple, universal truths, idealistic philosophies, and metaphysics, showing how these "threads" can be woven into the fabric of the existing society. We intend to impart this knowledge to those who can be instrumental in activating these changes on every level from the political, to the corporate, down to the lay person.

The Aim: To create New Future Centers throughout the world, one in every continent, eventually twelve.

The Purpose: To create an international network of centers, where more awakened individuals can meet for highly altruistic purposes. They will work to overcome civil and international strife for the security of the whole of humanity.

The Ideal: To allow the descent of the Supreme Consciousness and stabilization at the human level, to awaken the world consciousness in humanity.

****

These centers would be a training place whereby a person of sensitive idealism and open-mindedness can be trained in Psychology, Public Speaking, Yoga Philosophies, and Healing.

These people would be freelance individuals, dedicated to the highest principles. They would be *Universal Workers*.

All visible techniques would be employed, both ancient and modern, to make the appropriate changes necessary, from the individual to the group, nation, and the world.

The workers should be able to understand the basic concepts such as the Superconsciousness and Selfless service. They should try to accept the principle of a Universal mind as the container and giver of all ideas, theoretical and practical. A sense of world oneness must be generated in these centers. The cadre should be high-minded people with a sense of humbleness and duty for service.

The NFS would bring together the exceptional leaders of the world, recognized and not recognized, from every level of society, putting an emphasis on the participation of the corporate world, making sure that they contribute to the transformation of the world's economies *and* peoples.

Morality and ethics would be reestablished to promote and preserve the life on the Earth, including plants and animals, and to preserve all arts, culture, and language on the Earth.

Philosophies from India, including Yoga, which has existed for more than 5,000 years, would be studied. Yoga can be considered to be a method for attaining perfection of the body, mind, and spirit. "Yoga may be regarded as a system of psychology far more developed than is known in Western Science." — *The Tibetan Book of the Dead*

****

For those of us who have the opportunity to operate on higher levels of consciousness, our thoughts and ideals need support, not only from the forces above, but from each other.

We must all become channels.

We, alone, must bring about the changes in ourselves. We should not ask "God" to do it for us; for we are His fingers, and we must use them to make the proper and necessary changes on the Earth.

Spiritual forces and values must be reestablished for the New Future Society to be strong, not only economically, but for her peoples to be complete and truly free.

Preamble

What do we mean by the New Future Society?

A Society based on the equal rights of man, woman, and child for the discovery of Truth ... Truth that beholds the force of light; to make sure that the "necessary evils" in the existing society are removed.

To inspire the members of the existing society to strive for more than their dues...

To create a niche in the world for a revival of the ancient truths...

To seek the goodness in our hearts, to tell the tale of love...

To recognize that the spirit renders all earthly powers worthless, and that this is the way for a true transformation...

Beyond the normalities, we will create abnormalities of holy worth: a SACRED RACE of peoples worldwide that shares the knowledge of a new future society.

Wisdom

To allow the descent of the heavenly forces, we are chosen by ourselves to answer the prayer of the Supreme, who knows how to manifest the right changes on the Earth.

WISDOM is our motto:

WISDOM of the TRUTH

WISDOM of the LAW

WISDOM of the LOVE

WISDOM of the JOY

WISDOM of the PEACE

WISDOM of the right way of living, trying to find out who is more wise, more true, more accepting, and preparing for our own entrance into this wisdom.

This is "Soul Searching" and of the utmost importance in the New Future Society.

It is essential that a "knowing" pass from the wise to the unknowing among us.

The New Future Society will be wise and free.

New Future Ideals

What are the aims of the New Future *ideals*?

To give a practical manual to those ready for higher learning and for higher guidance.

To be able to initiate, *en masse*, people into action. Inner and outer action are of equal importance.

They can be instrumental for eventual revolutionizing of the Earth for greater harmony between nations and peoples.

A Revolution for Peace.
Take the idea of war. Is it not a waste?
Take the idea of conquering others. Is this not, too, a waste? We should seek authorization before we act with such extreme violence.

The face of the Earth will change greatly in this new millennium, and we should want to contribute to this change.
Why have we forgotten about inner questing? Why have we forgotten about our spirit and soul? Why have we forgotten to treat others (nations, peoples) with due respect?
Why must the technology reign supreme when there exists a wiser power and force in our lives?

When the dawn and dusk of Cyberculture has arrived and gone, we will still exist, the same as we were before and the same afterward. We will be bereft of any understanding of ourselves, unless we delve into our inner sanctum, our inner connection, our inner realm. For without directions for inner guidance, we cannot know what is true in us. We cannot know, because we think from false thoughts and emotions coming from the ego.

We should create a way for ourselves to live in *Truth* in society.

A Message from the Masters

The New Future aspect will encompass ideologies that may or may not come to fruition. Yet, on our plane, they exist. These ideologies will take one out of the humdrum existence into the fantasm that is the spiritual realm. On Earth we can make a paradise — if not around us, *inside of us.*

The New Future Ideologies are as follows:

- Pursuit of (one) Truth
- Pursuit of wisdom
- Pursuit of action for the Divine, bringing power reins back under *Divine control*
- Pursuit of *love*
- Pursuit of *freedom*
- Pursuit of *knowledge*
- Pursuit of *Victory* for Spiritual Forces

When we pursue these factors, the Divine play on Earth will be more realized.

New Future Centers
New Future School Programs
New Future Lectures
New Future Workshops
New Future Dialogues

The Dilemma

As we enter the new millennium, we have, as members of the world community, a *responsibility* to correctly assess the present situation, to analyze it, and conceive of the true and idealistic direction for the twenty-first century.

America, the lone Superpower, the "leader" of the world, forges ahead, and mostly the world follows. America, the Utopia, her "archetypes," "inspiring" millions. What could possibly be superior to this?

Yet, what does this Western nation resemble? What kind of people live there?

Materially, Americans are the biggest consumers on the Earth, clamoring to be individually satisfied, each man for himself in the race to reach the peak of fulfillment in every way. We find a morally bankrupt race of people, guided by the corporate structure: their goal, to create the highest profits, sending salesmen to every corner of the globe.

Western societies are decaying internally. The family structure is debilitated; people no longer have a sense of community or an orientation to their inner central being. All of these effects are results of the national mega egos, supported by bodies of influence who neither wish to change society nor care.

Once we admit the imperfections, we can start shaping a perfected society.

More leaders, at every layer, from the corporate world, to the political world, have to speak out, to recognize the present day dilemma that we are faced with. It is not only for the sanity and well-being of our children, but the world at large, as she watches America, for advice, solace, guidance, and for the Truth.

Our Responsibility

The longer we absolve ourselves from any responsibility, the more desperate the world situation will become. The activating agent or force that inspires true spiritual work may not necessarily be from around you — in the workplace or in the home initially. It has to come from within yourself. And where does it come from? It comes from the great master planner who wants change for the good on the Earth.

Yet, before we can really represent this force, we should purify ourselves from the shackles of all belief systems. We should seek Initiation and a transformation of our ego self.

* * *

Science and Its Poisonous Effect on the Human Appreciation of Its Spiritual Heritage

Since man has given himself justifiable, physical proof that there is order and potentially unlimited possibilities in the physical domain, he has surrendered to this outlook of the Universe and given himself pride in doing so. Yet, so quickly he has forgotten his heritage, which we can all agree comes from more than a gene pool.

Man has actually stopped, for one of the first times in history, exploring — exploring the fabric of his inner nature. He has forfeited this exciting and crucial field for external titillation. He has taken a step away from the wisdom of his forefathers, deeming their knowledge as secondary.

Our forefathers knew that this world was a Divine play, that it was a riddle, a passage into the highest realms of Illumination.

Let us not insult the wisdom of the ancients any longer. Let us not be fooled by the scientists' "discoveries."

Become your own laboratory and find out who you are — therein lies the true journey.

Time to Unite

"The Future starts today."

—Aristotle

"The message, expressed by a Western mind who has decanted the message of the East, and can transmit it, not through parables or hidden in allegories and myths, but in a clear and accessible language, this message is the key to the liberation of the world, the key to the ***Future****, to the survival of Humanity, the key to the balance of powers, and to the liberation of man."*

— Ananda Devi

Purity is one of the greatest qualities of the child. In children we can "see" the future, for they are closest to the Truth, and yet we hardly acknowledge their inherent wisdom, naturalness, and divinity. Their ideas for the new future world would be one of harmony, peace, sanctity, and light, seeing only goodness in their eyes. But when we grow up, we allow the imprints of the world, good and bad, to become a part of us; then, too readily, we accept war, violence, fear, and greed.

If we were put into a state of innocence again, a state of childlike wonderment, we would reject all that is false. We would see our society in a perfect state of bliss, creating perpetual happiness would be our aim.

Yet, far away from the idealism of our youth, we mock at others, their ways, nations, and their understanding. *We* are the ignorant ones then, not even fulfilling the promises we held sacred when we were children for ourselves, our family, city, nation, and the world.

It is time to unite in the 21st century, to make this world a place ready to receive the birth of new children, the birth of new souls. The psychology of the future citizens will have to change, moving away from concentration on the vital and on the emotions, toward an "inspirational" and spiritual way of living. We should not forget so easily our responsibility toward others, that we were born into this civilization made from the toil and hard work of our ancestors.

Why should we be the generation to accept of this so called "fate," including wars, greed, and violence? Is it not our role to reverse the current trends, to reverse this misconduct and folly? We should set our sights on the future, seeking the possibility in the creation of a world where self-interest is also in harmony with the interest of the whole.

There is a key to open the box of solutions, a way to prevent this tidal wave of resistance and despair. And this key is in all of us. In the human spirit, a spirit connected with the "all" spirit, the All-God, the all existence.

First, we must find our own inner spiritual revolution, to revolt against what is false, inducing what is true.

Freedom

"Freedom comes by a unity without limits; for that is our real being."

"Having realized infinite unity in ourselves, then to give ourselves to the world is utter freedom and absolute empire."

— *Sri Aurobindo*

Far beyond convention, we seek freedom. Is this obtainable, if we cling to the material values of Capitalism and her rogue masters?

Freedom is a state acquired when we alleviate ourselves of all burdens and attachments to earthly egoistic goals and aims. Ultimately, true freedom lies not in bettering our fellow man, by acquiring more than he, but by looking for the Truth and dwelling in its purpose and spirit. Freedom comes when we know who we are, when we are freed from all constraints, when we are master of all situations.

* * *

The Personable God

The Personable God is the entity that exists inside of you. The Personable God is the unknown Soul, the undiscovered force, the undeniable Truth that governs behind the outer mind and being. This God is compared with the All-God and force undeniably mighty and powerful.

Everything we do is not separate from this entity nor disharmonious. When we strive, as a nation, to unveil and realize this God, then the path to all solutions will be clear. Society today, with its ideals of freedom and democracy, has merely allowed forces of capitalism and greed to seize us. Let us address true freedom, true liberation, and find our Personable God.

True Sense of Liberty

Genius is the disclosure of maturity in its final, absolute shape. It is the ideal prototype of man fully unfolded. It is the reach of the archetype of man and his own re-entrance into the perfection of the living idea, the realm of essence.

We all have the capabilities to activate positive energies and forces inside of us to perpetuate and solve the problems facing society. We have to address this latent force and explain to the people that the true sense of Liberty is one of a union of all that is good, wise, and joyful: a union without anger, frustrations, falsehoods, and hatred.

The methods to achieve this are far and wide; the spectrum spans farther than we can imagine. Go into the realm of your mind and experiment. Now imagine a world created from perfection. A world of true liberty. One without greed, violence, hatred, and unlawfulness. Imagine that you could take part in this world, for its transformation, and live in this world. This is a *reality,* not a fantasy, unrealizable. We *can* create this; we can change the minds of those forces who pretend to know the "right" way to govern and rule and to fill the minds of the people.

True liberty comes not by filling the minds of the people, but by emptying them to see that the material world has its limitations. For the true power for transformation lies in the latent spiritual forces in man; this force and power is known in the East as the Serpent Power, the creative force. Existing society creates our personality, and even thoughts, for us. With inspiration, this awakening can easily connect us with the source of our life force and action.

En masse, we need to awaken this Serpent/creative power in the people, so they can unleash and realize what it is to know their own capabilities as individuals and the Society as a whole. They will see that the attachments to their beliefs need not be tampered with. We are *striving for an upliftment adjacent to these ideals*. We are seeking the unity of a nation, a people, a world for the New Future Society.

How can this be performed en masse*?*

By the instruction of the members of the New Future Society, who will see that the populace will come to understand the way for transformation; by inspiring them to find the "FIRE," the creatrix's tool; not to relish in the past, not to harbor old wounds, but to recognize the liberty of transformation, and of giving to the world.

The New Future Society is about bravery. Bravery to be different, to dare to question, to dare to proselytize. To dare to be truly free, outside and inside; and to dare to know the capabilities of yourself and the society around you. A society that does not dare, nor question, nor acknowledge its failings, will eventually wither and die. Do not allow this spiritual destiny to pass you by.

Allow yourself to *want* a New Future Society: TO DARE — THE WAY. TO KNOW — THE POSSIBILITIES. TO LIKE — TO CHANGE.

* * *

Stop the Apathy!

There are common misconceptions being told to every one of us. One of these being that the people who are materially rich have the power. This is a falsehood and one that can be countered.

We have to ask ourselves, where does true power come from? After all, material power is only a representation, a reflection of earthly achievements. Yet, what is concealed behind the glamorous exterior for the majority is a shallowness of wisdom and fragility. For they have not properly investigated their *true* role on the Earth. The true reason to be in a materially prosperous state is to enable the divine Light to utilize them and steer the world in the right direction.

We must make it our responsibility to inspire people and world leaders, ignite their curiosity to take the reins, not for their own earthly desires, but for the True path on the Earth — one of *enlightenment*.

The lightness of spirit will guide us above the maelstrom of problems derived from earthly life, into our God-like way of being. It is here that true methods and ways to cure the present dilemma can be solved. We must embrace these scientific methods, known as Yogic techniques, to act in this lightness of spirit. We must be held down by nothing. Allowing no petty or egoistic aims to divert us. We must surrender ourselves over to this actuality that there will be a New Future Society.

The Remedy

Western man's desire is the pursuit of fun and joy which is, in reality, due to the existence of the Ego and a separation from our selves and Truth. We strive *for* happiness, because, as a people, we are not living in this spirit. To remedy this we should conduct more experiments, cultivating the prolongation of the child spirit in man.

Where does the origin of happiness lie? It is with the withdrawal of the senses and hedonistic pastimes that we find solutions.

Perfection lies in the surrendered being and/or spirit.

To acknowledge the supernature on Earth, we must all make advances toward this end, with every detail of our action, in every minute of every day. We should align ourselves with the Ancestors of the Earth, the Masters of the Earth, who are able to transform this world if we would allow their work to manifest through us.

We should question not whether the Earth can be saved, but proceed in saving it. We should not question our magnitude and force, but act in the light of facing and conquering malevolent forces here on Earth. Destiny of man, at present, is indeed a misguided reality — so few on the Earth truly understand this. And yet, those few who do understand can be very effective in making and inspiring change.

If all factions of our existing society refuse to be converted in the effort to change for the good, then society will fall, and those who wish to exist with a spiritual intent will set up sister/daughter societies within the main skeleton. Which, if understood, and if the newly formed society has solutions for a pragmatic change, it will go forth.

How can the daughter, or New Future Society, improve on the existing framework? By emphasizing a one-minded approach to all activities, and by applying a healthy physical, mental, and psychological habitat for all members. By stressing the Archetypes — the Masters and their role — by adhering to Masters on the Earth level. Who are the leaders and Realized Souls to inspire and make cohesive the projects? The state of being of all members should be of spiritual adherents, spiritual aspirants based on the Yoga philosophy (of all core civilizations for purification and implementation of Divine law) on the Earth. We are all ready for this work; it is merely the case whether or not we want to deny ourselves our separate and greedy ego will.

The leaders of the New Future Society will be able to discern those who are ready for an even higher initiation for, after all, the Society, whether existing or "New Future," is a springboard for the preparation of the Soul's path.

There should be a readjustment of training of the mental being, for many of us are clear cut away from being true, intuitive beings. Happiness and our divine link are severed as long as the mental aspect is cultivated, while today the existing society continues to link intelligence with success and eventual material gain with societal standing. The New Future Society sees this currently held view as an obstacle, for inner happiness and harmony are not born out of intellectual cognition alone.

We should create a conducive atmosphere, spiritually speaking, to become the vehicles of divine Spirit.

K.H.
M.M.
D.K.

Implementation of Plans

On a grand scale, our work would involve the complete restructuring or reorganizing of Life known in the Western world, starting with the field of education. Whereby the child has a chance to live close to his true nature, so by the time he reaches adulthood, he would not be the product of a materialistic world, an automaton, but a free agent ready to contribute *to* the world, not necessarily to take *from* the world. The whole curriculum of the schools would move away from its science-based logic and register higher learning of the metaphysical to promote the true creative spirit in each person and his/her potential to contribute to society.

Interactive techniques will be essential. Giving the student the possibility to live, act, and create from his own inner "spiritual" truth versus society's truth and encourage active philosophy, analysis, and psychology: for example, examination of the individual by themselves and class members — introducing the concepts of becoming cosmically aware, concentrating more on philosophy of the ancient civilizations, in particular Eastern philosophies, metaphysics, and transcendental literature and art.

The next field of influence would be the way the society is led. In the field of politics, there would be a complete dissociation between the corporate interests and the policies regulating all domestic and foreign policy, separating the influence of military establishment. It is important to have systems of defense, but the influence and power that the military has established is disproportionate to the role it should be taking. We should discourage the emphasis and credo of money, materialism, and military might.

The corporate sector should be regulated, giving equally back to society either within our outside of the nation state wherever aid is required.

There should be universal plans — accords made to balance and regulate these corporations — making sure that a council from each nation has an influential contribution. We should try to move away from the monopolizing influence of the military and economic giants, giving respect to other nations that may well have viable plans of action. One world government should control and monitor certain issues, such as a peacekeeping force of negotiators where no one country could declare war without submitting proposals to these negotiators and would, for example, incur a fine of payment to be given to a world aid program equaling the same amount of money that it would take to go to war.

There should be a movement away from the fanatical side of all religions and their claims to become independent from whichever mother country. For now, it seems the militarily economic countries are encouraging independence, for therein lies the possibility of economic conquest.

There should be, as Plato wrote of, a Philosopher King — not religious, but a spiritual man or woman or council that rules alongside of the elected — one who seeks the interests of humanity and the world at large. He would have the power to change policy for the good and bring more harmony to the competitive form of politics existent today.

This philosopher ruler would embark in a sister program, encouraging more metaphysical, spiritual, and cultural pursuits in the society.

New Future Plan of Action

To promote World Consciousness, which will ensure the establishment of peace in the world and the possibility of a deliberate and constructive progress in a spirit of unity, this New Future Center will embrace an *Esoteric* as well as an *Exoteric* activity.

PART ONE
ESOTERIC PART

This part will comprise:

A group of several persons stabilized in the Soul Consciousness. Their main function will be to derive their powers and inspiration from the Comic Consciousness, to receive the Cosmic plan, and to transmit the right thoughts and impulses in order to implement Cosmic action in the world, in accordance with the necessities of Humanity, that is, to be the consecrated instruments of the Cosmic and the true embodiment of the Spirit of the Time.

This group will have an esoteric activity as well as an open activity, both combined, which means that the instrument on the human level will adjust itself in such a way that it will be the perfect expression of the dynamism of the Soul.

Such type of workers should be detected as soon as possible and a conscious link established among them; the vision and inspiration that they receive from the Cosmic plane being identical, they should work together in a spirit of unity thereby embodying Cosmic dynamism. Through their mediumship, the super-conscious activity of the Cosmic from which, behind the veil of ignorance, everything concerning our Earth plane and its evolution is worked out and elaborated, will become *conscious* on the human mental sphere; the result is that more individuals will be attracted to participate in the work. A constant and more accurate study of world affairs should be pursued by them. A precise work should be undertaken which will entail directing suggestions upon the conscious and subconscious collective mind of the nations.

Problems should be solved on those lines one after another; there is always, in the present, a problem which is of major importance and which is most urgent and vital to solve for the very security and welfare of Humanity. This is to be the instrument of the conscious aspect of Shakti in the world.

Apart from this esoteric activity, which can be performed only when the higher mental sphere of Humanity is attuned to the Cosmic Will, through the instrumentation of a few selected and consecrated channels, namely the Cosmic workers, a constant work of psycho-analysis of the Nations and of the various human groups should be undertaken, in order to remain constantly aware of the inner developments which are taking place within these nations of groups as wall as of the larger scheme of evolution of humanity as a whole. Contacts should be sought at the individual level with the instruments who are in charge of human affairs in the world, more especially with those who are consciously, or unconsciously, the instruments of the Cosmic in each nation of the world.

The detection of Cosmic workers, who are not as yet prominent on the international stage, but nevertheless who consciously or half-consciously are the trusted agents of the Cosmic, should be undertaken and actively pursued and the formation of new Cosmic workers who have not as yet attained that level should start as soon as possible.

To that effect, those who are already the dedicated agents of the Cosmic and who are available, should go throughout India and various parts of the world, guided by intuition, in order to detect and meet the agents of the Cosmic wherever they may be found, and to establish a conscious bond among as many as possible. Through such contacts, taken on the individual level, much can be achieved to help implement the work of the superconscious spheres.

Agents of the Cosmic, world workers, should be ready to go wherever there is a difficulty which produces international tension and threatens peace in the world. Their very presence and the personal contacts they would make with the representatives, temporal or Cosmic, of the nations, or the groups creating the tension, can greatly assist in bringing about a solution to the particular problem in the shortest possible time. Their presence will serve as an amplifier to the vibrations and thoughts of the Cosmic Mind, thereby constituting to make it active and creative in our world. Moreover, they will bring down and canalize from the Cosmic the necessary powers in order to control the situation. Wherever they may be, these agents are driving powers, their presence is essential when a difficulty arises in any part of the world, in order to overcome it, for the security of the whole of Humanity.

There is a plane of consciousness whence such intense powers can be drawn to change immediately, or in the shortest possible time, any situation in the world. These particular agents of this special plane are most urgently and vitally required in the world today. There is a power which can achieve in an instant that which requires much longer time through the channel of other forces. Through this power the normally long process of nature is shortened and creation becomes instantaneous.

Apart from this activity, a work in the philosophical field has to be undertaken in order to explain and justify, from a higher level of thought, the actual opposed ideologies which are respectively manifested in the East and West. Such was the mission of Sri Aurobindo. Unfortunately, the seed which he brought into the human mental sphere is in a slow process of development and very few at present can be enlightened by it. Powers of ignorance have been at work to create confusion and to misinterpret his thought and the true meaning of his teachings. Consequently, an re-translation of the idea which he intended to impress of the human Mental sphere has to be made. All this work can only be achieved if a larger number of individuals are being convinced of the necessity of becoming more dynamic, more active — in a word, "awakened" — to the life of the world.

Commentaries of the Bhagavad Gita should be made again, explaining it in the true light of the Spirit. A more esoteric significance of its message should be put forth and made evident to all, revealing, in all its magnitude, the Cosmic Action and how the individual can be initiated by the Lord Himself (*i.e.,* the conscious level of the Cosmic) in order to be the consecrated instrument of the Divine, for the implementation of the Divine Plan and will.

Yoga philosophy, in its most esoteric aspect, being as such a unique promoter of evolution for each individual, should be taught and propagated on the largest possible scale and should be introduced in schools. Schools of Yoga for teachers should be opened.

New translations and interpretations of the sacred Books are to be made in the true light of the Spirit. Scholars who can carry on this work should be found out, as well as thinkers, whose minds are attuned to the Cosmic. Their collaboration must be sought so that a coordination of work should be carried out in this particular field.

We must endeavor to awaken as many individuals as possible to the Cosmic Sense. Only a few in the world, at present, are consciously working on that plane and deriving their powers directly from it. Our efforts must be centralized and directed toward establishing a contact among them all. This kind of activity is a very new one in the field of experimentation of human consciousness. Consequently, those who are not yet completely dynamic on this plane have to be awakened and made active on that particular plane. As soon as such contacts with them are established they will cease to feel isolated; this will serve as a confirmation of their own intuition and it will strengthen them in their own individual effort.

The core of activity would consist in an attempt to stabilize the Cosmic Consciousness on our level in as many individuals as possible. This would be the preliminary step toward awakening, within the very heart of humanity, a World-Consciousness — the real center of gravity of the whole — which will contribute to the recognition of the essential unity of the human family, not only as a totality of national aggregates, but as one and indissoluble in its archetypal and basic structure. The awakening of a world-consciousness in humanity will have, as a necessary and inevitable consequence, the most determining impact on international problems by projecting on them a new light, thereby helping toward the establishment of peace in the world — the necessary prelude to a real transformation of the world.

Contacts with the Cosmic agents of the various nations of the world should be established with the purpose of working through them and using their mediumship, so as to affect the conscious and subconscious Mind of the nations and help these nations to find the correct attitude to adopt at each stage of their national life, so that world peace may be maintained and not constantly perturbed.

The immediate task of the proposed Center is to "detect" the Cosmic workers in each nation of the world — all following the same lines of thought and receiving identical messages insofar as they are more perfectly attuned to or identified with the Cosmic Mind. In each of them there is a similarity of purpose. The Will is identical, as the vision is the same. Only the distribution of work varies. It is already a world organization. To become more powerful and more effective, this world organization has to be discovered and its instruments consciously united on a world basis.

The problems created by the nations, which are not as yet awakened to a greater consciousness, are issued from their inadequacy to find out what is their real interest. Nations are not as yet completely aware and convinced that their own interest is not divorced from the interest of other nations, but identical. This identity should be stressed in our epoch more than ever before. Whatever happens in any part of the world now directly affects the rest of the world. Nations should receive suggestions along these lines of thought. They should be urged to realize that, in order to avoid destruction, there is no other way than to respect the interest of others. At every stage of their national life, they should be helped to find the right attitude and the correct impulse. This work can be achieved through the right instruments and channels of the Cosmic, in each nation, once a conscious contact has been established with them. Now more than ever before, personal and often narrow egoism of the nations must yield to the notion of common interest, so that ultimately the interest of each of them may be truly safeguarded. It is a question of logic and common sense. They have to be shown a new direction of thought so as to avoid engaging themselves any longer in the paths too often trodden. New patterns of conduct must be adopted. The vital interest of each nation is at stake. There is no other way out. The alternative is the re-awakening of vindictive selfishness, carriers of germs of destruction and death. This proves that there is a lack of a real controlling power in the world and that those who are spiritually in charge of human societies are not sufficiently aware of their responsibilities. They should abandon their present retreat and come down to the plane of the common man, making a deep and accurate study of the problem of human affairs in the most realistic manner so as to become the real dynamic agents of the Cosmic.

Humanity is like a gigantic child without a tutor, lacking the proper education and the necessary patterns of conduct. A group of the real intelligensia of the world should be organized to re-establish the equilibrium in the world and to bring some common sense into human relations. These few must be helped by the intelligensia in all countries of the world. It is a common and vital interest. Spiritualists should help the Cosmic workers in their task.

The proposed center aims at canalizing and diffusing these ideas on a world level. It proposes to give as many evidences as possible of the reality of the Spirit, as the essence of all manifestations.

PART II
THE EXOTERIC PART

A scientific study of the Spirit should be made in its manifold aspects, more especially in relation to the "nature" of man. A scientific teaching of Yoga should be expounded through this Organization. Yoga, the real means of evolution for each human being, should be propagated on the widest possible scale in the East as well as in the West. It should be introduced in schools; at least a beginning in this respect should be made in India.

DEPARTMENT OF YOGA

This will include a College of Initiation with methods of initiation as used in India as well as in Ancient Egypt. A more esoteric initiation in the art of Yoga will be given. This department will be reserved only to those who are ready to receive this particular training. Study will be made of the ancient forms of Yoga and the study of Yoga philosophy as expounded by Sri Aurobindo.

A special study will be made of:

i) how to achieve Cosmic Consciousness and thus become an instrument thereof in the world;
ii) formation of Cosmic Beings, adaptation to the Cosmic work, study of the Cosmic plane;
iii) experiences on the foregoing, how the Cosmic Mind monopolizes our former mental formation;
iv) the Cosmic Will and Action, Organization of the Cosmic workers, direction, distribution of the work, study of world problems on the social, economic and political fields in the light of the true consciousness;
v) psychological analysis of the nations, lines of thought received from the Cosmic Mind to be impressed on the human mental sphere;
vi) study of the penetration of these ideas in our world, the various reactions they provoke in relation to the human mental sphere;
vii) A study will be made of the penetration of an idea from the Cosmic into the Human mental sphere.

Preparation and Counsel

How can we prepare a person to be ready physically and psychologically for cosmic activities, and how do we treat individuals who come to the New Future Society?

Preparation

It is very important to prepare a loving and quiet surrounding where the individual can retreat from the outside world and enter into a new atmosphere, creating a healing sanctuary with spiritual objects of art and music. The individual should feel that he is in a sacred place.

The individual will most definitely require a period of purification and rejuvenation. We have found that our students require attention addressing their entire being. Here we propose methods for the health of the physical body.

i) Giving regular classes of Hatha and Tibetan Yoga
ii) Massage
iii) Magnetism, sending shakti/energy into the seven chakras and, if needed, the ailing area of the body.
iv) We are attentive to natural remedies for curing ailments, avoiding drugs and medicines as much as possible.
v) We endorse *Dr. Max Gerson's* therapy concentrating on detoxification of the body, utilizing colonic irrigation and enemas; some periods of fasting (allowing the body to rest whilst the toxins are eliminated) can be effective even for the most serious illnesses.
vi) Also, we advocate a daily regime of fresh vegetable and fruit juices, respecting the pioneers in this field, *Dr. Norman Walker,* and *Dr. John Heinerman* (see his book, *Encyclopedia of Healing Juices* where he describes at length how specific ailments can be cured with fresh juices).
vii) The body can be rejuvenated with these juices, as the fresh enzymes and nutrients are delivered in an easily digestible form. To maintain a healthy body we suggest daily consumption of organic carrot juices along with many other vegetables and herbs such as beets, celery and parsley.
viii) Raw food should be eaten as much as possible, for when we cook the food, most essential nutrients are lost.

ix) A daily dosage of vitamins and minerals are recommended, as well as adequate pure water. When possible, fresh raw goat's milk should be drunk instead of cow's milk. Eating foods that create a good alkaline constitution will benefit the body in many ways.

Indeed, each individual will require different applications. If they are suffering from either physical or mental exhaustion there should be a period of long rest, applying all the above dietary recommendations along with the concentration on specific ancient mantras that can purify the spirit, benefiting the mind and body.

Counsel

We consider that psychologically counseling the individual is essential, in order to assist in the dynamic purification, especially if they are troubled, to eradicate a particularly adverse aspect of their lives or past. However, our psychological counsel is always integrated with a metaphysical teaching, leading the individual out of his duality and confusion into an expanded, more universal, cosmic perspective. When the individual can view himself from this vantage point, true healing can occur, and new foundation is made, that is lasting and true.

Then we can attempt to take the individual to a higher plane of consciousness, using various different methods.

Primarily, through the mere presence of the Master, this can be performed. The master utilizes many esoteric techniques for this purpose. However, one of these techniques is described here. We call it Incubation or suspended animation, based on Egyptian forms of Initiation where the initiate is taken deep into the inner temple and in silence, preferably in the dark, the initiate turns his concentration inwards away from his five senses. With conscious suggestions, rhythmic breathing, visualizations and energy applied to the chakras, the initiate can leave his body and experience an elevation of his consciousness, entering entirely into the spiritual realm.

Regression

In order to unlock the psychological barriers that occur; a regression through this lifetime, and possibly to past lifetimes, can be extremely effective in allowing the individual to detach himself from the traumas of his past; the individual can now "see" his memory like an old movie, aiding the purification process.

Another aspect of regression is invaluable in taking the individual back to the child consciousness — to allow the opening and experience the spiritual child personality that is waiting beneath the surface of the adult ego intellect.

Surrendering ourselves to this state allows the individual to be momentarily free of all inhibitions, innocent and pure.

In fact, this may be considered as a form of hypnosis — yet, the person is perfectly conscious that this metamorphosis is occuring — they are now a two or three year old again, and more perfect and harmonious with their natural inner nature than the crushed and contrived, societally bound adult.

A prolongation of this regression occurred when Premananda Deva took Lakshmi Devi into this state, where she stayed for one week. It was during this time of regression that she was psychically cleansed and rested — wholly rejuvenated and again connected with her essential self.

This is a revolutionary cure for purification of psychological maladies — which we hope will be accepted more as it is understood in the field of psychology.

However, the bond that is created here is indeed very profound between the individual and the spiritual healer/teacher, much the same as a parent and a child. The individual again experiences a completeness and a purity that long since left during his lifetime.

Purification

During this process of the elimination of psychological traumas that prevent the adherent from ending their mental duality, the most rapid cures and forms of initiation (which in itself requires that the individual be purified) are through isolation. If the individual can be isolated from all effects of their lives, even family and friends, the rapidness of the cure is ensured. If the individual cannot consecrate themselves for a duration of a week or a month, for example, at the very least, then it will be much more difficult to ensure the elimination or integration of the two selves, for the ego consciousness is only encouraged and sustained by the human world that is essentially dual.

Initiation

We have spoken of methods for purifying the individual, however there are some exceptional people who can almost instantly be ready for direct Initiation and spiritual experiencing.

By surrendering to the Master, it is possible to attune oneself with the vibrations of the Master's consciousness and by becoming one with him will lift those select few directly out of all psychological traumas, bypassing the mind and emotions, producing an awakening in their psychic and spiritual selves, whereby they can experience early forms of Cosmic Consciousness.

However, it must be stated that after the initial experience great care must be taken to sustain the unity of mind and spirit, not allowing the ego consciousness to rule and project itself again. Here it is essential to protect the individual much as we would a rare flower — to be sure not to abort the sacred consciousness that has been granted by virtue of the Masters' command.

It is true that when someone comes to the New Future Society, every aspect, no matter how simple or profound, is always seen as a preparation for that individual's ascension and illumination. The subjects delineated here touch on the esoterism of our work; it is our goal to create New Future Centers where all of these techniques can be adhered to — where true schools of initiation will once again thrive and inspire.

DEPARTMENT OF HEALING

This Department will study:

i) special applications of Yoga to the art of healing;
ii) formation of scientific healers;
iii) study of their methods and their applications;
iv) magnetism;
v) how to cure all possible kinds of disease in oneself and in others.

This knowledge and science should become universal. The application of Yoga in the art of healing gives the possibility of recreating any part of the body according to the ideal physical and psychological human prototype. Study will be made of the possibilities of awakening the vital currents in a degenerated organism. This science should be taught on the largest possible scale and a training of scientific healers should be undertaken. A special school for teachers in the art of healing should be created.

DEPARTMENT OF PSYCHOANALYSIS

This Department will study the collective sub-consciousness of humanity through the different epics, their symbols, their similarity and significance.

Study will also be made:

i) in the analysis of the psychology of the child in general and as visualized by Jung;

ii) its discovery in the human complex; its unifying and liberating potentialities;

iii) historical study of the myth of the child — (*i.e.* Krishna as a child).

Study will be made in the cure of mental diseases by magnetism, creation of a state of receptivity in the patient.

Creation of a Center of Orientation for Youth; psychological study of youth by qualified persons trained in this science.

Discovery of the child Archetype. Special training for children to help them develop an awareness of their real identity, and unfold their potential.

Research should be conducted on the individual at the laboratory level, and on the group (dissemination of ideas within a group, study of the best possible factors for the dissemination of the ideas to be diffused within a group; psycho-analysis of the various human groups; reshaping of their system of thought; induction for new motivations; study of the various forms of frustration, leading to the adoption of behavior-patterns recognized as dangerous for the group itself or for the world at large, study of the methods to be used in order to liberate the group from these frustrations, study of the psychological configuration of each and every human group). Psychologists trained in this area could serve as counselors to any Government who would request their assistance in relation to a general or more particular problem. They would not be politicians nor even diplomats. They would make a thorough and totally objective study of the people in relation to the problem, using the material available and gathering their own material on the spot.

SOCIO-PHILOSOPHICAL DEPARTMENT

This department will try to:

i) elaborate a synthesis of all the contradictory tendencies manifested in the world at present, on the philosophical and mental planes;
ii) their analysis, and a comparative study of these will be made in the light of the Cosmic Consciousness;
iii) study of the three concepts: God, the Human Being, the Exterior World;
iv) their mutual links and true relations;
v) discovery of the true significance of the concept of God and of the secret link existing between men and the outer world;
vi) discovery of Paramatman;
vii) the way to become conscious of the one Reality;
viii) the significance of the human vehicle;
ix) study of the Bhagavad Gita;
x) the initiation of Arjuna into the consciousness of Krishna, initiation of Krishna-Arjuna as one and as executor of the Cosmic Will in the World;
xi) Gita being the revelation of the Cosmic Consciousness to Arjuna, impelling him to perform the Cosmic action.

Study will be made of the different ideologies prevailing in the world today in the spiritual, moral, social and political fields, in the light of True Consciousness.

Comparative study will be made of:

i) philosophies;
ii) their techniques — in India, in Ancient Egypt and in other civilizations;
iii) significance and utilization of statues: their power, their life, vibrations of thought, atmosphere created by thought, accumulation of power;
iv) "saturation" in one place, process of "incubation" as practiced in Ancient Egypt.

Research will be made on:

i) man of today in anticipation of man of tomorrow;
ii) the possibilities of extending man's field of action in the light of these studies.;

iii) increase of his freedom on the philosophical and psychological field, as well as in relation with the exterior world;
iv) reshaping man along new coordinates;
v) man eternally perfectible;
vi) constant discovery of his latent and still concealed powers, the Cosmic Consciousness being a higher level of consciousness in humanity.

The mission is to bring about a "world consciousness."

EDUCATION

This Department will include:
i) study of the powers of love, parallel development of the heart and the mind, to avoid egocentricity;
ii) development of *intuition*, which will give birth to a new system of education;
iii) comparative study of the different systems of education;
iv) science of the Spirit, studied in light of modern techniques;
v) development of young people.

CONCLUSION

The main object of this New Future Center is to preserve the true spirituality in the world. Those who are conscious of the reality of the Spirit should unite and combine their efforts to preserve the spiritual heritage among human beings. India should be helped in this transitory phase of her evolution so that by taking the fullest advantage of her present experiences, she may continue to be, as in the past, the *real leading light of the world.* A re-orientation of her conception of the world should be effected, thereby leading to the realization of a greater and all-embracing Truth, wherein the inner and the Outer Worlds may find their legitimate places. The true legitimacy of life in the world should be emphasized.

The world is evolving at such a speed that a conscious guiding and controlling power, reorganizing and unifying of all the spiritual powers in the world, must be created and should find a way of expression through a Central Body. The purpose of this activity is to attest the Reality of the Spirit, to transmit the spiritual heritage of the past to the next generations, as well as to give a proper place and an adequate understanding of the necessities of man in the modern age, socially and economically. In view of the many factors of disintegration which have been at work in the world, such as mass hysteria, satanism, atheism, moral disintegration, we must be alert so that the world should not fall into complete darkness. There is no other way out. It is the heritage of spirituality that we have to defend for the human race.

This manifold activity has also to help humanity in its present phase of evolution, to extricate her from her present confusion and the dilemma in which she finds herself, thereby helping the disintegration of the forces of antagonism — the creators of hatred and war. Therefore, those conscious of these vital necessities should unite and come together. A lack of cohesion and a real controlling power in humanity will sooner or later lead to disaster. It is not enough to praise the greatness of God if we are unable act as his instruments in the world. It is just a phantasmagoria if it leads nowhere. *Men of real spirituality should now become Realist.* Every ideology has its own supporters and tends to unity and cohesion, yet true spirituality represents a unity only on the spheres which have not been revealed to the human consciousness on a vast scale; the awareness of this unity must be developed.

The need of helping and serving the world is greater than ever before. To do so we must first learn how to think, we must develop the power of thoughts, practice the purification of the mind, be receptive to the higher planes of thought, and know how to utilize will power scientifically. The individual, after his reunion with the Cosmic Consciousness, becomes a channel of light and power. A stabilization of this higher consciousness should be sought and advocated on the human level.

Lectures should be delivered throughout the world asking for the cooperation of all the high-minded, enlightened people, so that the unity of the world should become a reality which would contribute to the welfare of all the nations of the world. A spirit of cooperation should be developed and the extension of economic and social assistance among the nations should be increased and planned on a world scale.

The conscious power of the mind of the masses should be utilized in a positive way and the sense of antagonism and selfish egotism should be eliminated as energies become directed toward more constructive channels and objectives. Much can be achieved in this direction regarding the solution of the latent problems of the world.

This Center aims to be a *magnet* for the minds who are still confused or in error in the world. It will operate on the Supramental Sphere as a controlling and guiding center from which everyone will be able to find solutions to problems as yet unsolved or not embraced in their proper light by the generality of Mankind.

The world is in great need of solutions to its problems; religions are no longer accepted as "taboos" in various countries.

Only a scientific approach to the problems of man may bring some new light and may be acceptable to the new generation. Let us think in terms of the world and no longer merely in terms of a nation, a party, a religion, or an individual.

Then, only, can we build a real *World Consciousness,* and a New Future Society so deeply needed now, more than ever.

Appendix

Times of India, Bangalore;
February 7, 1997

Nirvana in a cafe

The tug of Oriental spirituality proved too irresistible for this Californian teacher. Premananda Deva, earlier **John J. Kennedy**, experienced the power of soul consciousness when he met **Ananda Devi — Ms Lydie Bastien** in her former avatar — in 1960 at Cafe Nirvana. He moved to Paris four years later and set up *Kalidasa*, an Indian restaurant. In the meantime, he had also set up ashrams at New York and Paris. Throughout, the fascination for India remained undimmed. He's now in the city with wife **Lakshmi Devi** from England, propagating Ananda Devi's philosophy and offering a variety of healing methods for the body, mind and spirit.

Based near Seva Nagar in Bangalore, this couple believes that India's spirituality has a lot to offer. And this path can undo the many wrongs of the present-day world. Ananda Devi's book *The Illumined Mind* published by Minerva Press was released in the United Kingdom and is awaiting for distribution in this country after a tie-up with an Indian publisher. The book outlines her search into higher consciousness and why India is the country of the future. After her death in 1994, Premananda has been spreading her good word.

Premananda and Lakshmi Devi: Searching for higher consciousness through Indian spirituality

EXPRESS INDIA

September 18, 1998

Need For Indian Cultural Centre In Washington, DC

Express India News Serivice :
It is amazing that it took an American and a British yogi to realise and point out that there is no Indian Cultural Center in the world's capitol, despite such a large Indian community living in Washington, DC.

Premananda Deva and Lakshmi Devi or John and Sarah Kennedy came to Washington from India just a few months ago. They say they are happy to see the Indian community trying to build temples, but temples alone will not deliver for the second generation and a third generation of Indians in America.

Premananda, who has founded and managed Indian cultural centers in Paris and New York, along with his guru, a personal friend of Dr Radhakrishnan, who comapred her to Shri Aurobindo, Ananda Devi - says, "an Indian Cultural Center in Washington will enable all peoples to appreciates and enjoy the magnificient of the Indian culture and civilizatin, striving to fulfill those Indians in America who are looking for a cohesion of their peoples."Lakshmi Devi - his wife and disciple - emphasizes the need for the center for Indian kids who were born in America and find it tough to connect with their roots and heritage.

Lakshmi says the center is needed " to excite, stimulate and initiate the children, first generation Americans, who are, therefore, unable to appreciate the delicacies of the spirit - so separate are they from the rituals, temple worship, and even the concept of devotion to the archetypes of India, they are in reality strangers to their peoples, to their spirit and their souls."The couple is in a unique positon. As westerners - experienced and trained in the traditions of the East - they are truly a bridge between the East and West. They met in the Himalayan mountains, where she was initiated by him, and they have been travelling and working together for nearly five years."India for us is the closest civilization that understands the spiritual experience we have had" says Premananda. "Egypt, Babylonia, Greece and Rome all understood metaphysics and its important message, but India is the only living place on the Earth that still respects this way of life. We want to uphold truth in this world, and for us, India and her people are closest to this reality."

We should concentrate on this, adds Lakshmi Devi, because for generations there has been an understanding and an interwoven thread of divinity that will be lost, both in the West and in India, as even the urban children in India look to computerization, modernization as a salvation and glamorous way of life. We must be instrumental then in making the union of the Eastern spirit and the western world.Premananda believes the center should also hold the office of an Ambassador of philosopies - encouraging the western mind from all belief systems to taste the methodologies from the East and seek shelter in her nurturing ways.

Introducing PREMANANDA DEVA and LAKSHMI DEVI

The line of descent, lineage guru-disciple, was recognized from ancient civilizations up to the present day. Premananda Deva was initiated by guru-avatar Ananda Devi, who was enlightened by Sri Aurobindo and Sri Ramana Maharishi. Ananda Devi and Premananda Deva worked tirelessly for 34 years, promoting yoga philosophy and world peace.

Deva, after surrendering to Ananda Devi in the true yogic fashion, experienced the Descent of the Supramental in 1960, entering Nirvana. From the emanations of Ananda Devi's being, Deva integrated his powerful inner conscious experiences into his waking state. The training he received is unique, transforming his own disciple, Lakshmi Devi into a cosmically conscious being.

Deva is a synthesis of East and West, a master who is absorbed in the highest truth consciousness — an example of the cosmic mind on Earth. He is akin to the ancients who receive true questers for enlightenment.

Lakshmi Devi, disciple and medium, entered her Atman (Soul) soon after her Himalayan encounter with her guru Deva in 1994. World lecturers on yoga philosophy and their metaphysical experiences, they are dedicated instruments of the Brothers of the White Lodge, giving themselves over to the Master Plan of K.H. for a New Future Society.

HEALING CENTERS

New York	1958 – 1968
Paris	1963 – 1993
India	1994 – 1997
Washington, D.C.	1997 – Present

LECTURES AND SEMINARS

Deva and Lakshmi use *Initiation Yoga* in their lectures and seminars based on their own investigations and personal experiences. Their lecture topics include:

- ❖ Enlightenment in This Lifetime
- ❖ Spiritual Initiation
- ❖ The Soul's Realization
- ❖ Cosmic Consciousness
- ❖ Child Consciousness
- ❖ Our Inherent Qualities
- ❖ The Supramental Light
- ❖ Attaining Divine Perfection
- ❖ Yoga — Physical to the Metaphysical
- ❖ Living in True Surrender
- ❖ The Dual Nature of Man — True Self and Ego Self
- ❖ Stilling the Mind, Stopping All Thoughts
- ❖ The Celestial Archetypes

LECTURE TOURS

United States: San Francisco, Beverly Hills, Los Angeles (CA); New Orleans (LA); Rockville, Calverton (MD); Santa Fe (NM); Memphis (TN); Richmond, Virginia Beach (VA)

Europe: Athens; Prague; London; Paris; Rome; Berlin

Asia: *India*: Dharmsala; Amritsar, Punjab; Bangalore; Karnataka; New Delhi; Puri, Orissa
Nepal: Kathmandu; *Thailand:* Bangkok; Chiang Mai; Phuket

Africa: Indian Embassy; Cairo, Egypt

INDIVIDUAL TREATMENT

Not since J. Krishnamurti and Paramahansa Yogananda (*Autobiography of a Yogi*) has America received two Yogis who live in such high consciousness, Sat Chit Ananda.

Deva and Lakshmi have proven methods to arrest all sadness and depression, helping to create a completely integrated individual. To be in their presence is profound and transformative. They will impart methods for rejuvenating the body, stilling the mind, and liberating the self.

Transformation & Purification

- Regression, Child Consciousness, analysis, evaluation, and integration.

Metaphysical Initiation & Experiencing

- Esoteric methods for achieving one-mindedness and Cosmic Consciousness.

Yoga, Massage & Acupressure

Magnetism

- Healing energy from the hands, especially on the seven chakras.

Incubation

- Ancient Egyptian methods: images and subtle suggestions for healing.

Mediumism

- Incorporation of ancient entities.

RETREATS

Deva and Lakshmi also offer weekend retreats for individuals and small groups. Contact the New Future Society for details.

PUBLICATIONS

The Illumined Mind of Ananda Devi is a collection of writings of an extraordinary woman, a Westerner who experienced complete illumination, which for millennia was known only to Eastern mystics. The second book from the New Future Society is *New Future Society:* ***Spiritual Revolution.***

Glossary

Agni	fire, the fire god; flame of Divine Force.
Ananda	delight, bliss, spiritual ecstasy.
Arjuna	main character of the *Bhagavad-Gita*, chosen by Lord Krishna to be the perfect spiritual man.
Asanas	Hatha yoga postures.
Ashram	ancient name for sacred/spiritual center.
Astral	the Astral plane of existence is a more ethereal state; where we go when we sleep.
Asuras	demonical forces who are the enemies of the gods. The asuric nature is led by the ego.
Atma/Atman	Soul, our highest individual Divine Self, untainted by earthly ignorance and ego — pure wisdom.
Bhagavan	Lord
Bharat Mata	Great Mother India.
Bodhisattva	a Soul realized individual who returns to the Earth to assist others to realization.
Brahma	the great Father and Lord of all; creator of the world; the One.
Brahmin/ Brahminical/ Brahminic	the highest caste in India; the priest caste, keeper of the esoteric secrets; (*Brahminical* of the Brahmins).
Brahmacharya	applying Yogic discipline to live in a pure state of no desire (abstinence).
Buddhi	intuitive chakra in the middle of the forehead.
Chakra	seven centers of energy of the body.

Chela/Cheli	disciple
Cholan	as in Maha Cholan: a great teacher of the spiritual.
Darshan	receiving blessings from a spiritual Master.
Days of Ashok	referring to the reign of the great Emperor Ashok, who became the primary Buddhist missionary, and who spread Buddhism throughout Asia.
Deva	god; a divine realized mental being; Premananda Deva.
Devi	the female of a deva; Premananda Deva's guru, Ananda Devi.
Dharma	mission/duty
Disciple	spiritual student of a Master.
Esoterism	that which pertains to the secret unseen initiation rituals.
Exoterism	the outer rituals and procedures for worship.
Ganesh	Hindu god of protection and wisdom.
Gautama	the name of the original Buddha.
Gunas	three qualities of all created beings: *satva, raja, tamas.*
Guru	a spiritual Master and representative and vehicle of Divine Power and, therefore, entitled to receive implicit obedience from disciples.
Hinayana	the small wheel; microcosm of the Universe (*Buddhism*).
Isis	Egyptian Mother Goddess.
Jivatman	the union of the Jiva (human self) and Atman (Soul).
Ka	the Egyptian name for the Soul Dwelling in the human body.

Kali	goddess of destruction; the ultimate creative force in the universe.
Kundalini	the force related to the seventh chakra; the creative force.
Lakshmi	Hindu goddess, consort of Vishnu; the disciple of Premananda Deva.
Lila	Cosmic Play
Maha	great
Mahayana	the large wheel; macrocosm (*Buddhist*).
Moksha	the final liberation.
Paramatman	the Supreme Self; the Supreme Divine Being.
Prakriti	nature; creative consciousness; force of the Universal Reality; the one who is informed by Purusha.
Prana	breath; life force.
Pranayama	"prana": breath, "yama": god of death. By performing this breathing method one is meant to overcome death.
Pratyahara	a discipline where one withdraws from the senses, observing oneself in action.
Puja	a spiritual ceremony.
Purushottama	the highest Ultimate Soul.
Radha	Hindu goddess, favored mistress of Krishna.
Rajasic/Rajas	qualities of passion, activity; movement; violence.
Ram	a Hindu god.
Rishi	the sage; the seer.
Sadhak	the spiritual seeker or student.
Sadhana	advanced spiritual contemplation, becoming of one law of being and nature with the Supreme.
Samsara	illusion, appearance

Sannyasin	an ascetic, one who has inwardly renounced all.
Satva/Satvic	equilibrium, the quality that illumines.
Shakti	female energy force, universal force.
Shiva	Hindu god; Eternal Being; god of creation/ preservation.
Subconscient	subconscious
Superconsciousness	the highest Divine Consciousness
Supramental	the highest mental divine force that can descend inside of us, defined by Sri Aurobindo.
Swadharma	each and every one's duty or function.
Tamas/Tamasic	inertia, darkness, ignorance.
Vishnu	Hindu god; apex of the modern Hindu pantheon; preserver of the world.
Wu Wei	letting go (*Chinese*).
Yajna	sacrifice
Yuga	as Kali Yuga; four ages of time.

If you wish to contact the New Future Society, Premananda Deva and Lakshmi Devi, please do so at the following address:

New Future Society
5825 Royal Ridge Drive
Springfield, VA 22152
U.S.A.
(703) 923 – 0176
e-mail: newfuturesociety@yahoo.com
website: ww.geocities.com/newfuturesociety